AMERICAN SILVERSMITHS
—— and ——
THEIR MARKS

THE DEFINITIVE (1948) EDITION

Stephen G. C. Ensko

DOVER PUBLICATIONS, INC.
NEW YORK

Published in Canada by General Publishing Company, Ltd., 30 Lesmill Road, Don Mills, Toronto, Ontario.
Published in the United Kingdom by Constable and Company, Ltd., 10 Orange Street, London WC2H 7EG.

This Dover edition, first published in 1983, is an unabridged republication of the definitive third edition of the work as published by Robert Ensko, Inc., N.Y., in 1948 under the title *American Silversmiths and Their Marks III*.

International Standard Book Number: 0-486-24428-8

Manufactured in the United States of America
Dover Publications, Inc., 180 Varick Street, New York, N.Y. 10014

Library of Congress Cataloging in Publication Data

Ensko, Stephen Guernsey Cook, 1896-
American silversmiths and their marks.

Bibliography: p.
1. Silversmiths—United States—Biography. 2. Hall-marks. I. Title.
NK112.E66   1983   739.2'3722 [B]   82-17763

CONTENTS

4

ACKNOWLEDGEMENTS

I wish to express my sincere and grateful thanks to Dorothea E. Wyle and Vernon C. Wyle for invaluable help and inspiring cooperation in the preparation and progress of this work.

I appreciate the suggestions and friendly interest extended to me by Prof. John M. Phillips, Director, Yale University Art Gallery; Curator of The Mabel Brady Garvan Collection.

I desire to thank Kathryn C. Buhler, Museum of Fine Arts, Boston, for gracious assistance and constructive criticism.

To Helen Burr Smith I am deeply indebted for the scholarly work of Chapter III, listing silversmiths and showing their locations on the maps of New York, Boston, Philadelphia; and for research work and generous contributions of information and dates.

I am indebted for information to: C. Louise Avery, Metropolitan Museum, N. Y.; Lockwood Barr, Margaret M. Bridwell, E. Milby Burton, Charleston Museum, S. C.; Dr. George B. Cutten, Stephen Decatur, Carl W. Drepperd, Henry F. du Pont, Caroline R. Foulke, Harrold E. Gillingham, Jessie Harrington, Mrs. John Russel Hastings, John D. Hatch, Albany Institute of History and Art, N. Y.; Edwin J. Hipkiss, Museum of Fine Arts, Boston; Stanley Ineson, Walter M. Jeffords, Rhea M. Knittle, Dr. J. Hall Pleasants, Elizabeth B. Potwine, Mrs. Harold I. Pratt, Mrs. Alfred C. Prime, Beverley R. Robinson, Frank O. Spinney, Andrew V. Stout, Mr. and Mrs. Charles Messer Stow, R. W. G. Vail, New-York Historical Society; Mabel C. Weaks, Alice Winchester. To friends and acquaintances who have given me permission to use photographs, and have supplied marks and information, I wish to express my thanks and appreciation.

I am indebted for the use of illustrations to: Mrs. Adelyn B. Breeskin, Baltimore Museum of Art, Md.; Erwin Christiansen, Index of American Design, National Gallery of Art, Washington, D. C.; Downtown Assn., New York; Joseph Downs, Metropolitan Museum of Art, N. Y.; Helen S. Foote, Cleveland Museum of Art, Ohio; V. Isabelle Miller, Museum of the City of New York; Charles Nagel, Brooklyn Institute of Arts and Sciences, N. Y.; Russell A. Plimpton, Minneapolis Institute of Arts, Minn.; Robert H. Tannahill, Detroit Institute of Arts, Mich.; Josephine Setze, Art Gallery, Yale University.

To my wife Dorothea W. Ensko, I owe the greatest debt, for the many years that she has cheerfully given her assistance and generous encouragement.

STEPHEN G. C. ENSKO

New York.

To
S. M. K.
and
S. C. E.

INTRODUCTION

TUDY of American silver leads into many fields of interest and profit. One of them is history in general. Another is history in some of its subdivisions — economic, social, esthetic. Best of all, however, it leads to a better understanding and appreciation of the ethos of America.

Now ethos is a word which I believe ought to appear oftener in our thinking. The dictionary definition of it is "the character, sentiment or disposition of a community or people; the spirit which actuates manners and customs." More concretely, I think, the ethos of America is that characteristic inherent in its mentality, its customs and its handiwork which may be comprehended in the phrase the American Way of Life.

So thoroughly is the American ethos embodied in the works of American silversmiths that it has given to their product a typical identity and it never can be mistaken for that of any other country, though other nations may have influenced design and workmanship. Traces of English ostentation, French flourish and Spanish and Italian rococo fussiness may be found, but all these influences have been transmuted into American forthrightness and simplicity.

The same process is seen in the work of American cabinetmakers. Nobody mistakes a Philadelphia Chippendale chair for its English prototype or a Duncan Phyfe Federal period table for its English Regency model. Even the houses our ancestors built, though patterned after those of Georgian England, were so changed by the American ethos that we consider them typically American.

We learn from the earliest silver made in this country that the American spirit is no phenomenon of recent political origin. It started long before America was a nation.

The seventeenth century silversmiths of New England and New York followed English Jacobean and Restoration and Dutch styles, but altered and simplified their copies so that even the earliest known American silver had an individuality of its own — it signified an American ethos already initiated.

One of the contributing causes of the American spirit expressed by our silversmiths was the ingenuity and native skill demanded of them. In the seventeenth century the master silversmiths of London complained to the Guild Hall that their trade had become too specialized. Too many different craftsmen, they grumbled, must contribute to the making of a single piece — the hammerers, the planishers, the handle molders, the engravers. In America one journeyman silversmith accomplished all the kinds of work done in England by shop specialists.

Study of American silver in connection with certain phases of American history shows that it is a record of the economic and esthetic life of the colonies, all and each. At first, cups, tankards, beakers, porringers and other household utensils were made out of the silver acquired by the owner in trade or commerce. They were his equivalent of a savings bank.

INTRODUCTION

As wealth increased, household silver became an index of the owner's financial status and an indication of his manner of living. Pride of possession led him to have initials or armorial bearings engraved on his silver, and these, together with the maker's marks, are often an invaluable help to genealogists and other historians.

Study of the variations found in the silver produced in the various colonies is rewarding for the light it throws on local characteristics.

New England silversmiths followed more nearly the designs of England than did the craftsmen of other colonies, perhaps because New England's customs were more like those of Old England than any other colony — except Virginia. There the ties were so close that most of its silver as well as everything else was bought in London. Philadelphia, too, followed English styles (with modifications) but because of Quaker tolerance, design there in every branch of craftsmanship was more or less eclectic.

New York silver is considered to offer the best opportunity for tracing the process of Americanization at work. The city's earliest silversmiths, of course, were Dutch. Then came the English and the French Huguenots. Not one of these alien craftsmen continued the traditions learned in his apprenticeship in Europe. All succeeded in producing something typically American.

When the rococo and chinoiserie fashions flourished in the England of George II, New York silver remained simple, strong, almost stark. When England tired of fussy design toward the end of the eighteenth century and turned to the classics for inspiration, New York silversmiths, and those in the other centers, too, accepted the forms, but made modifications of ornament into a simplicity dictated by the American ethos.

All these suggestions as to the importance of the silversmith, with many others, are to be found in this book, which itself is the most complete study of American silver and its makers yet achieved. Mr. Ensko reckons American silver a manifestation of the American ethos, for he is convinced that it embodies the ingenuity, the spirit and all the other intangible factors that have made America what it is. He believes also that a study of the subject will quicken consciousness to grasp the need for preserving the American ethos, and in this I heartily concur.

CHARLES MESSER STOW.

AMERICAN
SILVERSMITHS
—————— *and* ——————
THEIR MARKS

Chapter I

NAMES OF EARLY AMERICAN SILVERSMITHS
1650-1850

THIS LIST of early American silversmiths has been compiled for the convenience of those desiring to know more about the craftsmen who fashioned early American silver. To facilitate reference the names have been listed in alphabetical order. All sources of available information have been used with a considerable amount of critical correction. In keeping with the original intention of this book only silversmiths and allied craftsmen who can be identified with known examples of their workmanship have been included in this list. With the names of silversmiths are earliest working dates; hyphenated double dates indicate births and deaths; and locations of business mentioned are followed by records of marriages, freemanships, apprenticeships, and other pertinent information.

* * * * *

To appreciate and understand the pieces of early American silver illustrated in this chapter it is necessary to know the lines and forms, and the styles of decoration of the various periods represented. This is not difficult if we keep in mind the influence of the early Chinese designs and the evolution into the Grecian shapes. In some instances we find the English and Continental prototypes of slightly later date, especially in the beginning of the eighteenth century, but generally speaking the designs and workmanship are more or less contemporary.

Presenting a simple picture of this development in the eighteenth century we note a globular bowl of 1725 changing into the elongated pear-shape of about 1750, and to the Grecian vase form of 1775. This considerable change in a span of fifty years is also to be found in the square tray conforming to the later fashionable curved outlines; the straight-sided, flat-top tankard acquiring a bulbous body and stepped-domed cover; all reflecting the general tendency to greater height and tapering line. For further study and educative interest the author refers the student to the bibliography included in this book.

A

JOHN W. ABBOTT
1790-1850

Portsmouth, N. H., 1839, at Market Square.

FRANCIS M. ACKLEY
1797

New York at 95 Warren Street; Bowery Lane; Henry Street; until 1800.

JOHN ADAM, JR.
1780-1843

Alexandria, Va., advertised after 1800. Was also noted Musician and Artist.

PYGAN ADAMS
1712-1776

New London, Conn., 1735. Son of Rev. Eliphalet Adams. Married Ann Richards, May 5, 1744. Capt. Adams held prominent public offices. General Assembly, 1753-1765. Died in New London.

WILLIAM L. ADAMS
1831

New York at 620 Greenwich Street; 10 Elm Street in 1835. Noted politician. President of the Board of Alderman, 1842-3. In Troy, 1844-1850.

EDWIN ADRIANCE
1809-1852

St. Louis, Ill., 1835. Born in Hopewell, N. Y. Son of Abraham Adriance and his Wife Anna Storm. Married Elizabeth O'Connor. Firm of Mead, Adriance & Co.; Mead & Adriance 1831.

GEORGE AIKEN
1765-1832

Baltimore, Md., in Calvert Street in 1787; 118 Baltimore Street in 1815. Married Sarah Leret McConnell 1803.

JOHN AITKEN
1785

Philadelphia, Pa., at 607 Second Street, 48 Chestnut Street 1791. No record after 1814. Advertised as, "Gold and Silversmith, Clockmaker, Musical Instrument Manufacturer and Copper-Plate Engraver".

JOHN B. AKIN
1820-1860

Danville, Ky., 1850.

CHARLES ALDIS
1814

New York at 399 Broadway; 23 Elm Street in 1815.

ISAAC ALEXANDER
1850

New York at 422 Grand Street.

SAMUEL ALEXANDER
1797

Philadelphia at South Second Street until 1808. Firm of Wiltberger & Alexander.

ALEXANDER & RIKER
1797

New York, at 350 Pearl Street until 1798.

ALLCOCK & ALLEN
1820

New York.

CHARLES ALLEN
1760

Boston, Mass.

CUPS

John Coney
1679

Edward Winslow
1710

John Coney
1718

Jacob Hurd
1725

Jeremiah Dummer
1700

Gerrit Onckelbag
1695

Samuel Vernon
1725

STANDING CUPS

Samuel Edwards 1739

Jeremiah Dummer
1700

Paul Revere
1782

FLAGON

Edward Winslow
1713

JOHN ALLEN   1671-1760
Boston, Mass., 1695. Son of Rev. James Allen. Married Elizabeth Edwards. Partner
of John Edwards.

ALLEN & EDWARDS   1700
Boston, Mass. John Allen and John Edwards in Partnership.

JERONIMUS ALSTYNE   1787
New York. At Maiden Lane until 1797. Married Eyda Beekman.

WILLIAM ANDERSON   1746
New York. Apprenticed 1717 to noted Simeon Soumaine, Freeman of July 1, 1746.

ANDRAS & RICHARDS   1797
New York at 166 Broadway. Dissolved in 1799.

WILLIAM ANDRAS   1795
New York at 40 William Street. Partner of Samuel Richards.

ANDRAS & CO.   1800
New York.

JOHN ANDREW   1747-1791
Salem, Mass., at "Sign of Golden Cup", 1769. Cambridge, at "Sign of the Anchor",
1775. In Windham, Me., 1789. Married Elizabeth Watson.

HENRY ANDREWS   1800
Philadelphia at 65 South Second Street. In Boston 1830.

JOSEPH ANDREWS   1800
Norfolk, Va.

N. ANDRUS & CO.   1834
New York.

ISAAC ANTHONY   1690-1773
Newport, R. I., 1715. Born, April 10, 1690, son of Abraham and Alice Wodell
Anthony. Advertised as a Goldsmith in the *Boston Gazette*, March 21, 1737.
Died in Newport, 1773.

JOSEPH ANTHONY, JR.   1762-1814
Philadelphia, Pa., 1783. Born in Newport, R. I., January 15, 1762, son of Joseph
and Elizabeth Sheffield Anthony. Married Henrietta Hillegas, December 29, 1785.
Advertised at Market Street, 1783-1796, where he admitted his sons in the business
in 1810.

JOSEPH ANTHONY & SONS   1810
Philadelphia, at 94 High Street until 1814, with sons, Michael and Thomas.

GEORGE B. APPLETON   1850
Salem, Mass.

ALLEN ARMSTRONG 1806
Philadelphia at 4 North Second Street, 225 Arch Street, 1817.

THOMAS ARNOLD 1739-1828
Newport, R. I., 1760. Prominent citizen. Continued in trade until 1796.

EBENEZER J. AUSTIN 1733-1818
Charlestown, Mass., after 1760 where he was born. Hartford, Conn., after 1764. New York, 1788, listed as Revolutionary Pensioner in 1818.

JOSIAH AUSTIN 1718-1780
Charlestown, Mass., 1745. Landowner in 1765. Married Mary Phillips in 1743. Worked with Samuel Minott in 1768.

NATHANIEL AUSTIN 1734-1818
Boston, Mass, 1760. Shop in Fourth Ward. Born in Charlestown, Mass. Married Ann Kent in 1759. Directory, 1796-1816. Died in Boston, October 18, 1818.

AUSTIN & BOYER 1770
Boston, Mass. Josiah Austin and Daniel Boyer.

JOHN AVERY 1732-1794
Preston, Conn. Selftaught silversmith, opened shop in 1760. Appointed Justice of Peace. His four sons, John, Robert, Samuel and William, were silversmiths.

SAMUEL AVERY 1760-1836
Preston, Conn., 1786, continuing father's business with brothers.

SAMUEL AYRES 1805
Lexington, Ky. Advertised, *Kentucky Gazette,* 1790, "In Shop on Main Street, nearly opposite Mr. Collins Tavern". Offers shop for sale in 1819. Died, September, 1824.

B

C. BABBITT 1815
Taunton, Mass.

SAMUEL BABCOCK 1788-1857
Middletown, Conn., 1812 North of Episcopal Church. Born in Saybrook where he was Collector of Customs.

A. BACHMAN 1848
New York.

DELUCINE BACKUS 1792
New York at 12 Crown Street. Firm of Cady & Backus.

B. M. BAILEY 1824-1913
Ludlow, Vt., 1848. Apprenticed to Robert H. Bailey in Woodstock. Later in Rutland. Died in Brooklyn, N. Y.

E. E. BAILEY 1825
Portland, Me. Firm of E. E. & S. C. Bailey.

E. E. & S. C. BAILEY 1830
Portland, Me.

E. L. BAILEY & CO. 1835
Claremont, N. H.

HENRY BAILEY 1800
Boston, Mass., directory 1803.

LORING BAILEY 1780-1814
Hingham, Mass., 1801. Born in Hull. Married, 1807. Caleb Gill, Levitt Gill and Samuel Norton served apprenticeships. Nicknamed "Thankful Loring" by townspeople.

ROSWELL H. BAILEY 1825
Woodstock, Vt. Apprenticed to his brother-in-law and cousin B. M. Bailey.

WILLIAM BAILEY 1818
Utica, N. Y.

BAILEY & CO. 1848
Philadelphia, Pa.

BAILEY & KITCHEN 1833
Philadelphia until 1846.

ELEAZER BAKER 1764-1849
Ashford, Conn. 1785, advertised as clock and watchmaker and gold and silversmith.

GEORGE BAKER 1825
Providence, R. I., and Salem, Mass.

STEPHEN BAKER 1830
New York.

EBENEZER BALCH 1723-1808
Hartford, Conn., 1750. Born in Boston. In Wethersfield in 1756.

EBENEZER BALDWIN 1810
Hartford, Conn., until 1819.

H. E. BALDWIN & CO. 1825
New Orleans, La.

JABEZ C. BALDWIN 1777-1819
Boston, Mass., 1800. Partner of John B. Jones in 1813.

JEDEDIAH BALDWIN 1793
Hanover, N. H. Advertised, *Spooners Journal,* October 7, 1793: "Clocks and watches made and repaired together with plate and jewelry in their various branches. The subscriber most respectfully informs the inhabitants of the town of Hanover, and the towns adjacent and the public at large, that having served a regular apprenticeship at the above branches of the business, he now proposes carrying them on in the town of Hanover, in the vicinity of Dartmouth College, a few rods south of the printing office. He hopes for the patronage and employment of those who have occasion for his labor in any of the above branches, but expects no further than he may be found by his fidelity, punctuality and moderate charges to merit them. N.B. The highest price given for old Gold, Silver, Brass, Copper and Pewter. A load of coal is wanted." Later in Portsmouth, Northampton, Mass., Rochester, N. Y. Died, 1839.

STANLEY S. BALDWIN · 1820
New York, at Franklin Square.

BALDWIN & CO. · 1830
Newark, N. J.

BALDWIN & JONES · 1813
Boston, Mass., Jabez Baldwin & John Jones. Directory 1816-1820.

JEDEDIAH & STORRS BALDWIN · 1800
Rochester, N. Y.

BALL, BLACK & CO. · 1850
New York.

BALL & HEALD · 1812
Baltimore, Md.

JOHN BALL · 1763
Concord, Mass., advertised in *Boston News Letter,* March 17, as goldsmith, until 1767.

SHELDON BALL · 1821
Buffalo, N. Y., until 1836.

BALL, TOMPKINS & BLACK · 1839
New York. Successors to Marquand Co., 1851; Ball, Black & Co., 1876.

WILLIAM BALL · 1759
Philadelphia, Pa., advertised, *Pennsylvania Journal,* November, 1759, as Silversmith. Notice in May, 1761, "going to England". Returned in 1765 and located on Front Street, corner of Market until 1771.

WILLIAM BALL, JR. · 1763-1815
Baltimore, Md., 1785. Advertised dissolution of the partnership of Johnson & Ball in 1790. Located at the "Sign of the Golden Urn", in 1793. Listed in Directory at Market Street, 1796-1815. Married Elizabeth Dukehart in 1790.

ADRIAN BANCKER · 1703-1772
New York, 1725. Born October 10, son of Everett, Mayor of Albany, and Elizabeth Abeel. Married in New York, January 31, 1728, Gertrude E. Van Taerling. Served apprenticeship with Hendrick Boelen. Freeman, 1731. Advertised at Bridge Street in 1766. Appointed Collector of South Ward 1733-6. Died August 21, 1772.

JOHN J. BANGS · 1825
Cincinnati, O., until 1829.

CONRAD BARD · 1825
Philadelphia, Pa., at Chestnut Street until 1850. Firms of Bard & Hoffman; Bard & Lamont.

BARD & LAMONT · 1841
Philadelphia, Pa., at Mulberry Street until 1845.

GEORGE BARDICK · 1790
Philadelphia, Pa. Census List of 1790. Located at Wagner's Alley, next shop to brother John.

BARKER & MUMFORD   1825
Newport, R. I.

JAMES BARRETT   1805
New York.

SAMUEL BARRETT   1775
Nantucket, Mass.

DAVID BARRIERE   1806
Baltimore, Md. Son of Anthony Barriere. Apprenticed to Lewis Buichle, 1799.

BARRINGTON & DAVENPORT   1806
Philadelphia, Pa., at 112 South Second Street.

JAMES MADISON BARROWS   1828
Tolland, Conn. Born Mansfield 1809.

STANDISH BARRY   1763-1844
Baltimore, Md., 1784. Born, November 4, son of Lavallin Barry. Apprenticed to
David Evans. Married 1788 to Agnes Thompson. Advertised at Market Street in
1784. Dissolved partnership with Joseph Rice, 1787. Listed at Baltimore Street and
later North Gay Streets, 1796-1808, when he became merchant. Was prominent in
public affairs. Colonel of First Rifle Regiment.

ROSWELL BARTHOLOMEW   1781-1830
Hartford, Conn., 1805. Born in Harwinton. Apprenticed to Beach & Ward. Partner
of James Ward, 1804. Firm of Ward, Bartholomew & Brainard.

ISRAEL BARTLETT   1748-1838
Newbury, Mass., in 1800 and later in Haverhill. Elected State Senator.

NATHANIEL BARTLETT   1760
Concord, Mass.

SAMUEL BARTLETT   1750-1821
Boston, Mass., 1775. Born in Concord. Married, Mary Barrett, 1775. Elected
Register of Deeds in Cambridge in 1795 which office he held until he died.

ERASTUS BARTON & CO.   1822
New York, at 166 Broadway.

JOSEPH BARTON   1764-1832
Stockbridge, Mass., 1790; Utica, N. Y., 1804.

WILLIAM BARTON   1769
Philadelphia, Pa., advertised in *Penn. Chronicle,* June 1769 on Front Street, at the
"Sign of the Golden Cup and Crown". Also, Bartram.

WILLIAM BARTRAM   1769
Philadelphia, Pa.

FRANCIS BASSETT   1774
New York.

BASSETT & WARFORD   1806
Albany, N. Y.

A. T. BATTEL 1847
Utica, N. Y. Firm of Davies & Battel.

HENRY BAYEAU 1801
Troy, N. Y., until 1812.

BAYLEY & DOUGLAS 1798
New York at 136 Broadway.

SIMEON A. BAYLEY 1789
New York at Old Slip; 94 Market Street in 1794. Firm of Bayley & Douglas.

JOHN BAILY 1755
Philadelphia, Front Street. New York, 1762.

A. BEACH 1823
Hartford, Conn.

MILES BEACH 1742-1828
Hartford, Conn., 1775. Dissolved partnership of Beach & Ward, 1798. Colonel
in Revolutionary War. Chief of Fire Department, 1789-1805.

BEACH & SANFORD 1785
Hartford, Conn. Col. Miles Beach and Isaac Sanford continued in partnership on
Main Street, until 1788.

BEACH & WARD 1789
Hartford, Conn. Miles Beach and James Ward. Advertised, *American Mercury,*
May 24, 1790; "Continued to carry on the Silver and Gold Smith's Business, Brass
Founding, Clock and Watchmaking, and etc. at their shop south of the Bridge."
Last Notice, January 17, 1795.

CALEB BEAL 1746-1801
Hingham, Mass., 1796; Boston, 1796-1800.

DUNCAN BEARD 1765
Appoqenimink Hundred, Del. Noted Mason. Died 1797.

E. BEARD 1800
Philadelphia, Pa. Brother of Andrew.

E. A. BEAUVAIS 1840
St. Louis, Mo.

RENE BEAUVAIS 1838
St. Louis, Mo., until 1898.

PHILLIP BECKER 1764
Lancaster, Pa.

JOHN BEDFORD 1757-1834
Fishkill, N. Y., 1782, advertised on Main Street.

JAMES W. BEEBE 1835
New York at 89 Race Street.

JAMES W. BEEBE & CO. 1844
New York.

TANKARDS

Henry Hurst
1700

Robert Sanderson
1675

Cornelius Vanderburgh
1690

Simeon Soumaine
1715

Edward Winslow
1700

Peter Van Dyke
1725

Samuel Vernon
1710

TANKARDS

John Coney
1715

John Coddington
1715

Jacob Hurd
1730

Adrian Bancker
1730

Philip Syng
1750

Paul Revere
1790

Samuel Minott
1770

WILLIAM BEEBE   1850
New York at 102 Reade Street.

CLEMENT BEECHER   1778-1869
Berlin, Conn., advertised in 1801. Born in Cheshire where he returned in 1818.

JOSEPH BELL   1817
New York, until 1824.

S. W. BELL   1837
Philadelphia, Pa.

B. BEMENT   1810
Pittsfield, Mass.

A. C. BENEDICT   1840
New York at 28 Bowery Lane.

BENEDICT & SQUIRE   1839
New York.

BARZILLAI BENJAMIN   1774-1844
New York, 1825. Born in Milford, Conn. Later in New Haven at Chapel and
State Streets. Shop formerly occupied by Robert Fairchild. Firms of Benjamin
& Co.

EVERHARD BENJAMIN   1807-1874
New Haven, Conn. 1830. Son of Barzillai, whose business he continued after 1829.
Partner of George H. Ford.

EVERHARD BENJAMIN & CO.   1830
New Haven, Conn.

JOHN BENJAMIN   1743
Stratford, Conn. Apprenticed to Robert Fairchild. Gilded rooster on old Episcopal
church steeple, in 1743. Married (1) Mary Smith, 1725, (2) Lucretia Backus.
Town Treasurer, 1777. Colonel in the Revolution after 1782. Died, September
14, 1796.

THOMAS BENTLEY   1764-1804
Boston, Mass., at Distill House Lane, 1789-1798. Apprenticed to Stephen Emery,
directory 1796-1803 at Salvation Alley.

THAUVET BESLEY   1727
New York, Freeman in 1727. Advertised, *New York Post Boy*, November 1746,
"House on Golden Hill". Mentioned in 1749. Died, 1757.

FRANCIS BICKNELL   1818
Rome, N. Y., until 1831.

HENRY BIERSHING   1790-1843
Hagerstown, Md., 1815-1843.

BIGELOW & BROTHERS   1840
Boston, Mass. John, Alanson and Abram O. in business in Washington Street.

JOHN BIGELOW   1830
Boston, Mass. Advertised on Washington Street next to Old State House.

ANDREW BILLINGS 1743-1808

Poughkeepsie, N. Y., 1773. Born in Stonington, Conn. Property owner in 1788. Listed with wife and nine children in First Federal Census. President of Village in 1803.

DANIEL BILLINGS 1795

Preston, Conn., shop at Poquettannock Village.

CHARLES BILLON 1821

St. Louis, Mo.

JOHN STILLES BIRD 1794-1887

Charleston, S. C., 1825.

CHRISTIAN BIXLER 1784

Easton, Pa. Apprenticed to John Keim of Reading, Pa.

JAMES BLACK 1795

Philadelphia, Pa., until 1819, at Second and Chestnut Streets.

FREDERICK STARR BLACKMAN 1810-1898

Danbury, Conn., 1830.

FREDERICK S. BLACKMAN & CO. 1840

Danbury, Conn.

JOHN CLARK BLACKMAN 1808-1872

Bridgeport, Conn., 1827. Son of Frederick.

JOHN CLARK BLACKMAN & CO. 1835

Bridgeport, Conn.

JOHN STARR BLACKMAN 1777-1851

Danbury, Conn., 1805, shop south of the Court House. Son Frederick, succeeded to business.

ASA BLANCHARD 1808

Lexington, Ky., at Mill and Short Streets. Died 1838.

JURIAN BLANCK, JR. 1666

New York. Baptised, April 9, 1645. Admitted to Membership of the Dutch Reformed Church in 1668. Appointed City Censor of Weights and Measures in 1672. Married Hester Vanderbeek, October 25, 1673. Taxed for property in New York and Brooklyn in 1679. Witness to Baptism of Grandson, December, 1699.

BLEASOM & REED 1830

Portsmouth, N. H.

JONATHAN BLISS 1800

Middletown, Conn.

JOHN BLOWERS 1710-1748

Boston, Mass., advertised 1738, 1746 *Boston Gazette*. Born in Beverly, son of Rev. Thomas Blowers. Married to Mary Slater.

CHARLES LOUIS BOEHME 1774-1868

Baltimore, Md., advertised, 1799 at 15 Market Street. Directory, 1801-1812.

HENRICUS BOELEN   1697-1755
New York, 1718. Baptized May 5, son of Jacob. Married Jannette Waldron, June 19, 1718. Member of Dutch Church, 1725. Was willed father's business in 1729. His will proved, September, 1755.

JACOB BOELEN   1657-1729
New York, 1680. Born in Amsterdam and emigrated with parents in 1659. Admitted as a member to the Dutch Church, 1676. Married Katharina Klock, May 21, 1679. Appointed Alderman of North Ward, 1695-7-1701, and held other important offices. Admitted freeman, 1698. His shop near Hanover Square, willed to his son, Henricus. Died, April 4, 1729.

JACOB BOELEN, II   1733-1786
New York, 1755. Son of Henricus. Married, April 4, 1764, (1) Magdalena Blauw, (2) Mary Ryckman, August 31, 1773. Headed list petitioning Governor, dated, November 27, 1783.

JACOB BOELEN, III   1785
New York.

EVERADUS BOGARDUS   1698
New York, born, 1675, Freeman, July 5, 1698. Married, Ann Dally, June 3, 1704.

NICHOLAS J. BOGERT   1801
New York at 10 Lombard Street.

TIMOTHY BONTECOU   1693-1784
New Haven, Conn., 1725. Born in New York of Huguenot descent. Learned his trade in France. In 1735, in Stratford he became member of the Church of England. Married second wife in 1736. Advertised in New Haven on Fleet Street. Became Warden of Trinity Church in 1765. Shop offered for sale in 1775. Died as result of injuries received during British Invasion in 1784.

TIMOTHY BONTECOU, JR.   1723-1789
New Haven, Conn., 1760. Born in Stratford. Trained as silversmith by father.

JEREMIAH BOONE   1791
Philadelphia, Pa. Advertised with Joseph Anthony and John Cooke in 1798. Located at 30 South Second Street; 132 Chestnut Street until 1796.

EZRA B. BOOTH   1805-1888
Rochester, N. Y., 1838-1850. Born in Vermont. In partnership with Erastus Cook.

E. BORHEK   1835
Philadelphia, Pa.

ZALMON BOSTWICK   1846
New York at 128 William Street.

SAMUEL BOSWORTH   1816
Buffalo, N. Y., until 1837.

GIDEON B. BOTSFORD   1776-1866
Woodbury, Conn., 1797. His shop and home now owned by the Episcopal Diocese of Connecticut.

ELIAS BOUDINOT 1706-1770

Philadelphia, Pa., 1730. Born in New York, July 8, 1706, son of Elias and Marie Catharine Carre Boudinot. When fifteen years old was apprenticed to Simeon Soumaine, for seven years. Removed to Antigua where he was married August 8, 1729 to Susannah LeRoux, in 1733 to Catherine Williams. From Antigua he removed to Philadelphia where he advertised until 1752. In Princeton, N. J., 1753-1760. After 1761 is in Elizabethtown, where he died, July 4, 1770. Father of the Hon. Elias Boudinot.

HELOISE BOUDO 1827

Charleston, S. C. Continued the business of her husband, Louis, until 1837, when her daughter, Erma Leroy, advertised for patronage.

LOUIS BOUDO 1786-1827

Charleston, S. C., 1810. Born in St. Domingo. Partnership with Manuel Boudo dissolved in 1810. Advertised at Queen and King Streets, 1809-1827. His widow, Heloise continued the business.

STEPHEN BOURDET 1730

New York. Married, Hannah Earle, widow of Peter Stoutenburgh, in 1720, in Reformed Church, Hackensack, N. J. Admitted to Freedom of New York City, August 4, 1730, as a Silversmith.

JOHN BOUTIER 1805

New York, directory until 1824. His widow continued until 1826.

C. BOWER 1828

Philadelphia, Pa., directory until 1833.

ELIAS BOWMAN 1834

Rochester, N. Y.

SAMUEL BOWNE 1780

New York at 81 John Street. Married Mary Steeker, November 7, 1778. Died, 1819.

GERADUS BOYCE 1814

New York at 101 Spring Street until 1830. Firm of Boyce & Jones.

JOHN BOYCE 1801

New York, at Bowery Lane.

BOYCE & JONES 1825

New York. Geradus Boyce and William Jones advertised at 101 Spring Street.

JOSEPH W. BOYD 1820

New York.

BOYD & MULFORD 1832

Albany, N. Y. William Boyd and John H. Mulford dissolved partnership in 1842. Succeeded by Boyd & Hoyt.

DANIEL BOYER 1726-1779

Boston, Mass., 1750. Married Elizabeth Bulfinch. Served as Court Clerk, 1754-8. Sergeant of the Artillery Company, 1762. Advertised, *Massachusetts Gazette*, October 30, 1766, "Opposite the Governors'." Located near the Province House in 1773.

BOYER & AUSTIN 1770

Boston, Mass. Daniel Boyer and Josiah Austin in partnership.

JEFFREY R. BRACKETT 1840

Boston.

THEOPHILUS BRADBURY 1815

Newburyport, Mass., advertised April 4, as working silversmith.

ABNER BRADLEY 1753-1824

Watertown, Conn., 1778. Born in New Haven where he learned his trade. Brother of Phineas. Revolutionary hero, retiring as Colonel of Militia, after serving at Crown Point, Ticonderoga and in the Danbury Raid in 1778.

LUTHER BRADLEY 1772-1830

New Haven, Conn., 1798.

PHINEAS BRADLEY 1745-1797

New Haven, Conn., 1770. Brother of Abner. House and shop on Crown Street. Was Captain in Revolutionary War.

ZEBUL BRADLEY 1780-1859

New Haven, Conn., 1810. Apprenticed to Marcus Merriman. Became a partner of the company in 1806. Worked with Merriman, Jr., 1826-1848.

BRADLEY & MERRIMAN 1826

New Haven, Conn. until 1847.

E. BRADY 1825

New York.

S. BRAMHALL 1800

Plymouth, Mass.

AIME & CHARLES BRANDT 1800

Philadelphia, Pa., until 1814.

AMABLE BRASIER 1790

New York at 79 Queen Street. Philadelphia at 12 South Third Street, 1794-1828. Spelled Brasher.

EPHRAIM BRASHER 1744-1810

New York, 1766. Married Ann Gilbert, November 8, 1766. Member of the Gold and Silversmiths Society, 1786. Minted the famous "Brasher Doubloon". Advertised at 5 Cherry Street. Firm of Brasher & Alexander.

WILLIAM BREED 1750

Boston, Mass.

BENJAMIN BRENTON 1695-1749

Newport, R. I. Freeman, 1717. Born September 8. Married Mary Butts, November 12, 1719. Died April 2, 1749.

JOHN BREVOORT 1715-1775

New York. Freeman, 1742. Son of Elias and Margaret Sammans Brevoort. Married Louisa Kockerthal in 1739. Whitehead Hicks, Mayor of New York, son-in-law, was granted letter of administration of will, March 3, 1775.

C. BREWER & CO.   1815
Middletown, Conn.

CHARLES BREWER   1778-1860
Middletown, Conn., 1810. Born in Springfield, Mass. Apprenticed to Jacob
Sargeant of Hartford. Firm of Hart & Brewer, 1800-1803. Later Brewer & Mann.

ABEL BREWSTER   1797
Norwich, Conn. Sold business to Judah Hart and Alvan Willcox in 1805 because
of illness.

JOHN BRIDGE   1751
Boston, Mass. Born, 1723. Sergeant of Artillery Company, 1748. Constable, 1752.

TIMOTHY BRIGDEN   1774-1819
Albany, N. Y., 1813 until 1816 at 106 Beaver Street. Member of the Albany
Mechanics' Society.

ZACHARIAH BRIGDEN   1734-1787
Boston, Mass., 1760. Born in Charlestown. First wife, daughter of Thomas
Edwards, died, May 30, 1768. Married Elizabeth Gillem, January 2, 1774. Adver-
tised shop on Corn Hill. Died March 11. Estate appraised by Benjamin Burt.

ABRAHAM BRINDSMAID   1815
Burlington, Vt. Firm of Brindsmaid & Hildreth.

BRINDSMAID & HILDRETH   1830
Burlington, Vt.

JOHN BROCK   1833
New York.

L. BROCK   1830
New York.

ROBERT BROOKHOUSE   1779-1866
Salem, Mass., 1800, at Old Paved Street. Purchased the Benjamin Pickman Man-
sion on Washington Street, built in 1763, from last owner, Elias Hasket Derby.
Retired from silversmithing in 1819.

SAMUEL BROOKS   1793
Philadelphia, Pa., advertised, *Federal Gazette,* June 10, 1793, "At 29 South Front
Street, not to be excell'd by any of his profession on the Continent. . . ."

S. & B. BROWER   1810
Albany, N. Y., until 1850.

S. DOUGLAS BROWER   1832
Troy, N. Y., until 1836. Albany directory 1837-1850.

BROWER & RUSHER   1834
New York.

D. BROWN   1811
Philadelphia, Pa.

JOHN BROWN 1785
Philadelphia, Pa., at Third Street between Spruce and Union Streets. At 36 North Front Street, 1796. Listed until 1824.

R. J. BROWN & SON 1833
Boston, Mass.

ROBERT JOHNSON BROWN 1813
Boston, Mass. Robert Brown & Son, after 1833.

R. R. BROWN 1830
Baltimore, Md.

SAMUEL C. BROWN 1825
New York.

WILLIAM BROWN 1810
Baltimore, Md.

WILLIAM BROWN 1849
Albany, N. Y.

BROWN & KIRBY 1850
New Haven, Conn.

LIBERTY BROWNE 1801
Philadelphia, Pa., at 102 North Front Street. Listed as Collector of Taxes at 119 Chestnut Street in 1813. Firm of Browne & Seale.

BROWNE & SEAL 1810
Philadelphia, Pa. Liberty Browne and William Seal dissolved partnership the following year.

CHARLES OLIVER BRUFF 1735-1787
New York, 1763, January 3, advertised, *The New York Mercury,* also in 1767, "For making silver tankard, 3 S. per ounce. For making a silver tea-pot, £ 4. For making a Sugar-pot, 35 S. For making a milk-pot, 24 S. For making a Soup-spoon 20 S. For making six table-spoons 21 S. For making six tea spoons 10 S. For making tea-tongs, bows or others 10 S. For making a pair of carved silver buckles 8 S. I design to put the stamp of my name, in full, on all my works; and will work as cheap as any in the city." Elizabeth, N. J., 1760-1765. Continue to advertise at "the Sign of the Tea-pot, Tankard, and Ear-ring, opposite to the Fly-Market", until 1776. Married Mary LeTellier, October 20, 1763. Retired to Nova Scotia, 1783-1787.

JOSEPH BRUFF 1730-1785
Easton, Md., 1755. Advertised at Talbot Court House, Penna. Gazette, 1767.

THOMAS BRUFF 1760-1803
Easton, Md., 1785, inherited shop from father, Joseph. Advertised in Chestertown, 1791-1803.

PHILLIP BRYAN 1802
Philadelphia, Pa., at 116 Plumb Street.

J. B. BUCKLEY   1807
Philadelphia, Pa., at 31 North Front Street. Firm of Buckley & Anderson.

ABEL BUEL   1742-1825
New Haven, Conn., 1770. Apprenticed to Ebenezer Chittenden. Noted engraver
and inventive genius. Born in Clinton. Married Master's daughter in 1764.
(2) Lettice Devoe of New York in 1775. Convicted of counterfeiting in New
London. Firm of Buel & Greenleaf, in 1798.

SAMUEL BUEL   1742-1819
Middletown, Conn., 1777. Born in Killingsworth. Advertised in Hartford, July 4,
1780, *Connecticut Courant;* "Removal from Middletown, . . . wanted a good
journey-man, goldsmith, . . . Highest wages given, paid in gold, silver, or Continental Bills." Died in Westfield, Mass.

LEWIS BUICHLE   1798
Baltimore, Md., 1802.

G. W. BULL   1840
Farmington, Conn.

BULLES & CHILDS   1840
Hartford, Conn.

BUMM & SHEPPER   1819
Philadelphia, Pa.

BENJAMIN BUNKER   1751-1842
Nantucket, Mass., 1780. Born March 17, son of William and Mary Bunker. Took
part in Penobscot Expedition. Became Prisoner of War in Revolution. Died,
April 14, 1842.

A. F. BURBANK   1845
Worcester, Mass.

NICHOLAS BURDOCK   1797
Philadelphia, Pa., at Waggoner's Alley.

DAVID I. BURGER   1805
New York, at 62 James Street; Mott Street, 1818-1830. Son of John.

JOHN BURGER   1780
New York. Member of the Gold and Silversmith's Society, and Geneva Society
of Mechanics and Tradesmen, 1786. Married, Sarah Baker, January 20, 1767.
Advertised at 153 Water Street, 207 Queen Street, 1789. His sons, David and
Thomas, joined him in business in 1805 at 62 James Street.

THOMAS & JOHN BURGER   1805
New York, at 62 James Street.

THOMAS BURGER   1805
New York, at 62 James Street.

ELA BURNAP   1784-1856
Boston, Mass., 1810. Listed in New York, 1817, Rochester, 1825. Born in Connecticut.

CHARLES A. BURNETT   1793
Alexandria, Va., and Georgetown, D. C., until 1822.

BEAKERS

I. B.
1690

Jeremiah Dummer
1700

Moody Russell
1719

Jacob Hurd
1740

Cornelius Vanderburgh
1685

Myer Myers
1775

John W. Forbes
1833

Garret Eoff
1825

John Kitts
1845

CUPS

John Coney
1700

Simeon Soumaine
1710

John Coney
1710

Henricus Boelen
1730

Isaac Anthony
1730

Philip Syng
1730

Samuel Minott
1770

Paul Revere
1792

William Gale
1830

BURNETT & RYDER 1795
Philadelphia, Pa.

ALBERT CHAPIN BURR 1806-1832
Rochester, N. Y., 1826 until 1832. Apprenticed to Erastus Cook.

CHRISTOPHER A. BURR 1810
Providence, R. I., at 73 North Main Street; 42 Westminster Road, 1824.

CORNELIUS A. BURR 1816-1863
Rochester, N. Y., 1838-1850, continued his brother's business. Son of General Timothy Burr and his Wife, Mary Chapin. Married Mary L. Lyon in 1847. Died in Brooklyn. Firm of C. A. Burr & Co.

EZEKIEL BURR 1765-1846
Providence, R. I., 1793. Born, April 14, 1765, son of Ezekiel and Elsie Whipple Burr. Married Lydia Yates, July 9, 1786. Located with brother William, South of the Baptist Meeting House. Advertised at 5 Benefit Street, 1822. Of the firm of Burr & Lee, 1815.

NATHANIEL BURR 1780
Fairfield, Conn.

WILLIAM BURR 1793
Providence, R. I., advertised with brother Ezekiel, January 3, 1793, *United States Chronicle,* "Informs the public that they carry on the business of gold and silversmiths in its various branches, a few doors south of the Baptist Meeting House, and directly opposite Capt. Richard Jackson's, where they have for sale; silver spoons of different kinds and sizes, gold necklaces and a variety of plated buckles."

SAMUEL BURRILL 1704-1740
Boston, Mass., 1733.

BENJAMIN BURT 1729-1805
Boston, Mass., 1750 on Fish Street. Son of John Burt. Married, Joan Hooten. Purchased silversmith's tools from widow of Zachariah Brigden. Estate appraised at $4788.52.

JOHN BURT 1691-1745
Boston, Mass., 1712. Son of William and Elizabeth Burt. Married, Abigail Cheever. Father of silversmiths, William, Samuel and Benjamin. His estate was valued at £ 6460.

SAMUEL BURT 1724-1754
Boston, Mass., 1750. Son of John Burt. Married, Elizabeth White; later Elizabeth Kent of Newbury.

WILLIAM BURT 1726-1752
Boston, Mass., 1747. Son of John Burt. Married, Mary Glidden.

BENJAMIN BUSSEY 1757-1842
Dedham, Mass., 1778.

THOMAS D. BUSSEY 1773-1804
Baltimore, Md., 1792. Directory, 1796-1803.

CHARLES P. BUTLER 1765-1858
Charleston, S. C., at King Street, 1790-1802. Born in Boston, Mass.

JAMES BUTLER   1713-1776
Boston, Mass., 1734. Married (1) Elizabeth Davie, (2) Sarah Wakefield. Captain of Militia, 1748.

BUTLER & McCARTY   1850
Philadelphia, Pa., at 105 North Second Street.

BUTLER, WISE & CO.   1842
Philadelphia, Pa .

JAMES BYRNE   1784
Philadelphia, Pa., advertised, *Carey's Penna. Herald,* January 25, 1785; "Jeweller and Silversmith, East side of Front Street, three doors above Chestnut-street. Acknowledges with gratitude the kind encouragement he has received since his commencement in business; and begs leave to inform his friends and the public, that he has now for sale the following articles, which will be found on trial equal to any in this city." In New York at Fly Market until 1797.

THOMAS BYRNES   1766-1798
Wilmington, Del., 1793. Son of Joshua and Ruth Woodcock Byrnes. Apprenticed to Bancroft Woodcock. Married, Sarah Pancoast, July 10, 1795. Advertised in *Delaware Gazette.*

C

ALEXANDER CAMERON   1813
Albany, N. Y., until 1834.

ELIAS CAMP   1825
Bridgeport, Conn.

CHRISTOPHER CAMPBELL   1808
New York, at 394 Greenwich Street, 43 Hudson and 41 Roosevelt Streets, until 1812.

JOHN CAMPBELL   1829
Fayetteville, N. C. Advertised, *Carolina Observer,* 1831. Of firm of Selph & Campbell; Campbell & Prior.

ROBERT CAMPBELL   1799-1872
Baltimore, Md., 1819 on Market Street. Firm of Richards & Campbell.

R. & A. CAMPBELL   1835
Baltimore, Md. Robert and Andrew worked until 1854.

THOMAS CAMPBELL   1800
New York, 1800. Philadelphia in 1828.

L. B. CANDEE & CO.   1830
Woodbury, Conn.

CHARLES CANDELL   1795
New York at 19 Cliff Street.

CANFIELD & HALL 1800
Middletown, Conn.

SAMUEL CANFIELD 1780
Middletown, Conn. Advertised until 1797. Sheriff, 1787. Firm of Canfield & Foot. Last in New York.

GEORGE CANNON 1767-1835
Warwick, R. I., 1800. Advertised in *The Inquirer.* 1825-1835 in Nantucket, Mass.

J. CAPELLE 1850
St. Louis, Mo.

WILLIAM CARIO 1721-1809
Boston, Mass., 1738, advertised in *Boston Gazette,* "Shop at South-end of the Town, over against The White Swan. " In Portsmouth, N. H., before 1748. Married Abigail Peavey, 1759; Lydia Coxcroft, April 16, 1768. In New Market until 1790. Died in Newfields in 1809. House still standing.

GEORGE CARLETON 1810
New York.

ABRAHAM CARLISLE 1791
Philadelphia, Pa., Census List. Advertised, 1791-1794 at Brooks Court and North Front Street.

JOHN CARMAN 1771
Philadelphia, Pa. Advertised, *Penna. Journal,* August 22, 1771; "Goldsmith and Jeweller. At the Golden Lion, corner of Second and Chestnut Streets." In Kingston, N. Y., 1774-1775.

CHARLES CARPENTER 1790
Norwich, Conn.

JOSEPH CARPENTER 1747-1804
Norwich, Conn., 1775. Married Eunice Fitch, 1795. Advertised in Canterbury, 1797, and returned to Norwich, 1804.

JOHN & DANIEL CARREL 1785
Philadelphia, Pa. Advertised, *Penna. Evening Herald,* February 5, 1785, "Two doors above the Old Coffee House, on Market Street."

WILLIAM CARRINGTON 1830
Charleston, S. C. Died 1901.

THOMAS CARSON 1815
Albany, N. Y., until 1850. Member of the Albany Mechanic's Society. Partner of Green Hall, 1813-1818.

CARSON & HALL 1810
Albany, N. Y. Thomas Carson and Green Hall dissolved partnership in 1818.

LEWIS CARY 1798-1834
Boston, Mass., 1815. Apprenticed to Churchill & Treadwell. Member of the Massachusetts Charitable Mechanic's Association, 1828. Had many apprentices.

GIDEON CASEY   1726-1786
Warwick, R. I., 1763. Son of Samuel and Dorcas Ellis Casey. In partnership with
brother Samuel in 1753. Married, Jane Roberts, July 31, 1747; Elizabeth Johnson,
May 11, 1760.

SAMUEL CASEY   1723-1773
South Kingstown, R. I., 1750. Notice in *Boston News Letter*, October 1, 1764.
"His house at South Kingstown, R. I., was destroyed by fire, including 'Drugs,
Medicines, etc.' . . . occasioned by a large Fire being kept the Day preceding in
his Goldsmith's Forge."

STEPHEN CASTAN & CO.   1819
Philadelphia, Pa.

THOMAS CHADWICK & HEIMS   1815
Albany, N. Y.

JAMES CHALMERS   1749
Annapolis, Md. Advertised in *Maryland Gazette*, March 19, 1752. "Removed into
South-East Street." Advertised until 1768. Was innkeeper in conjunction with
goldsmith business.

JOHN CHAMPLIN   1745-1800
New London, Conn., 1768, advertised until 1780.

STEPHEN CHANDLER   1812
New York at Chatham Square; Hester Street in 1823.

ALBERT CHAPIN BURR   1820
Rochester, N. Y., until 1832.

CHARTERS, CANN & DUNN   1850
New York at 53 Mercer Street.

CHAUDRON & CO.   1807
Philadelphia, Pa., at 12 South Third Street until 1811.

CHAUDRON & RASCH   1812
Philadelphia, Pa. Simon Chaudrons and Anthony Rasch at Third Street.

JOHN HATCH CHEDELL   1806-1875
Auburn, N. Y., 1827. Apprenticed to William Nichols of Cooperstown in 1820.

GEORGE K. CHILDS   1828
Philadelphia, Pa., at 34 Dock Street.

PETER CHITRY   1814
New York at White and Elm Streets; Burrows and Henry Streets, 1820-1825.
Formerly of Philadelphia.

EBENEZER CHITTENDEN   1726-1812
New Haven, Conn., 1765. Born in Madison. In partnership with son-in-law,
Abel Buel, 1770. Associated with Eli Whitney, inventor of the cotton gin. Warden
of Trinity Church.

JOSEPH CHURCH   1794-1876
Hartford, Conn., 1815. Apprenticed to Jacob Sargent and Horace Goodwin. Shop
at Ferry Street in 1818. Sold business to C. C. Strong and L. T. Wells, former
apprentices. Frederick E. Church, the landscape painter, was his son.

CHURCH & ROGERS 1825

Hartford, Conn., on Main Street, partnership of Joseph Church and William Rogers.

JESSE CHURCHILL 1773-1819

Boston, Mass., 1795, at 88 Newbury Street until 1810. Member of Massachusetts Charitable Mechanics Association, 1810. Firm of Churchill & Treadwell.

CHURCHILL & TREADWELL 1805

Boston, Mass. Partnership dissolved in 1813. Hazen and Moses Morse, Lewis Cary, and Benjamin Bailey served apprenticeships to this firm.

A. L. CLAPP 1802

New York.

F. H. CLARK & CO. 1850

Memphis, Tenn.

GABRIEL D. CLARK 1813-1896

Baltimore, Md., at Calvert and Water Streets, 1830.

GEORGE C. CLARK 1824

Providence, R. I., at 27 Cheapside Street until 1847. In partnership with Jabez Gorham, Christopher Burr, William Hadwen and Henry Mumford, for five years.

I. CLARK 1754

Boston, Mass.

I. & H. CLARK 1821

Portsmouth, N. H.

J. H. CLARK 1815

New York.

JOSEPH CLARK 1791

Danbury, Conn., shop located near the Printing Office. Served in Revolution in 1777. In Newburgh, N. Y., 1811. Died in Alabama, 1821.

LEVI CLARK 1801-1875

Norwalk, Conn., 1825. Born in Danbury. Apprenticed to father-in-law, John S. Starr Blackman.

LEWIS W. CLARK 1832

Watertown, N. Y., 1832-1836; Utica, N. Y., until 1838.

CLARK, PELLETREAU & UPSON 1823

Charleston, S. C.

THOMAS CLARK 1725-1781

Boston, Mass., 1764, advertised on South side of the Court House.

WILLIAM CLARK 1750-1798

New Milford, Conn., 1775. Born in Colchester. One of the founders of the Union Library, 1796.

CLARK & ANTHONY 1790

New York.

CLARK & BROTHER 1825
Norwalk, Conn.

CLARK & PELLETREAU 1819
New York.

JONATHAN CLARKE 1705-1770
Newport, R. I., 1734, later of Providence.

AARON CLEVELAND 1820
Norwich, Conn.

BENJAMIN CLEVELAND 1767-1837
Newark, N. J., 1800.

WILLIAM CLEVELAND 1770-1837
Norwich. Conn., 1791. Born in Norwich. Apprenticed to Thomas Harland. Partner of John P. Trott. 1792. Married Margaret Falley, 1793. Returned from New York. Was Deacon in First Congregational Church in 1812. His son, Richard, was father of President Cleveland. In Worthington, Salem, Mass., also Zanesville, Ohio. Died in Little Rock, N. Y. Firm of Cleveland & Post.

CLEVELAND & POST 1815
Norwich, Conn., William Cleveland and Samuel Post.

JOHN CLUET 1725
Kingston, N. Y. Also near Albany, probably Fonda or Schenectady. Of the firm Van Sanford & Cluet.

ISAAC D. CLUSTER 1850
St. Louis, Mo.

C. COEN & CO. 1810
New York.

DANIEL BLOOM COEN 1787
New York at 31 Maiden Lane until 1805. Married Deborah Ogilvie, niece of John Ogilvie, silversmith. Also spelled Coan.

EPHRAIM COBB 1708-1777
Plymouth, Mass., 1735. Married Hannah Allen.

JOHN COBURN 1725-1803
Boston, Mass., 1750, "at head of Town Dock." *Boston News Letter.* Married, 1765, (1) Elizabeth Greenleaf, (2) Catharine Vans, daughter of first Dutch citizen of Boston. Shop in King Street. Sergeant of artillery in 1752. Town Warden and Census Taker. Died in Boston.

JOHN CODDINGTON 1690-1743
Newport, R. I., 1712. Son of Nathaniel and Susanna Hutchinson Coddington. Married, May 23, 1715. Member of the House of Deputies, 1721-1729. Sheriff, 1733-5. Colonel of Militia. Mentioned as goldsmith in will.

COE & UPTON 1840
New York.

HENRY COGSWELL   1846
Salem, Mass., until 1853.

THOMAS COHEN   1814
Chillicothe, Ohio.

E. COIT   1825
Norwich, Conn. Died 1839.

COIT & MANSFIELD   1816
Norwich, Conn. Thomas C. Coit and Elisha H. Mansfield dissolved partnership
in 1819.

THOMAS CHESTER COIT   1791-1841
Norwich, Conn., 1812. Learned trade in Canterbury. Partner of Elisha H. Mansfield,
1816-1819. In Natchez, Miss., 1826. Died in New York. Firm of Clark & Coit.

ALBERT COLE   1844
New York at 6 Little Green Street.

EBENEZER COLE   1818
New York at 96 Reade Street.

BENJAMIN COLEMAN   1795
Burlington, N. J.

C. C. COLEMAN   1835
Burlington, N. J.

NATHANIEL COLEMAN   1765-1842
Burlington, N. J., 1790. Apprenticed to James Roe of Kingston for seven years
until 1783. Member of the Society of Friends. Married, Elizabeth Lippincott, 1791.

SAMUEL COLEMAN   1805
Burlington, N. J. Son of Thomas and Elizabeth Coleman. Married Elizabeth
Hampton, daughter of Benjamin and Ann Hampton of Wrightstown, Pa., June 6,
1807.

SIMEON COLEY   1767
New York. Advertised, *New York Gazette,* March 16, 1767, "Goldsmith from
London at Shop near the Merchants Coffee House." Dissolved partnership with
William Coley, 1766. After a public meeting charging Coley with daring infrac-
tions of the Non-importation Agreement, Coley advertised that he intends to leave
the city in 1769.

WILLIAM COLEY   1767
New York. Notice of partnership dissolved with Simeon Coley, September 11,
1766. Listed at 191 Washington Street, 1801; 64 Ann Street, 1804.

THOMAS COLGAN   1771
New York. Apprenticed to Thomas Hamersley, 1764.

ARNOLD COLLINS   1690
Newport, R. I. Married (1) in 1690, (2) Amy Ward, 1692. Received commission
to make Seal of Colony, "Anchor and Hope," in 1702. Contributed to building
the Baptist Church, 1729. Proprietor of Common Council. Died, 1735.

SELDEN COLLINS, JR.   1819-1885
Utica, N. Y., directory, 1837-1850.

COLLINS & JOHN W. FORBES   1825
New York.

COLTON & COLLINS   1825
New York.

DEMAS COLTON, JR.   1826
New York.

JOHN CONEY   1655-1722
Boston, Mass., 1676. Son of John and Elizabeth (Nash) Coney, born January 5. Married three times, Sarah Blackman, second wife, 1683, Mary Atwater Clark, Widow of Captain John Clark, November 8, 1694. Located in 1688 at Court Street, 1699 near Town Dock, 1717 at Ann Street. Died August 20, wife, Mary, administered his estate. Notice in *Boston Gazette*, November 5/12, 1722. "This Evening the remaining part of the Tools of the late Mr. Coney are to be sold."

T. CONLYN   1845
Philadelphia, Pa.

J. CONNING   1840
Mobile, Ala.

JOHN H. CONNOR   1835
New York at 6 Little Green Street. Firm of Eoff & Connor.

RICHARD CONYERS   1688
Boston, Mass. Willed tools to his apprentice, Thomas Millner, 1708.

BENJAMIN E. COOK   1825
Northampton, Mass. Born 1803. Partner of Nathan Storrs, 1833. Later Troy, N. Y.

ERASTUS COOK   1793-1864
Rochester, N. Y., 1815-1864.

JOHN COOK   1795
New York at 51 Ann Street; 236 Broadway, 1806. Boston, Mass., Directory 1813. Firm of Cook & Co.

JOSEPH COOK   1785
Philadelphia, Pa. Advertised, until 1795, at his "Ware-House on Second Street". Located on Third and Market Streets where he offers a large and general assortment at the Federal Manufactory and European Repository, for 15 s per ounze. In *Penna. Packet,* July 8, 1795, "Wanted immediately, Journeymen Goldsmiths, Small-workers, and other Mechanics. Foreman to instruct apprentices, and do every duty incumbent, shall receive a handsome salary for his services, with board and lodging in the house." Also spelled Cooke.

OLIVER B. COOLEY   1828
Utica, N. Y. Died 1844.

JOSEPH COOLIDGE, JR.   1747-1821
Boston, Mass., 1770. Advertised, "Shop located opposite Mr. William Greenleaf, Foot of Cornhill." *Boston News Letter*. Mentioned as, "one of the Boston Tea Party." Merchant in Directory 1789.

SPOUT CUPS

John Coney
1700

Jacob Boelen
1710

Jeremiah Dummer
1700

Allen & Edwards
1710

John Coburn
1760

John Coney
1715

PITCHERS

Paul Revere
1800

William Thompson
1815

Ebenezer Moulton
1811

Isaac Hutton
1800

John Crawford
1825

William Forbes
1835

B. & J. COOPER 1810
New York.

FRANCIS W. COOPER 1846
New York at 102 Reade Street.

COOPER & FISHER 1850
New York.

JOSEPH COPP 1757
New London, Conn. Married, Rachael Dennison in 1757. Advertised shop was entered by burglars in 1776.

CHRISTIAN CORNELIUS 1810
Philadelphia, Pa., at 8 Pewter Platter Alley until 1819.

WALTER CORNELL 1780
Providence, R. I.

JACQUES W. CORTELYOU 1781-1822
New Brunswick, N. J., 1805. Born June 16. Married Rachael Van Harlingen. Died of typhus fever, December 8.

LOUIS COUVERTIE 1822
New Orleans, La., at 29 St. Peter, below Royal Street.

JOHN COVERLY 1766
Boston, Massachusetts.

THOMAS COVERLY 1760
Newport, Rhode Island.

WILLIAM D. COWAN 1808
Philadelphia, Pa., at 10 German Street.

WILLIAM COWELL 1682-1736
Boston, Mass., 1703. Advertised as a "Goldsmith." *Boston News Letter,* August 3, 1736. Married Elizabeth Lilby. Retired shortly after son finished apprenticeship to become an innholder. Estate was appraised by Jacob Hurd.

WILLIAM COWELL, JR. 1713-1761
Boston, Mass., 1734. Continued father's business on his retirement. Advertised in *Boston News Letter,* 1741; and *Boston Gazette,* 1761. Samuel Edwards and William Simpkins, silversmiths, appraised his estate.

RALPH COWLES 1840
Cleveland, Ohio.

J. & I. COX & CLARK 1831
New York, until 1833.

JOHN & JAMES COX 1817
New York at 15 Maiden Lane until 1853.

JOHN CRAWFORD 1815
New York until 1820, at 92 John Street; Philadelphia, in 1837.

NEWTON E. CRITTENDEN   1826-1872
Cleveland, Ohio, 1847.

JONATHAN CROSBY   1764
Boston, Mass. Born in 1743. In directory at Fish Street, 1796.

WILLIAM CROSS   1695
Boston, Mass. Born 1658 in London, son of English minister. Apprenticed to
Abraham Hind, at Sign of Golden Bell, Fenchurch Street, London.

I. B. CURRAN   1835
Ithaca, N. Y.

EDMUND M. CURRIER   1830
Salem, Mass.

CURRIER & TROTT   1836
Boston, Mass., at 139 Washington Street.

JOHN CURRY   1831
Philadelphia, Pa., at 72 Chestnut Street. Firm of Curry & Preston.

CURRY & PRESTON   1831
Philadelphia, Pa., at 72 Chestnut Street.

CURTIS, CANDEE & STILES   1831
Woodbury, Conn.

LEWIS CURTIS   1774-1845
Farmington, Conn., 1797. Born in Coventry. Apprenticed to Daniel Burnap. Adver-
tised his shop was robbed in 1797. Removed to St. Charles, Mo., 1820. Died at
Hazel Green, Wis.

CURTIS & DUNNING   1828
Woodbury, Conn.

CURTIS & STILES   1835
Woodbury, Conn.

A. CUTLER   1842
Boston, Mass.

EBEN CUTLER   1846
Boston, Mass.

D

PHILLIP DALLY   1779
New York at 59 Queen Street in 1787. Son of John Dally, shipwright. Married
Charity Hunt, July 27, 1779. Partner of Jabez Halsey.

PEYTON DANA   1800-1849
Providence, R. I., 1821.

THOMAS DANE   1723-1796
Boston, Mass., 1745.

JOHN DARBY   1801
Charleston, S. C., at 10 Beaufair Street; at 27 Archdale Street, 1831.

JOHN F. DARROW   1818
Catskill, N. Y.

JONATHAN DAVENPORT   1789
Baltimore, Md., until 1793 when listed in Philadelphia.

JOHN DAVID   1736-1794
Philadelphia, Pa., 1763. Son of Peter with whom he worked. Advertised in
Penna. Gazette, at Second Street corner of Chestnut, near Drawbridge, in 1772.

JOHN DAVID, JR.   1785
Philadelphia, Pa., at 928 South Front Street. Partner of Daniel Dupuy, 1792-1805.

PETER DAVID   1691-1755
Philadelphia, Pa., 1730. Advertised, "Goldsmith, . . . in Front Street. . . ."
American Weekly Mercury, April, 1739. Born in New York, son of John,
Huguenot refugee. Married Jeanne Dupuy and removed to Philadelphia. Adver-
tised, 1738 and 1750 at Second Street. Married Margaret Parham, July 28, 1753.
Died, October 21, 1755.

EDWARD DAVIS   1775
Newburyport, Mass. Died, 1781.

ELIAS DAVIS   1805
Boston, Mass., at 11 Union Street, to 1825.

JOSHUA G. DAVIS   1796
Boston, Mass., until 1840.

DAVIS, PALMER & CO.   1842
Boston, Mass., directory 1846.

SAMUEL DAVIS   1801
Plymouth, Mass. In Boston, at Marlboro Street, 1807. Directory until 1842.

THOMAS ASPINWALL DAVIS   1825
Boston, Mass., until 1830.

DAVIS, WATSON & CO.   1820
Boston, Mass. Partners, Samuel Davis, Edward Watson, Bartlett M. Bramhill.

DAVIS & BROWN   1809
Boston, Mass., until 1820.

DAVIS & WATSON   1815
Boston, Mass.

CHARLES DAVIDSON   1805
Norwich, Conn. Son of Brazillai.

JOHN DAY   1820
Boston, Mass., to 1825.

JAMES DECKER 1833
Troy, N. Y., to 1848.

DE FOREST & CO. 1827
New York.

JABEZ DELANO 1763-1848
New Bedford, Mass., 1784.

JOHN DeLARUE 1822
New Orleans, La.

ANDREW DEMILT 1805
New York.

JOHN DENISE 1798
New York.

JOHN & TUNIS DENISE 1798
New York.

DENNIS & FITCH 1836
New York.

OTTO PAUL DePARISIEN 1763
New York, advertised, April 25, *New York Gazette:* "Goldsmith from Berlin, makes all sorts of plate, plain and chased, in the neatest and most expeditious manner; likewise undertakes chasing any piece of old plate at his House, the lower end of Batto-Street." Admitted Freeman, January 31, 1764. Notices, 1765, 1769. In 1774 "Silversmith, in the Fly, in this City, took Fire by means of his furnace." Located in Dock Street, later at Queen Street, 1787-1789. Son, Otto W., joined business. Commissioned by Corporation Council of the city to make a gold box, for which he was paid £ 32/18/16.

OTTO PAUL DePARISIEN & SON 1789
New York at 60 Queen Street until 1791.

PIETER DeRIEMER 1738-1814
New York, 1763. Baptised in the Dutch Reformed Church, January 23, 1739, son of Steenwyck and his wife Catharine Roosevelt. Married Elsie Babbington, May 10, 1763. Freeman, January 31, 1769. Probably apprenticed to his grandfather Nicholas Roosevelt. In Poughkeepsie, 1796-1809. Died, October 2, 1814, in Hyde Park.

DANIEL DESHON 1697-1781
New London, Conn., 1730. Born in Norwich. Apprenticed to René Grignon who willed him his tools. Completed his service with John Gray. Married Ruth Christophers.

JOHN DEVERELL 1764-1813
Boston, Mass., 1785.

MICHAEL DeYOUNG 1816
Baltimore, Md., until 1836.

AARON DIKEMAN 1824
New York.

G. E. DISBROW 1825
New York.

ISAAC DIXON 1843
Philadelphia, Pa.

JOHN DIXWELL 1680-1725
Boston, Mass., 1710. Born in New Haven, Conn., son of Col. John; (one of the Judges of Charles I of England. The regicide fled to the Colony where he married). Married three times. One of the founders and officers of the North Church. Son Basil, 1711-1746 was a silversmith. Mentioned and advertised in *Boston News Letter*, 1713 and 1722.

JOSHUA DOANE 1740
Providence, R. I. Died 1753.

EZEKIEL DODGE 1792
New York at 31 Little Dock Street.

JOHN DODGE 1818
Catskill, N. Y., 1818-1819.

NEHEMIAH DODGE 1795
Providence, R. I., advertised a shop near the Church, where he makes and sells all kinds of smith's work. Located at 41 Benefit Street in 1824.

SERIL DODGE 1765-1803
Providence, R. I., 1793, February 21, *United States Chronicle;* "At the sign of the Arm and Gold Ear-ring, at his new shop opposite the Market, . . . offers a great variety of goldsmith's and jewelry ware."

D. N. DOLE 1810
Newburyport, Mass.

J. DOLL 1820
New York, 1820.

AMOS DOOLITTLE 1754-1832
New Haven, Conn., 1780. Born in Cheshire. Apprenticed to Eliakim Hitchcock. Silversmith and engraver. Died in New Hampshire.

JOSHUA DORSEY 1793
Philadelphia, Pa., at 22 North Third Street and 44 Market Street; 14 Green Street until 1804. Brother of Samuel.

ROBERT DOUGLAS 1740-1796
New London, Conn., 1766, at shop next door to Capt. Hurlbuts. Served in Revolutionary War. Died in Canterbury.

JEREMOTT WILLIAM DOUGLASS 1790
Philadelphia, Pa., at 257 South Front Street until 1793.

GEORGE CHRISTOPHER DOWIG 1765
Philadelphia, Pa., at Second Street. Advertised, *Maryland Gazette;* July 7, 1789; "Having fully determined upon quitting the Business of a Silversmith, purposes to dispose of his remaining Stock in Trade by Lottery, which will positively be the last." In Market Street, Baltimore, until 1791.

G. R. DOWNING   1810
New York.

DOWNING & BALDWIN   1832
New York.

DOWNING & PHELPS   1810
Newark, N. J.

JOSEPH DRAPER   1825
Wilmington, Del., at 77 Market Street. Succeeded by Emmor Jefferis in 1832.

T. P. DROWN   1803
Portsmouth, N. H. Son of Samuel Drown. Advertised until 1816.

BENJAMIN DROWNE   1759-17)3
Portsmouth, N. H., 1780. Brother of Samuel.

SAMUEL DROWNE   1749-1815
Portsmouth, N. H., 1770.

ABRAHAM DUBOIS   1777
Philadelphia, Pa., advertised May 20th, *Penna. Evening Post;* "For sale at his
house in Second Street, four doors below Arch Street. . . ." Listed at 65 North
Second Street, 1785-1807. Admitted sons to business in 1805.

JOSEPH DUBOIS   1790
New York at 17 Great Dock Street and 81 John Street until 1797.

PHILO DUBOIS   1842
Buffalo, N. Y., until 1848.

TUNIS D. DUBOIS   1797
New York, at 90 John Street, 11 Pearl Street in 1799.

JAMES DUFFEL   1790
Georgetown, S. C., until 1800. In New York at 349 Pearl Street, 1801.

DUHME & CO.   1839
Cincinnati, Ohio.

JEREMIAH DUMMER   1645-1718
Boston, Mass., 1666. Born, September 14, 1645, son of Richard and Frances Burr
Dummer. Apprenticed to Hull & Sanderson. Married Hannah Atwater, sister of
John Coney's wife, in 1672. Was a member of the Old South Church. Later joined
the First Church and became a Deacon. Freeman, April 21, 1679. Appointed
Captain of Artillery Company, 1679-80. Constable, 1675. Justice of Peace, 1693-
1718. Owned interests in eleven ships, 1697-1713. Died in Boston, May 24, 1718.

JOHN BAPTISTE DUMOUTET   1761-1813
Philadelphia, Pa., 1793 at 71 Elm Street, 79 North Third Street, 1796, 55-57
South Second Street, 1800-1816. In Charleston, S. C. later.

DUNBAR & BANGS   1850
Worcester, Mass.

CARY DUNN   1765

New York. Freeman. Advertised, *New York Gazette,* March, 1770, "Shop, between New Dutch Church and the Fly Market." Listed at Maiden Lane and William Street, 1786. Dunn & Sons, 1787-1791. Member of the Gold and Silversmith's Society. In Morristown, 1778; Newark, N. J., 1782.

BARNARD DUPUY   1828

Raleigh, N. C. Advertised, *The Star,* 1833-1840, as silversmith on Fayetteville Street.

DANIEL DUPUY   1719-1807

Philadelphia, Pa., 1745. Born in New York, April 3, son of Dr. John Dupuy and Anne Chardavoine. Apprenticed to brother-in-law Peter David. Married, Eleanor Cox, September 6, 1746. Advertised for custom until, 1780, "Shop below Friends Meeting House in Second Street." Two sons, John and Daniel in business, 1792-1805. Memorandum book covers his life, 1740-1807.

DANIEL DUPUY, JR.   1753-1826

Philadelphia, Pa., 1785. Born, May 3. Married Mary Meredith, June 5, 1788. Advertised at 16 South Second Street, 1782-1812. Partner with brother John. Died in Daly, Pa.

DANIEL DUPUY & SONS   1784

Philadelphia, Pa., with sons, Daniel and John, at 114 Sassafras Street.

WILLIAM B. DURGIN   1850

Concord, N. H.

W. C. DUSENBURY   1819

New York until 1835.

DANIEL DUYCKINCK   1798

New York at 75 Fair and 10 Dutch Streets until 1800.

TIMOTHY DWIGHT   1654-1692

Boston, Mass., 1675. Born in Dedham. Apprenticed to John Hull. William Rouse and Thomas Savage appraised his estate.

E

SETH EASTMAN   1820

Concord, N. H.

JAMES EASTON   1807-1903

Nantucket, Mass., 1828. Born in Providence. Apprenticed to William Hadwen from whom he purchased the business. Married Sarah C. Wyer. Delegate to the Constitutional Convention. Died, February 20. Firm of Easton & Sanford.

NATHANIEL EASTON   1815

Nantucket, Mass.

EASTON & SANFORD   1830

Nantucket, Mass., James Easton and Frederick C. Sanford, advertised in *The Inquirer,* April 10, 1830. Located in 1833 at 62 Main Street. Partnership dissolved, May 1, 1838.

JAMES B. EATON
Boston, Mass. Directory 1805-1809. Charleston, S. C., 1829.

1805

TIMOTHY EATON
Philadelphia, Pa., at 9 Cherry Street.

1793

THOMAS STEVENS EAYRES
Boston, Mass., 1785. Apprentice and son-in-law of Paul Revere. In Worcester, 1791-1793.

1760-1803

JOHN EDWARDS
Boston, Mass., 1691. Born in Limehouse, England. Came to Boston with father in 1688. Married Sybil Newmann, 1700, later Abigail Fowle. Was Sergeant of the Artillery Company, 1704. Held town offices until 1727. Notice, *Boston Evening Post*, April 14, 1746, "John Edwards, goldsmith, 'a Gentleman of a very fair Character and well respected by all that knew him,' died April 8, 1746, aged 75 years." Sons, Thomas, Samuel, and grandson Joseph Jr., were silversmiths.

1671-1746

JOSEPH EDWARDS, JR.
Boston, Mass., 1758. Advertised, *Boston News Letter*, March 21, 1765, "whereas the shop of the Subscriber was last Night broke open and the following Articles stolen, viz: . . . Whoever will make Discovery of the Thief or Thieves, so that they may be brought to Justice, and that I may recover my Goods again, shall receive TWENTY DOLLARS Reward, and all necessary Charges paid by Joseph Edwards, Jun'r."

1737-1783

SAMUEL EDWARDS
Boston, Mass., 1729. Son of John. Married Sarah Smith, October 4, 1733. Received commissions from General Assembly for presentation pieces. Appointed Assessor, 1760. "Esteemed as a Man of Integrity." Sold property to R. Boyleston in 1742. Estate administered by brother Joseph.

1705-1762

THOMAS EDWARDS
Boston, Mass., 1725. Son of John. Freeman of New York, May 25, 1731. Married, Sarah Burr, November 20, 1723. Advertised 1747. Captain of Artillery Company. His wife Sarah, executrix of estate.

1701-1755

ALFRED ELDERKIN
Windham, Conn., 1792. Born in Killingworth. Partner of Elderkin & Staniford, dissolved in 1792. In Red Hook, N. Y.

1759-1833

JEREMIAH ELFRETH, JR.
Philadelphia, Pa., 1752. Son of Jeremiah and Sarah Oldman Elfreth. Married Hannah Trotter, August 27, 1752. Advertised at North Second Street.

1723-1765

GEORGE ELLIOTT
Wilmington, Del., 1835, when he purchased the shop of Charles Canby to whom he was apprenticed.

1810-1852

PETER ELLISTON
New York at Vesey Street; 187 Broadway, 1795-1800.

1791

JOHN AARON ELLIOTT
Sharon, Conn. Born 1788.

1815

BOWLS

Cornelius Kierstede
1710

Jacob Hurd
1738

Cornelius Vander Burgh
1690

William Homes
1763

Samuel Bowne
1790

PORRINGERS

Peter Van Dyke
1715

Hull & Sanderson
1660

Benjamin Burt
1760

Jan Van Nieukirke
1715

Johannis Nys
1715

Andrew Billings
1775

Tobias Stoutenburgh
1740

John B. Jones
1815

STEPHEN EMERY   1752-1801
Boston, Mass., 1775. Married 1777. Mentioned with Joseph Loring in Selectmen's Records in 1788. Located at 5 Union Street, 1789; Fish Street, 1796.

THOMAS KNOX EMERY   1781-1815
Boston, Mass., 1802. Son of Stephen. Married Mary Parker. Member of the Massachusetts Mechanics Association, 1806. At 32 Ann Street in 1813. Joseph Foster and Jesse Churchill appraised his estate.

EDGAR M. EOFF   1850
New York at 83 Duane Street.

GARRET EOFF   1779-1858
New York, 1806. Born, August 29, 1779, son of Garret and Sarah Heyer Eoff. Apprenticed to Abraham G. Forbes until 1798. Advertised at 39 Warren Street and 23 Elm Street until 1814; at 3 New Street in 1819. Of the firms, Eoff & Howell, Eoff & Connor, Eoff & Phyfe, Eoff & Moore.

EOFF & CONNOR   1833
New York.

EOFF & HOWELL   1805
New York at 2 Wall Street.

EOFF & MOORE   1835
New York at 51 Morton Street.

EOFF & PHYFE   1844
New York at 5 Dey Street.

EOFF & SHEPHERD   1825
New York.

EOLLES & DAY   1825
Hartford, Conn.

HENRY ERWIN   1817
Philadelphia, Pa., at 191 South Second Street; 33 North Third Street, 1824.

JAMES ERWIN   1809
Baltimore, Md. In New York in 1815 at 200 Church Street.

HENRY EVANS   1820
New York.

ROBERT EVANS   1768-1812
Boston, Mass., 1798. Married Mary Peabody. Died intestate. Rufus Farnam, administrated estate and Hazen Morse listed as one of the appraisers.

JOHN EWAN   1786-1852
Charleston, S. C., 1823.

WILLIAM H. EWAN   1849
Charleston, S. C.

JAMES EYLAND   1795-1835
Charleston, S. C., 1820.

F

JOSEPH FAIRCHILD
1824

New Haven, Conn.

ROBERT FAIRCHILD
1740

Durham, Conn., 1740, where he learned and practiced his trade, at the corner of Church and Chapel Streets. Represented the Town in the General Assembly, 1739-1745. Auditor of the Colony, 1740. Appointed Captain of Artillery Company, in 1745. Returned to Stratford, 1747, where he was born, 1703; New Haven, 1772.

ROBERT FAIRCHILD, Jr.
1738-1794

New York, 1775. Died in New York, November 15, 1794.

CHARLES FARIS
1764-1800

Annapolis, Md., 1793. Son of William and Priscilla Woodward Faris. Advertised in *Maryland Gazette*, September 12, 1793, ". . . at Church Street, where he opened a Shop." In 1799 elected Councilman.

WILLIAM FARIS
1728-1804

Annapolis, Md., 1757, March 7, advertised his shop near the Church. His account records and book of designs, 1773-1804, are interesting.

CHARLES FARLEY
1812

Portland, Me. Partner of Eleazer Wyer, 1828-1832.

HENRY FARNAM
1799

Boston, Mass. Born in Norwich, Conn., 1773. Apprenticed with brother Rufus to Joseph Carpenter. Advertised until 1833.

RUFUS FARNAM
1796

Boston, Mass. Born in Norwich, Conn., 1769. Served apprentice with brother Henry to Joseph Carpenter. Advertised until 1833. Firm of Farnam & Ward.

RUFUS & HENRY FARNAM
1807

Boston, Mass. He and his brother apprenticed to Joseph Carpenter. Later located in Hanover, N. H.

THOMAS FARNAM
1825

Boston, Mass., at 87 Washington Street, 1825. Directory until 1830. Son of Rufus.

FARNAM & WARD
1816

Boston, Mass.

JOHN C. FARR
1824

Philadelphia, Pa., until 1840.

FARRINGTON & HUNNEWELL
1837

Boston, Mass. John Farrington and George W. Hunnewell at 8 William's Court; at 4 Court Avenue in 1850.

JOHN W. FAULKNER
1835

New York, N. Y.

ABRAHAM FELLOWS   1786-1851
Troy, N. Y., 1809. Born in Rhinebeck, N. Y. Son of Philip Fellows and his wife Hannah Milledoler. Member of Trojan Greens in War of 1812, for which he received grant of 160 acres of land. Sold business to Dennis & Fitch. In Albany, 1841-1844. Died in Buffalo.

I. W. & J. K. FELLOWS   1834
Lowell, Mass. Ignatius W. and James K. Fellows.

JAMES K. FELLOWS   1832
Lowell, Mass., at Merriman Street until 1834.

FELLOWS & STORM   1839
New York.

J. S. FELT   1825
Portland, Me.

FENNO & HALE   1840
Bangor, Me.

ZIBA FERRIS   1786-1875
Wilmington, Del., 1810, opened a shop at corner of Fourth and Market Streets where he continued until 1860. Taught son, Ziba, Jr., and Thomas Megar.

PETER FEURT   1703-1737
Boston, Mass., 1732,and New York.

PETER FIELD, JR.   1805
New York. Directory until 1837.

GEORGE FIELDING   1731
New York, Freeman, April 13, 1731. Notice appears in *New York Gazette*, November 17, 1755. ". . . Mr. Fielding, Gold-Smith, formerly lived at corner of Broad and Princes Streets. . . ." In Albany in 1765.

J. P. FIRENG   1810
Burlington, N. J.

THOMAS FISHER   1797
Philadelphia, Pa., at German Street; Baltimore and Forest Streets in 1803.

DENNIS M. FITCH   1840
Troy, N. Y.

JAMES FITCH   1821
Auburn, N. Y., until 1826. Firm of Graves & Fitch, 1816-1821.

JOHN FITCH   1743-1798
Trenton, N. J., 1774. Born in Hartford, Conn. Married Lucy Roberts, December, 1767. Account book records employment of seven silversmiths, James Greaves, John Wilson, John Cochran, Joseph Toy, James Wilson, Frederick Burgy and Samuel Stout. Shop on King Street until 1776. Traveled to Northwest and engraved a map of the territory. In New York in 1782.

JOHN FITE   1810
Baltimore, Md.

JOSIAH FLAGG 1765
Boston, Mass.

FLETCHER & GARDINER 1809
Boston, Mass., Directory until 1810; Philadelphia, Pa., 1815. Thomas Fletcher and Sidney Gardiner at Third and Chestnut Streets until 1822.

THOMAS FLETCHER 1813
Philadelphia, Pa., at Chestnut and Fourth Street until 1850. Firms of Fletcher & Gardiner, Fletcher & Bennett.

ABRAHAM GERRITZE FORBES 1769
New York. Freeman. Married Jane Young, May 17, 1789. Located at 75 Bowery Lane, 1790; 118 Broadway, 1795. Marshal of the city, 1799.

COLIN V. G. FORBES 1816
New York at 72 Gold Street; Collect and Pump Streets in 1823.

COLIN V. G. FORBES & SON 1835
New York at 59 Vandam Street.

COLIN & JOHN W. FORBES 1825
New York.

GARRET FORBES 1808
New York at 316 Broadway. Joined with William G. Forbes at 90 Broadway, 1805-1809. Advertised in 1820 as a weigher and silversmith.

JOHN W. FORBES 1802
New York at 415 Pearl Street; various addresses on Broadway. Was Government measurer and weigher, in 1835.

WILLIAM FORBES 1830
New York at 2 Green Street; 277 Spring Street in 1850.

WILLIAM G. FORBES 1773
New York. Freeman, February 3. Married Catharine Van Gelder. Member of the Gold and Silver Smith's Society, 1786. Listed at 88 Broadway until 1789. Joined the Mechanic's Institute in 1802. At 90 Broadway with Garret Forbes, 1805-1809.

JABEZ W. FORCE 1819
New York at 1 Staple Street.

SAMUEL FORD 1797
Philadelphia, Pa., at 39 Arch Street. Married Eleanor Ford, 1802, in Baltimore, Md. Advertised at Green and Charles Street, 1802-1803.

GEORGE B. FOSTER 1838
Salem, Mass., Boston, 1842-1854.

JOHN FOSTER 1811
New York at 189 William Street; 53 Pearl Street, 1815. Partner of Thomas Richards.

JOSEPH FOSTER 1760-1839
Boston, Mass., 1785. Apprenticed to Benjamin Burt. Deacon of the Old South Church. Advertised at 171 Ann Street and later at Fish Street.

NATHANIEL & THOMAS FOSTER   1820
Newburyport, Mass., at 21 State Street until 1823.

THOMAS FOSTER   1820
Newburyport, Mass., at 21 State Street, until 1823.

FOSTER & RICHARDS   1815
New York. John Foster and Thomas Richards.

LOUIS FOURNIQUET   1795
New York, at 53 Ann Street until 1798; 42 William Street, 1800-1823. Firm of
Fourniquet & Wheatley.

NATHANIEL FRANCIS   1804
New York at 55 John Street; 79 Fulton Street in 1819.

GEORGE FRANCISCUS   1776
Baltimore, Md. Married Margaret Schley. Member of the Ancient and Honorable
Mechanical Society. His son, George Jr., continued the business at 4 Market Place
and other addresses until 1818. Died 1791.

GEORGE FRANCISCUS, JR.   1810
Baltimore, Md. Son of George and Margaret Franciscus. Continued his father's
business at 4 Market Street until 1818.

JACOB FRANK   1793
Philadelphia, Pa., at Front Street between Market and Arch Streets.

FREEMAN & WALLIN   1850
Philadelphia, Pa.

BENJAMIN C. FROBISHER   1792-1862
Boston, Mass., 1836, at 69 Washington Street.

FROST & MUMFORD   1815
Providence, R. I.

DANIEL CHRISTIAN FUETER   1754
New York. Listed on the register at Goldsmith's Hall, London, England, "Dan.
Christ. Fueter, Chelsea, next door to the 'Man in the Moon'," December 8, 1753.
Advertised in New York, May 27, 1754, "Near the Brew-house, facing Oswego
Market." In 1763 returned to City and located in Dock Street. In 1769 with son
Lewis Fueter who continued after father returned to Switzerland.

LEWIS FUETER   1770
New York. Freeman, March 28, 1775, son of Daniel C. Fueter, advertised in the
New York Gazette, ". . . at the Coffee-House Bridge . . . guilding in all its
branches. . . . He thinks himself obliged, in the name of his father, as well as
for himself, to return thanks to the respectable public for the many favours done,
and to assure those who shall honor him with their commands, that he will make
it his utmost endeavor to deserve their Countenance and encouragement." Queen
Street in 1774.

G

GREENBURY GAITHER   1822
Washington, D. C.

JOHN L. GALE 1819
New York at 177 William Street.

WILLIAM GALE 1799-1867
New York at Green Street, 1820; 29 Liberty Street until 1825. His son William joined him in 1823. Firms of Gale & Stickler, Gale, Wood & Hughes, Gale & Hayden, Gale & Willis, Gale & Mosely.

WILLIAM GALE, JR. 1825
New York.

WILLIAM GALE & SON 1823
New York at 63 Liberty Street; 116 Fulton Street, 1850.

GALE & HAYDEN 1846
Charleston, S. C.

GALE & MOSELY 1830
New York at 116 Fulton Street.

GALE & STICKLER 1823
New York at 104 Broadway.

GALE & WILLIS 1840
New York.

GALE, WOOD & HUGHES 1830
New York. Founded by William Gale, Jacob Wood and Jasper W. Hughes, at 116 Fulton Street. Charles Wood and Stephen T. Fraprie became apprentices. Dissolved in 1845 with retirement of Gale.

BALDWIN GARDINER 1814
Philadelphia, Pa., at Chestnut and Third Streets. Firm of Fletcher & Gardiner of New York.

B. GARDINER & CO. 1836
New York.

JOHN GARDNER 1734-1776
New London, Conn., 1760. Son of Jonathan and Mary Gardner. Inventory of estate lists silversmith's tools.

S. GARRE 1825
New York.

ELIAKIM GARRETSON 1785
Wilmington, Del. Married Lydia Windle, 1783.

PHILIP GARRETT 1811
Philadelphia, Pa., at High Street.

THOMAS C. GARRETT 1829
Philadelphia, Pa., until 1840.

J. GASKINS 1830
Norfolk, Va.

W. W. GASKINS   1806
Norfolk, Va.

JAMES GEDDES   1760
Williamsburg, Va. Son of James Geddy, gunsmith, whose house he occupied after
his father died in 1743. Advertised as a Goldsmith, Silversmith and Jeweller.
Notice appeared in the *Virginia Gazette,* ". . . objection of his Shop's being too
high up Town, . . . the Walk may be thought rather an amusement than a Fatigue."

JOSEPH GEE   1785
Philadelphia, Pa. Advertised in 1788.

NICHOLAS GEFFROY   1761-1839
Newport, R. I., 1795.

GEORGE S. GELSTON   1833
New York at 189 Broadway until 1836. Firms of Gelston & Co., Gelston &
Treadwell, Gelston, Ladd & Co.

HUGH GELSTON   1794-1873
Baltimore, Md., 1816. Married Rebecca G. Durham. In partnership with James
Gould.

GELSTON, LADD & CO.   1836
New York.

GELSTON & CO.   1837
New York.

GELSTON & TREADWELL   1836
New York.

JOHN D. GERMON   1782
Philadelphia, Pa. Advertised, *Independent Gazetteer,* July 13, 1782, for a "runaway
negro." Mentioned with Joseph Gee as a standard bearer in the Federal Procession
in Philadelphia in 1788. Located at 33 North 3rd Street until 1804; Quay Street
until 1816.

TIMOTHY GERRISH   1753-1813
Portsmouth, N. H., 1775.

GERRISH & PEARSON   1800
New York.

JOHN W. GETHEN   1811
Philadelphia, Pa., at 170 South Front Street, until 1818.

WILLIAM GETHEN   1797
Philadelphia, Pa., at 14 Combes Alley; 172 South Front Street, 1806-8.

PETER GETZ   1782
Lancaster, Pa. Self taught mechanic of singular ingenuity. Mentioned for office of
Chief Coiner for the Mint in 1792.

CAESAR GHISELIN 1670-1734

Philadelphia, Pa., 1700. French Huguenot naturalized in London, September 29, 1698. In Philadelphia in 1701 from record of William Penn's account book, until 1711. Married Catherine Reverdy. Warden of St. Anne's Church, Annapolis, Md., April 19, 1720. John Steele, goldsmith, left him £ 100 in his will, dated January 20, 1721. Died in Philadelphia, February 13, 1733.

WILLIAM GHISELIN 1751

Philadelphia, Pa. Son of Nicholas and grandson of Caesar Ghiselin. Advertised in *Penna. Gazette,* November, 1751. "Goldsmith, is removed from his late dwelling house in Second Street . . . to the house a little below the Church, in second St. where he continues Business as usual."

JOHN GIBBS 1790

Providence, R. I. Business continued by his wife, Eliza Gibbs, in partnership with brother-in-law and apprentice, in 1798, year of death.

MICHAEL GIBNEY 1844

New York at 1 Trinity Place.

WILLIAM GIBSON 1845

Philadelphia, Pa., at Third and Plum Streets.

CHRISTOPHER GIFFING 1815

New York at 64 Partition Street; Chapel Street, 1819-1825.

E. GIFFORD 1825

Fall River, Mass.

SAMUEL GILBERT 1798

Hebron, Conn.

WILLIAM W. GILBERT 1767

New York. Married Catharine Cosine, May 28, 1767. Notice that shop was robbed of near £ 200, in plate, August 27, 1770. City Alderman of West Ward, 1783-1788. Elected State Senator, 1809. Died 1818.

CALEB GILL 1774-1855

Hingham, Mass., 1798. Born August 14. Apprentice to Loring Bailey. Married Katy Beal, 1798. Selectman for many years. Advertised shop on South Street. Died in July, 1855.

BENJAMIN CLARK GILMAN 1784

Exeter, N. H. Born 1763, son of John and Jane Deane Gilman.

JOHN WARD GILMAN 1771-1823

Exeter, N. H., 1792.

JOHN B. GINOCHIO 1837

New York.

D. GODDARD & CO. 1850

Worcester, Mass.

D. GODDARD & SON 1845

Worcester, Mass.

TEAPOTS

John Coney
1710

Unmarked
1700

Peter Van Dyke
1710

Jacob Hurd
1730

Myer Myers
1750

Elias Boudinot
1750

Joseph and Nathaniel Richardson
1775

Daniel Van Voorhis
1790

TEAPOTS

Paul Revere
1785

Philip Dally
1790

William G. Forbes
1800

Paul Revere
1790

William B. Heyer
1815

Thomas Fletcher
1835

PHILIP GOELET   1708-1748
New York. Freeman, May 25, 1731. Baptized February 1, son of Jacobus and
Jannette Coussar Goelet. Married Catharina Boelen, March 28, 1730. Member of
the Dutch Church, February 17, 1730. Was Assessor, Collector and Constable of
the West Ward. Died before April 4, 1748, date of proving of will.

JOSEPH GOLDTHWAITE   1706-1780
Boston, Mass., 1731, when notice of removal from "Mr. Burrill's shop to the
House adjoining the Sign of the Red Lyon." Married February 8, 1727, Martha
Lewis. In 1730, First Sergeant of Artillery Company. In 1745 appointed Captain
in siege of Lewisburg. Constable in 1744. Died in Weston, Mass., March 1780.

D. T. GOODHUE   1840
Boston, Mass.

JOHN GOODHUE   1822
Salem, Mass. to 1855.

HENRY GOODING   1820
Boston, Mass., until 1854.

JOSIAH GOODING   1840
Boston, Mass., directory until 1859.

BENJAMIN GOODWIN   1756
Boston, Mass.

H. & A. GOODWIN   1811
Hartford, Conn.

GOODWIN & DODD   1812
Hartford, Conn. Horace Goodwin and Dodd.

ALEXANDER S. GORDON   1795
New York, at 40 William Street until 1800.

GEORGE GORDON   1800
Newburgh, N. Y., until 1824.

JABEZ GORHAM   1815
Providence, R. I. Born 1792. Apprenticed to Nehemiah Dodge, 1807. Attaining
his majority joined in partnership with Christopher Burr, William Hawden,
George C. Clark, and Henry G. Mumford for five years. Firms of Gorham & Beebe,
1825, Gorham & Webster, 1831-1841. Located at 12 Steeple Street with son,
founding the Gorham Manufacturing Co.

JABEZ GORHAM & SON   1842
Providence, R. I., at 12 Steeple Street.

MILES GORHAM   1757-1847
New Haven, Conn., 1790.

GORHAM & THURBER   1850
Providence, R. I.

GORHAM & WEBSTER   1831
Providence, R. I.

GORHAM, WEBSTER & PRICE 1835
Providence, R. I.

JAMES GOUGH 1769
New York.

JAMES GOULD 1816
Baltimore, Md., at Market Street, 1816-1821. Son of Josiah and Abigail Williams Gould. Married Eliza Leech. Apprenticed to Jabez Baldwin. Removed to Boston, Mass. In partnerships with Hugh Gelston, later A. Stowell, Jr., and William H. Ward. Died in Boston, 1874.

GOULD & WARD 1850
Baltimore, Md.

WILLIAM GOWDEY 1757
Charleston, S. C. Advertised "Imported English Goods", 1763. Member of South Carolina Society. Died 1798.

WILLIAM GOWEN 1777
Medford, Mass. Born in Charlestown, Mass., September 13, 1749. Married Eleanor Cutler, April 29, 1772.

THOMAS GRANT 1731-1804
Marblehead, Mass., 1754. Married Margaret Burbier, July 2, 1754.

WILLIAM GRANT, JR. 1785
Philadelphia, Pa., at 115 North Third Street; at Green and Third Streets, 1798-1814. Listed in directory, "Goldsmith, deaf and dumb, but can read and write."

G. GRAY 1839
Portsmouth, N. H.

JOHN GRAY 1692-1720
Boston, Mass., 1713. Near Old South Meeting House in 1717. Advertised settlement of brother Samuel's estate. Married Mary Christophers, in 1714. Later in New London, Conn.

ROBERT GRAY 1830
Portsmouth, N. H. Died in 1850.

SAMUEL GRAY 1684-1713
New London, Conn., 1710. Born in Boston, Mass. Brother of John. Married Mrs. Lucy Palmers, 1707.

SAMUEL GRAY 1732
Boston, Mass. Purchased land for shop, 1732, deed witnessed by William Simpkins and Basil Dixwell.

GREGG, HAYDEN & CO. 1846
Charleston, S. C., until 1852.

BENJAMIN GREENE 1712-1776
Boston, Mass., 1733. Worked with brother Rufus.

RUFUS GREEN 1707-1777
Boston, Mass., 1730. Married Catharine Stambridge in 1731. Advertised, *Boston News Letter,* 1733, "Stolen, a spoon, marked with the Crest of Tyger's Head."

DAVID GREENLEAF 1737-1800
Norwich, Conn., 1763. Born in Bolton, Mass. Apprenticed to Rufus Lathrop.
Married Mary Johnson. Served in Revolutionary War. In Coventry, 1778-1800,
where he died.

DAVID GREENLEAF, Jr. 1765-1835
Hartford, Conn., 1788. Born in Norwich, Conn. Married Nancy Jones, 1787.
Advertised, Northeast of State House. Partner of Abel Buel, 1798.

PETER GRIFFEN 1825
New York.

GRIFFEN & HOYT 1830
New York.

GRIFFEN & SON 1832
New York.

DAVID GRIFFETH 1768
Portsmouth, N. H.

WILLIAM GRIGG 1765
New York. Freeman, October 1. Married Helena Stout, September 29, 1766.
In Albany, 1770-1778. Returned to New York, 1791-5, at Maiden Lane and
William Street. Died 1797.

RENE GRIGNON 1691
Oxford, Mass. Huguenot silversmith who settled in Greenwich; Boston, 1696,
became an Elder in the French Church. Left Deerfield because of Massacre of 1704.
In Norwich, 1708,where he died in 1715. Inventory of his estate lists silversmith's
tools which he willed to Daniel Deshon.

WILLIAM GRISWOLD 1820
Middletown, Conn.

FREDERICK EDWARD GUINAUD 1814
Baltimore, Md.

ENOS GUNN 1792
Waterbury, Conn. Born in Guntown in 1770.

WILLIAM GURLEY 1804
Norwich, Conn. Born in Mansfield, 1764.

BENJAMIN GURNEE 1820
New York at 98 Reade Street; at 125 Church Street, 1835. Firm of Gurnee & Co.

JAMES GUTHRE 1796-1877
Wilmington, Del. Advertised in *The American Watchman,* 1822, "Gold and
Silversmithing. The subscriber, James Guthre, having purchased the stock of G. J.
Wolf, continues the Gold and Silver business at the same stand, No. 41 Market
Street; Come Friends and the Public, Come look at my Ware. Both Silver and Gold
I have plenty to spare. And such an Assortment I constantly keep, That for Cash
I can always supply you cheap."

GUTHRE & JEFFERIS 1840
Wilmington, Del.

H

HADDOCK, LINCOLN & FOSS 1850
Boston, Mass.

WILLIAM HADWEN 1791-1862
Nantucket, Mass., 1820. Born in Newport. Married Eunice Starbuck, 1822. Active until 1828, when he was succeeded by his apprentice, James Easton.

NELSON HAIGHT 1839
Newburgh, N. Y., until 1852.

ABRAHAM B. HALL 1806
Geneva, N. Y., until 1839.

CHARLES HALL 1742-1783
Lancaster, Penna., 1765, advertised, *Penna. Gazette*, July 4, "Goldsmith, in Lancaster. . . ." In 1777, ". . . Stolen out of a window . . . Four Silver Tea Spoons and a Cream Jug, having no other mark than the maker's name, C. H." In 1779, "Stolen . . . Eight Silver table spoons stamped on the handle C. Hall . . . a flower on the back of the bowl." Brother of David Hall.

DAVID HALL 1765
Philadelphia, Pa., advertised in Second Street. Clerk of the "Heart and Hand Fire Company". Continued as silversmith and merchant until he died, 1779.

JOSEPH HALL 1781
Albany, N. Y. Purchased freedom in 1781.

HALL & ELTON 1841
Geneva, N. Y.

HALL & HEWSON 1828
Albany, N. Y. until 1847.

HALL, HEWSON & BROWER 1850
Albany, N. Y.

HALL & MERRIMAN 1825
New Haven, Conn.

JABEZ HALSEY 1762-1820
New York, 1789 at 58 Queen Street; at 105 Liberty Street, 1795. Firm of Dally & Halsey.

BENJAMIN HALSTED 1764
New York. Freeman. Born 1734, son of John Halsted and his wife Susannah Blanchard. Advertised 1766 in partnership with brother Matthias. Elizabethtown, N. J. Notice appears in *New York Gazette*, same year. Married Sarah Tredwell, October 22, 1765. Member of the Gold and Silversmith's society, 1786. Advertised at Maiden Lane and Nassau Street, 1786-1789; 67 Broad Street, 1795-1805. Admitted son to business, 1799.

JAMES HAMILL 1816
New York at 200 Church Street. Firm of Hamill & Co.

WILLIAM HAMLIN
1772-1869

Providence, R. I., 1795. Born 1772 in Middletown, Conn. Apprenticed in Middletown, where he opened shop and established a business.

THOMAS HAMMERSLEY
1756

New York. Born 1727. Advertised in the *New York Gazette;* in 1757, removed from the Change in Dock Street to Hanover Square. Married Sarah Colgan, 1761. Last notice, 1764.

JOHN HANCOCK
1732-1784

Boston, Mass., 1760. Born in Charlestown, Mass., October 10. Married Martha Sparhawk, November 20, 1760. Died Maryland, 1772.

W. W. HANNAH
1840

Hudson, N. Y., until 1848.

GEORGE HANNERS
1697-1740

Boston, Mass., 1720. Married Rebecca Pierson. Taught his son, George Jr. the trade. Advertised, *Boston News Letter,* July 11, 1720; "Goldsmith, at his House at the Dock-Head. . . ." Died in Boston, estate appraised at £ 2670.

GEORGE HANNERS, JR.
1721-1760

Boston, Mass., 1744. Married Sarah Foster.

J. HANSELL
1825

Valley Forge, Pa.

NEWELL HARDING
1796-1862

Boston, Mass., 1822. Apprentice and brother-in-law of Hazen Morse. Introduced power in rolling of silver. Member of the Massachusetts Charitable Mechanics Association, 1830. Ward & Rich bought the business in 1832.

N. HARDING & CO.
1842

Boston, Mass.

STEPHEN HARDY
1781-1843

Portsmouth, N. H., 1805. Married Mary B. Hill, daughter of Daniel Hill. Sold land in new fields to William Cario in 1790.

THOMAS HARLAND
1735-1807

Norwich, Conn., 1775. Born in England where he learned his trade. Emigrated and settled in Norwich, 1773. Married Hannah Clark in 1779. Last advertised in 1796.

HARRIS & STANWOOD
1842

Boston, Mass.

HARRIS & WILCOX
1844

Troy, N. Y. Directory, 1847-1850.

ELIPHAZ HART
1789-1866

Norwich, Conn., 1810. Born in New Britain. Worked with brother Judah. Died in Norwich.

JONATHAN HART
1810

Canandaigua, N. Y., until 1815.

JUDAH HART   1777-1824
Middletown, Conn., 1799. Born in New Britain. Partner of Charles Brewer, 1800-
1803. Worked with Jonathan Bliss until he removed to Norwich, 1805, and leased
a shop with Alvin Willcox, until 1807. Griswold, 1816; Brownsville, Ohio, 1822.

WILLIAM HART   1818
Philadelphia, Pa., at 19 North Third Street. Later Baltimore, Md.

HART & BREWER   1800
Middletown, Conn., Judah Hart and Charles Brewer, until 1803.

HART & SMITH   1815
Baltimore, Md., at 100 Baltimore Street.

HART & WILCOX   1805
Norwich, Conn. Leased shop of Abel Brewster until 1807.

ALEXANDER R. HASCY   1835
Albany, N. Y., until 1850.

IRA HASELTON   1821
Portsmouth, N. H., directory until 1827.

JOHN HASTIER   1726
New York. Freeman, 1726. Advertised, *New York Journal,* 1735, in Queen Street.
Notice appears, 1739, of counterfeiters whom he apprehended. Last, 1758, May 15,
New York Gazette, "Run away on Monday last from John Hastier, of this City,
Goldsmith, a lusty well-set Negro Man named Jasper. . . ."

MARQUETTE HASTIER   1771
New York.

B. B. HASTINGS   1835
Cleveland, Ohio, until 1846.

H. HASTINGS   1815
Ohio.

SAMUEL HAUGH   1675-1717
Boston, Mass., 1696. Apprenticed to Thomas Savage in 1690.

WILLIAM HAVERSTICK   1781
Philadelphia, Pa., advertised in Second Street, between Arch and Race Streets.
Listed at 76 North Second Street, 1791-1793.

NATHANIEL HAYDEN   1805-1875
Charleston, S. C., 1832. Born in Connecticut. Firm of Eyland & Hayden.

HAYDEN & GREGG   1838
Charleston, S. C. Nathaniel Hayden and William Gregg dissolved in 1863.

PETER P. HAYES   1788-1842
Poughkeepsie, N. Y., 1826-1842.

HAYES & ADRIANCE   1816
Poughkeepsie, N. Y., until 1826. Peter P. Hayes and John Adriance.

HAYS & MYERS   1770
New York. Andrew Hays and Myer Myers.

JOSEPH HEAD   1798
Philadelphia, Pa., at Lombard and Seventh Streets.

J. S. HEALD   1810
Baltimore, Md.

JOHN HEATH   1761
New York. Freeman, March 3. Married Edith Pell, October 18, 1760. Advertised,
The New York Mercury, January 3, 1763, ". . . Goldsmith, in Wall Street."

LEWIS HECK   1760
Lancaster, Pa.

DAVID HEDGES, Jr.   1779-1856
Easthampton, N. Y., 1810. Born June 14. "House and Shop next Door, South of
Clinton Academy, East Hampton." Colonel in Militia. Represented Suffolk County
in the Assembly, 1825-33. Supervisor, 1812-1814.

NATHANIEL HELME   1761-1789
Little Rest, R. I., 1782. Son of Judge James and Esther Powell Helme, born
December 24, in South Kingston. Died November 19.

DANIEL HENCHMAN   1730-1775
Boston, Mass., 1753. Son of Rev. Nathaniel. Married Elizabeth, daughter of Jacob
Hurd. Advertised June 12, 1773, *New England Chronicle,* ". . . And as his work
has hitherto met with the Approbation of the most curious, he flatters himself that
he shall have the Preference by those who are Judges of Work, to those Strangers
among us who import and sell English Plate to the great Hurt and Prejudice of the
Townsmen who have been bred to the Business. Said Henchman will make any
kind of Plate they want equal in Goodness and Cheaper than any they can import
from London, with the greatest Dispatch." Nathaniel Hurd, Daniel Boyer and
Zachariah Brigden appraised his estate.

A. A. HENDERSON   1837
Philadelphia, Pa.

ADAM HENDERSON   1794-1859
Poughkeepsie, N. Y., 1837.

AHASUERUS HENDRICKS   1678
New York. Also Albany. Swore allegiance to the King in 1675. Married Neeltje
Jans, widow of Adam Oncklebag in 1676. Taxed for owning property in 1677.
Appointed to report on water supply of City, 1686. Constable of the North Ward
in 1687. Freeman in 1698. Died 1727.

CHARLES HEQUEMBOURGH, Jr.   1788-1875
New Haven, Conn., 1810. Son of Charles and Mercy Cook Hequembourgh. Married Mehitable Emery Fabian Morse, October 11, 1810. Sergeant in War of 1812-
1814. Advertised on Church Street 1809-1820. Located in various cities. Justice of
Peace in St. Louis, Mo. Died in Webster Groves, Mo., August 17, 1875.

WILLIAM HEURTIN 1731
New York. Freeman, April 6, 1731. Married Susannah Sibylla, daughter of Rev. Joshua and Sibylla Charlotta Kocherthal. Child baptized before 1729. Mentioned with John Moulinar in Dutch Reformed Church controversy. Died intestate in Newark, N. J., before 1765, wife appointed administrator.

ABRAHAM HEWS, JR. 1823
Boston, Mass.

HEYDORN & IMLAY 1810
Hartford, Conn.

WILLIAM BRAISTED HEYER 1776-1827
New York, 1798. Married Sarah Hackstaff, July 23, 1810. Advertised 1808, May 7, *American Citizen,* "Dissolution of Partnership with J. L. Gale, Jr." Served in War of 1812, to December 3, 1814, in Capt. John V. B. Varrick's Company. Listed at 47 Warren Street until 1827.

HEYER & GALE 1807
New York at 29 Park Street, dissolved 1807 by William B. Heyer and John L. Gale.

HIGBIE & CROSBY 1820
Boston, Mass.

JAMES HILL 1770
Boston, Mass. Claimed the house of Nathaniel Austin for a loss in 1775. Estate sold in 1798 when lien was cancelled in 1799.

WILLIAM F. HILL 1810
Boston, Mass.

BENJAMIN HILLER 1687-1745
Boston, Mass., 1711. Married Elizabeth Russell. Witnessed deed for John Coney, 1709. Connected with Artillery Company, 1716. Deacon of Church in 1719.

D. B. HINDMAN & CO. 1833
Philadelphia, Pa., until 1837.

HORACE HINSDALE 1782-1858
New York at 146 Broadway, 1805 to 1807. Later Newark, N. J. In partnership with John Taylor. Later, firm of Palmer & Hinsdale.

HINSDALE & ATKIN 1836
New York.

ELIAKIM HITCHCOCK 1726-1788
New Haven, Conn., 1757, also of Cheshire. Advertised in 1776. Member of the Second Company of Governor's Foot Guard.

JOSHUA HOBART 1810
New Haven, Conn., at Crown Street. Removed to Boston. Worked with Allen Fitch.

NATHAN HOBBS 1792-1868
Boston, Mass., 1815 at 1 Dock Street, and other addresses until 1850.

JOHN HODGE 1800
Hadley, Mass.

COFFEE POTS

Peter Van Dyke
1715

Edward Winslow
1700

John Burt
1735

Philip Syng
1765

David Hall
1760

Samuel Williamson
1790

HOT WATER KETTLES AND STANDS, CHAFING DISH, DISH CROSS

Cornelius Kierstede
1710

Joseph Richardson
1760

Adrian Bancker
1725

Samuel Tingley
1765

JAMES M. HOFFMAN 1820
Philadelphia, Pa.

LITTLETON HOLLAND 1770-1847
Baltimore, Md., 1800, at 217 Baltimore Street.

WILLIAM HOLLINGSHEAD 1754
Philadelphia, Pa. Advertised, *Penna. Gazette,* until 1774. Listed corner of Arch
and Second Streets until 1785.

JULIUS HOLLISTER 1818-1905
Oswego, N. Y., 1846.

ROBERT HOLLOWAY 1822
Baltimore, Md., at 115 High Street.

ADRIAN B. HOLMES 1801
New York at Church Street until 1830.

E. HOLSEY 1820
Philadelphia, Pa.

WILLIAM HOMES 1717-1783
Boston, Mass., 1739. Married Rebecca Dawes, July 14, 1733. Mentioned as Master
Goldsmith, 1739. Advertised in *Boston Gazette.* 1759, ". . . near the Draw-
Bridge. . . ." Held public offices, Warden, Grain Purchaser. Justice of the Town.
Captain of Artillery Company.

WILLIAM HOMES, Jr. 1742-1825
Boston, Mass., 1783. Worked in father's shop. Married Elizabeth Whitwell.
Advertised at Ann Street, 1789-1813. Spelled Holmes in directory, in 1796.

EDWARD HOLYOKE 1817
Boston, Mass., directory until 1825. Mentioned in Thomas Revere's estate.

HOOD & TOBEY 1849
Albany, N. Y.

JOSEPH W. HOPKINS 1730-1801
Waterbury, Conn., 1760, opened shop where he also practiced law. Appointed
Judge of the Probate Court.

STEPHEN HOPKINS 1721-1796
Waterbury, Conn., 1745.

HARLEY HOSFORD 1820
New York at 103 Fulton Street.

DAVID HOTCHKISS 1848
Syracuse, N. Y.

HOULTON & BROWNE 1799
Baltimore, Md., at 123 Baltimore Street.

HOULTON, OTTO & FALK 1797
Philadelphia, Pa.

GEORGE C. HOWE 1825
New York.

G. C. HOWE & CO. 1837
New York.

JAMES HOWELL 1802
Philadelphia, Pa., at 27 Key's Alley until 1804; 50 South Front Street, 1807.

J. HOWELL & CO. 1810
Philadelphia, Pa.

PAUL HOWELL 1810
New York at 34 George Street to 1812.

SILAS W. HOWELL 1798
Albany, N. Y. Advertised, *Albany Register,* December 10, "Tea cadys, tea trays, waiters, spoons, etc. at his shop opposite City Hall, Court Street." Firm of Howell & Arnold. Removed to New Brunswick, N. J.

GEORGE B. HOYT 1830
Albany, N. Y., 1830-1850, at 35 Market Street, later 395 Broadway. Firms of Hoyt & Kippen, Boyd & Hoyt.

HENRY E. HOYT 1820
New York at 121 Cherry Street.

S. HOYT 1817
New York.

S. HOYT & CO. 1842
New York.

CHRISTOPHER HUGHES 1744-1824
Baltimore, Md., 1771. Married Peggy Sanderson, 1779. Advertised partnership with John Cornan. *Maryland Journal,* 1774. Portrait painted by Charles Willson Peale.

EDMUND HUGHES 1804
Middletown, Conn. In partnership with John Ward. Firms of Hughes & Bliss, Hughes & Francis, 1807-1809.

JEREMIAH HUGHES 1783-1848
Annapolis, Md., 1805. Married Priscilla Jacob, 1807. After 1820 became editor of *Maryland Republican.*

WILLIAM HUGHES 1744-1791
Baltimore, Md., 1785. In *Maryland Journal,* until 1791, "From Dublin, Ireland, after seventeen years, located at corner of Market & Calvert Streets, Goldsmith and Jeweller."

PHILIP HULBEART 1750
Philadelphia, Pa., advertised in *Penna. Gazette,* November, 1761. Notice, 1764, "the estate of the deceased, P. Hulbeart."

JOHN HULL   1624-1683

Boston, Mass., 1645. Born in Market Harboro, Leicestershire, England, 1624.
In Boston, 1635. Married Judith Quincy, May 11, 1647. Freeman, May 2, 1649.
A Founder of the First Church in Boston. In his diary he records, "After a little
keeping at school I was taken to help my father plant corn, which I attended to
for several years together; and then by God's good hand I fell to learning by help
of my brother and to practice the trade of goldsmith. In 1652, the General Court
ordered a mint to be set up, and they made choice of me for that employment,
and I choose my friend Robert Sanderson to be my partner, to which the Court
assented. In 1659, 1st of May, I received in my house Jeremie Dummer and Samuel
Paddy, to serve me as apprentices for eight years. In 1673, I accepted Samuel Clark,
as an apprentice for eight years." Held many responsible offices, 1652-1678. Died
in Boston, October 1, 1683.

HULL & SANDERSON   1652

Boston, Mass. See John Hull and Robert Sanderson.

RICHARD HUMPHREYS   1772

Philadelphia, Pa., from Wilmington, Delaware, 1771. Notice in 1772, *Penna.
Packet,* (signed by Philip Syng) ". . . recommends him as a person qualified to
serve them on the best terms, and whose fidelity in the above business will engage
their future confidence and regard." Advertised until October 31, 1781, selections
of silver and jewellery. Listed at 54 High Street, 1786-1791.

PHILIP HUNTINGTON   1770-1825

Norwich, Conn., 1795. Married Theophila Grist, 1796. Town Clerk, 1801-1823.

RICHARD HUNTINGTON   1823

Utica, N. Y., until 1850. Born 1786.

S. HUNTINGTON   1850

Portland, Me.

BENJAMIN HURD   1739-1781

Boston, Mass., 1760. Son of Jacob and Elizabeth Mason. Married Priscilla Crafts,
1774. Brother-in-law of Daniel Henchman. Received estate from brother Nathaniel.

JACOB HURD   1702-1758

Boston, Mass., 1723. Son of John and Elizabeth Tufts Hurd, born in Charlestown,
February 12. Married Elizabeth Mason, May 20, 1725. Constable of City in 1736.
Member of the Ancient and Honorable Artillery Company, 1743. Advertised, near
the Town House and in Pudding Lane. Died in Roxbury where he retired in 1755.
Father of Benjamin and Nathaniel. Estate was appraised by Samuel Edwards and
William Simpkins.

NATHANIEL HURD   1729-1777

Boston, Mass., 1755. Son of Jacob and Elizabeth Mason Hurd. Attended Latin
School in 1738. Was Clerk of the Market, 1759-1761; Scavanger in Ninth Ward,
1760-1. Advertised, 1765-6.

HENRY HURST   1665-1717

Boston, Mass., 1690. Married Mary Billings. Estate appraised by John Dixwell
and Thomas Millner.

STEPHEN HUSSEY   1818

Easton, Md. Advertised, *Republican Star,* July 7, "Stephen Hussey, Gold and
Silversmith, Respectfully informs the Citizens of Easton, that he has taken the shop
lately occupied by William Needles, where he intends carrying on the business
in their various branches with punctuality, neatness and dispatch."

JACOB HUTCHINS 1774
New York.

NICHOLAS HUTCHINS 1777-1845
Baltimore, Md., 1810, at 1 Water Street until 1829. Married Suzanna Ayres, 1816.

SAMUEL HUTCHINSON 1828
Philadelphia, Pa., to 1839.

ISAAC HUTTON 1767-1855
Albany, N. Y., 1790. Son of George and Anna Maria Viele Hutton. Probably apprenticed to John Folsom. Purchased house on Market and Water Streets, September, 1791. Was prominent citizen, elected to public offices, occupied important positions; Treasurer of Albany Mechanics Society, 1793. Married Margaret Lynott, 1797. In partnership with younger brother until he retired in 1817.

JOHN STRANGEWAYS HUTTON 1720
New York. Freeman, November 8. Married Elizabeth Van Dyke, May 25, 1729.

GEORGE HUYLER 1819
New York.

HYDE & GOODWICH 1830
New Orleans, La.

HYDE & NEVINS 1815
New York, until 1819.

HENRY HYMAN 1799
Lexington, Ky., advertised in *Stewart's Kentucky Herald.*

I

JOHN INCH 1721-1763
Annapolis, Md., 1745. Advertised, *Maryland Gazette;* "Removed from South East St. to the House on the Point near the Guns. N.B. The said Inch has taken out License, and keeps a good Entertainment for Man & Horse: He sells Punch every day, and also retails rum, Wine, Cyder, etc." December 13, 1749. "He has likewise to sell, Ten Proved good swivel guns (planted near his House ever since the News of the Surrender of Fort Duquesne) with a Quantity of Shot to fit them." March 8, 1759. Notice, "Monday Morning last Died here, aged 42 years, Mr. John Inch, Goldsmith of this City, and Yesterday his Funeral was solemnized in a very decent Manner being attended by a Procession of the Brethren of the Lodge, properly Cloath'd and a great number of others." March 17, 1763. His widow, Jane Inch, administered estate and continued the business.

J

JACCARD & CO. 1850
St. Louis, Mo.

A. JACKSON 1840
Norwalk, Conn.

DANIEL JACKSON 1782
New York.

JOHN JACKSON   1731
New York. Freeman, April 6.

JOSEPH JACKSON   1803
Baltimore, Md., at 13 South Street. Married Mary Robinson. Last record on
Harrison Street until 1813.

GEORGE JACOB   1775-1846
Baltimore, Md., 1802.

ABEL JACOBS   1816
Philadelphia, Pa.

A. JACOBS & CO.   1820
Philadelphia, Pa.

MUNSON JARVIS   1742-1825
Stamford, Conn., 1765. Advertised as silversmith and ironmonger. As a loyalist
his shop was confiscated in 1783, when he removed to St. Johns, N. B.

HENRY J. JAVAIN   1835
Charleston, S. C., in King Street. Died in 1838.

EMMOR JEFFERIS   1804-1892
Wilmington, Del., 1827. Born in Chester County, Pa. Married Ann Robinson, 1827.
Located at 77 Market Street in 1832.

EPHRAIM JEFFERSON   1788-1844
Smyrna, Del., 1815.

JOHN C. JENCKES   1777-1852
Providence, R. I., 1798. Advertised, *United States Chronicle*, May 17, 1798.
"Gold and Silver Smith and Jeweller, has taken the shop formerly occupied by
Mr. John Gibbs, in company with the widow, Eliza Gibbs, under the firm of
John Jenckes & Co., where he intends prosecuting business carried on by the late
John Gibbs." At Friendship Street in 1824.

I. & H. JENKINS   1815
Albany, N. Y. Ira and Herman Jenkins.

JOHN JENKINS   1777
Philadelphia, Pa., at 16 Green Street in 1791.

JACOB JENNINGS   1729-1817
Norwalk, Conn., 1763. Advertised, *Boston Gazette*, "Whereas the Shop of the
Subscriber, living in Norwalk, in the Colony of Connecticut, was broken open on
the Sixth Day of April Instant at Night, and robb'd of the following Things,
viz, a Silver Cream Pot, 6 large Spoons, 2 or 3 Dozen Tea Spoons, and other sundry
articles. . . . Twenty Dollars Reward."

JENNINGS & LANDER   1848
New York.

DAVID JESSE   1670-1705
Boston, Mass., 1695. Born in England. Married Mary Wilson, of Hartford, Conn.,
in 1698. Member of the Brattle Street Church, 1704. A Member of the Artillery
Company in 1700. Died January 3, 1705.

CHAUNCEY JOHNSON   1825
Albany, N. Y., until 1841.

MAYCOCK W. JOHNSON   1815
Albany, N. Y.

JOHNSON & BALL   1790
Baltimore, Md.

SAMUEL JOHNSON   1780
New York. Assistant Alderman, 1783. Member of the Gold and Silversmiths
Society, 1786. Shop at Crown Street, 1789; 99 Liberty Street, 1795. Commissioned
by Council of the City to do work in Gold. Will proved, February 15, 1796, Cary
Dunn mentioned as witness.

JOHNSON & REAT   1810
Richmond, Va., and Baltimore, Md.

JOHNSON & RILEY   1785
Baltimore, Md., advertised at "Sign of the Golden Coffee Pot" in Market Street.
Dissolved the following year.

A. JOHNSTON   1830
Philadelphia, Pa.

WILLIAM B. JOHONNOT   1766-1849
Middletown, Conn., 1787, advertised "opposite Mrs. Bigelow's Tavern." Apprenticed to Samuel Canfield, 1782-1787. In Windsor, Vt., 1792.

JONES, BALL & CO.   1850
Boston, Mass.

JONES, BALL & POOR   1840
Boston, Mass.

ELISHA JONES   1827
New York.

JOHN B. JONES   1782-1854
Boston, Mass., 1813, at 10 Newbury Street; 37 Market Street, 1822. Firms of Jones
& Ward, Jones, Ball & Poor.

JOHN B. JONES & CO.   1838
Boston, Mass.

JONES, LOWS & BALL   1839
Boston, Mass.

PHILIP JONES   1843
Wilmington, Del.

WILLIAM JONES   1694-1730
Marblehead, Mass., 1715.

JONES & HUTTON   1840
Wilmington, Del., at 131 Market Street until 1843.

JONES & WARD   1815
Boston, Mass.

HIRAM JUDSON   1824
Syracuse, N. Y., until 1847.

K

J. KEDZIE   1809-1889
Rochester, N. Y., 1830.

JOSEPH KEELER   1786-1824
Norwalk, Conn., 1810.

THADDEUS KEELER   1805
New York at 350 Pearl Street until 1813.

TIMOTHY KEITH   **1805**
New York.

TIMOTHY & W. KEITH   1829
Worcester, Mass.

CHARLES KENDALL   1787
New York. Married Elizabeth Hallett, November 21, 1780. Advertised at 42 Crown
Street until 1792; 77 Chambers Street 1797. Various spellings, Kindle, Kendal,
Kenab, Kendle.

JAMES KENDALL   1768-1808
Wilmington, Del., 1785, on Market Street until 1802. Son of Jesse and Mary
Marshall Kendall. His estate was appraised by John White and Thomas McConnell.

WILLIAM KENDRICK   1824-1880
Louisville, Ky., 1840. Married Maria S. Schwing, 1842. In partnership with James I.
Lemon until 1842.

SAMUEL KEPLINGER   1770-1849
Baltimore, Md., 1812 at 60 North Howard Street.

JAMES KETCHAM   1807
New York, at 391 Pearl Street and 216 Water Street in 1823. Utica, 1847.

THOMAS KETTELL   1760-1850
Charlestown, Mass., 1784. Born February 23. Married Mary Soley, March 1, 1807.
Was a Clerk in the Middlesex Canal Company. Attendant of the First Church.
Died September 17, 1850.

ROBERT KEYWORTH   1833
Washington, D. C., at Pennsylvania Avenue between 9th and 10th Streets, West.

KIDNEY, CANN & JOHNSON   1850
New York.

KIDNEY & DUNN   1844
New York.

CORNELIUS KIERSTEDE 1674-1757
New York, 1696. Born December 25, and baptized January 5, 1675, son of Hans and Joanna Loockermans Kierstede. Married (1) Elizabeth ....; (2) Sarah Ellsworth, daughter of Clement and Anna Maria Engelbrecht Ellsworth, in 1708. Appointed Freeman, May 30th, 1702. After 1725 removed to New Haven, Connecticut, where he advertised at Church Street.

LEWIS A. KIMBALL 1837
Buffalo, N. Y.

WILLIAM KIMBERLY 1790
New York at 35 Crown Street; 7 Fly Market in 1792. Advertised, October 5, 1795, *The American Mercury;* "Three journeymen that can work at different branches of the gold and silversmith's trade." Notice of large importation in 1797. Later proprietor of hardware store. Probably in Baltimore, 1804-1821, where he married Elizabeth Webb. Died in 1821.

THOMAS R. KING 1819
Baltimore, Md.

THOMAS KINNEY 1786-1824
Norwich, Conn., 1807, at Shetucket Street. Thomas, Jr. in Cortlandt, N. Y., 1836. Spelled Kinne.

DAVID I. KINSEY 1845
Cincinnati, Ohio, until 1848.

E. & D. KINSEY 1845
Cincinnati, Ohio, at Main and Walnut Streets.

JESSE KIP 1660-1722
New York, 1682. Baptized in Dutch Reformed Church, December 19, 1660, son of Jacob Hendrickson Kip and Maria de la Montague Kip. Married Maria Stevens, September 30, 1695. Held public offices with other silversmiths in the North Ward. Died in Newtown, April, 1722.

GEORGE KIPPEN 1790-1845
Bridgeport, Conn., 1815. Born in Middletown. Apprenticed to Charles Brewer. In partnership with Barzillai Benjamin. In 1824 advertised at corner of Beaver and Broad Streets. Worked with Elias Camp. Last record, with George A. Hoyt.

SAMUEL KIRK 1793-1872
Baltimore, Md., 1815. Born in Doylestown, Pa., of Quaker ancestry. Apprenticed to James Howell, 1810. Opened shop, August 5, 1815, when he advertised for trade. At 212 Market Street in 1816. Partnership with Smith until 1820. Petitioned for modification of Baltimore Assay Law. In 1846 admitted son, Henry Child Kirk into business, founding S. Kirk, Sons, Co., Inc.

KIRK & SMITH 1817
Baltimore, Md., until 1821.

PETER KIRKWOOD 1790
Chestertown, later Annapolis, Md., 1800.

JOHN KITTS 1838
Louisville, Ky. Associated with Lemon & Kendrick, 1841. In partnership with William D. Scott, 1843. Formed John Kitts & Company, 1859-1878.

TEA SETS

Abraham Dubois, 1790

Paul Revere, 1799

Jacob G. Lansing, 1765

Daniel Van Voorhis, 1790

TEA SETS

Shepherd & Boyd, 1815

Joel Sayre, 1808

John Sayre, 1825

John Crawford, 1825

JOSEPH KNEELAND   1698-1740
Boston, Mass., 1720.

PETER L. KRIDER   1850
Philadelphia, Pa.

KRIDER & BIDDLE   1850
Philadelphia, Pa.

JACOB KUCHLER   1806
Philadelphia, Pa., at 84 North Second Street; at 8th Street, 1813; 4 College Avenue, 1831.

O. KUCHLER   1850
New Orleans, La.

L

JACOB LADOMUS   1843
Philadelphia, Pa., until 1850.

JOHN JOSEPH LAFAR   1781-1849
Charleston, S. C., 1805, worked with brother Peter. City Marshall in 1819. Lieutenant in Charleston Regiment of Artillery.

VINCENT LAFORME   1850
Boston, Mass.

VINCENT LAFORME & BROTHER   1850
Boston, Mass.

EBENEZER KNOWLTON LAKEMAN   1799-1857
Salem, Mass., 1830.

JOHN LAMOTHE   1822
New Orleans, La., at 52 Royal Street.

AARON LANE   1753-1819
Elizabeth, N. J., 1784. Died in New York.

EDWARD LANG   1742-1830
Salem, Mass., 1763.

JEFFREY LANG   1708-1758
Salem, Mass., 1733. Advertised as a goldsmith in *Boston Evening Post,* June 10, 1745. His sons, Richard, Nathaniel and Edward were silversmiths.

NATHANIEL LANG   1736-1826
Salem, Mass., 1760.

RICHARD LANG   1733-1820
Salem, Mass., 1770.

WILLIAM LANGE   1844
New York at 6 Little Green Street.

JACOB GERITTSE LANSING   1736-1803
Albany, N. Y., 1765.

JACOB GERITTZE LANSING   1700
Albany, N. Y.

MARTIN M. LAWRENCE   1832
New York.

SAMUEL J. LEA   1815
Baltimore, Md., at 238 Baltimore Street until 1822. Lieutenant in Union Volunteers.

CHARLES LEACH   1765-1814
Boston, Mass., 1789. "Shop on Ann Street, three doors below Draw-Bridge."

NATHANIEL LEACH   1789
Boston, Mass., on Kilby Street. Directory 1800.

JOHN LEACOCK   1748
Philadelphia, Pa. Advertised, *Penna. Gazette,* "Goldsmith Removed from Second
Street to the Sign of the Cup in Water Street where he continues." In Front Street,
1753-1759, lists a large selection of imported goods at the sign of the "Golden
Cup." Last record, November 19, 1796.

SAMUEL W. LEE   1785-1861
Providence, R. I., 1815. Born in Connecticut. Dissolved partnership of Burr & Lee
and removed to Rochester, N. Y., 1816. Firm of Schofield & Lee, 1822. Died in
Wisconsin.

NICHOLAS LEHURAY   1809
Philadelphia, Pa., until 1831.

NICHOLAS LEHURAY, JR.   1821
Philadelphia, Pa., until 1846.

BENJAMIN LEMAR   1775
Philadelphia, Pa., at Front between Chestnut and Walnut Streets. Died in 1785.

MATHIAS LEMAR   1790
Philadelphia, Pa. On Census List for 1790. Listed at 81 Market Street and other
addresses until 1798. Spelled Lemaire, Lamar.

G. LENHART   1845
Bowling Green, Ky.

JOHN LENT   1787
New York. Married Sarah Ogilvie, niece of John Ogilvie, Silversmith. Advertised, *Impartial Gazetteer,* August 2, 1788. "Goldsmith, silversmith and jeweller
. . . carries on the above business in all its various branches, in the newest and
most fashionable manner, 61 Beekman Street." After 1791 located at 69 Maiden
Lane.

ALLEN LEONARD   1830
New York at 154 Division Street.

SAMUEL T. LEONARD 1786-1848
Chestertown, Md., 1805. Born, November 22. Died, September 7. Firm of Lynch & Leonard, 1810.

LEONARD & WILSON 1847
Philadelphia, Pa., on R. Road.

PETER LERET 1779
Philadelphia, Pa. Advertised in Carlisle, Pa., until 1787. Baltimore, Md., 1787- 1802.

BARTHOLOMEW LE ROUX 1687
New York on West Side of Broadway and Beaver Lane. Freeman, June 6, 1687. Married in 1688. Assistant Alderman, 1702-1712.

BARTHOLOMEW LE ROUX 1717-1763
New York, 1738. Son of Charles. Freeman, May 15, 1739. Will, dated August 13, 1757, leaves estate to brother Charles and sisters; proved March 30, 1763.

CHARLES LE ROUX 1689-1745
New York, 1710. Freeman, February 16, 1724. Elected Deacon of New York School. Appraised Lottery with Peter VanDyke in 1727. Assistant Alderman of East Ward, 1735-1738. Commissioned by Common Council for presentation pieces.

JOHN LE ROUX 1716
New York. Born, 1695, son of Bartholomew. Freeman, January 8, 1723. Later in Albany.

EDWARD P. LESCURE 1822
Philadelphia, Pa., at 75 Union Street until 1850.

JOHN LETELIER 1770
Philadelphia, Pa., at Second Street between Market and Chestnut Streets. In 1777, opposite the Coffee House. Listed in 1793 at 172 North Front Street. Same year, December 21, *Delaware, Gazette,* "John Le Telier, Gold and Silversmith, Late from Philadelphia, Hath Commenced business in Market-street, Wilmington, opposite Captain O'Flin's, the sign of the Ship, where he intends carrying on his business in its various branches, such as Coffee and tea urns, coffee pots, tea pots, Sugar dishes, cream urns, Canns and tankards, spoons of all kinds, shoe and knee buckles; likewise, makes and mends all kinds of swords and hangers. Those who will please to favor him with Custom, may depend upon having their work done in the neatest and most expeditious manner, and on the most reasonable terms."

KNIGHT LEVERETT 1703-1753
Boston, Mass., 1736. Apprenticed to Andrew Tyler. Married to Abigail Brittolph. Sergeant of Artillery Company, 1736. Held public offices, 1742-1748.

JONES LEVY 1835
New York.

HARVEY LEWIS 1811
Philadelphia, Pa., at Second Street; at 143 Chestnut Street, 1822.

ISAAC LEWIS 1773-1860
Huntington, Conn., 1796. Removed to Ridgefield, 1809.

J. H. LEWIS   1810
Albany, N. Y.

LEWIS & SMITH   1805
Philadelphia, Pa., at 2 South Second Street until 1811.

GABRIEL LEWYN   1770
Baltimore, Md., in Gay Street where he leased house, May 4. Vestry records of St. Thomas' Parish, 1772. Last record, 1780.

JACOB G. L. LIBBY   1820
Boston, Mass., until 1846.

JOHN LIDDEN   1850
St. Louis, Mo.

A. L. LINCOLN   1850
St. Louis, Mo.

ELIJAH LINCOLN   1794-1861
Hingham, Mass., 1815.

LINCOLN & FOSS   1850
Boston, Mass.

LINCOLN & GREEN   1810
Boston, Mass.

LINCOLN & READ   1835
Boston, Mass., until 1846.

CLARK LINDSLEY   1850
Hartford, Conn., at 22 Hudson Street.

PAUL LITTLE   1760
Portland, Me. Located with John Butler from Newbury, 1761. Advertised at corner of Middle and King Streets in 1771, where Capt. Daniel Tucker was apprenticed at eleven years of age. Little claimed £ 685 property damage after the destruction of Portland in 1775.

WILLIAM LITTLE   1775
Newburyport, Mass., where he advertised as silversmith in Newburyport Herald.

ALFRED LOCKWOOD   1817
New York, until 1831.

FREDERICK LOCKWOOD   1828
New York, until 1845.

JAMES LOCKWOOD   1799
New York at 36 Lombard Street; and 53 Read Street until 1807.

ADAM LOGAN   1803
New York at Cherry Street and Chatham Square until 1823.

BARTHELEMY EDWARD LOMBARD   1800-1830
Charleston, S. C., 1828.

HENRY LONGLEY   1810
New York at 178 Broadway.

LONGLEY & DODGE   1810
Charleston, S. C., at Broad Street.

G. LOOMIS & CO.   1850
Erie, Pa.

BENJAMIN LORD   1796
Pittsfield, Mass., advertised December 5, *Western Star,* located opposite the Meeting House on the road to Lanesborough.

JABEZ C. LORD   1825
New York at 177 William Street until 1835. Firm of Lord & Smith.

ELIJAH LORING   1744-1782
Barnstable, Mass., 1765.

HENRY LORING   1773-1818
Boston, Mass., 1800. Son of Joseph and Mary Atkins Loring. Married Sarah Stewart.

JOSEPH LORING   1743-1815
Boston, Mass., 1775. Born in Hull. Son of Caleb and Rebecca Lobdell Loring. Married Mary Atkins. Advertised in Union Street. Served in Revolution, later 1791 in Artillery Company. Mentioned as Bondsman with Stephen Emery, July 24, 1788. Jesse Churchill appraised estate.

ROBERT LOVETT   1818
Philadelphia, Pa., until 1824, when removed to New York, until 1830.

JOHN J. LOW   1825
Boston, Mass.

JOHN J. LOW & CO.   1830
Boston, Mass.

JOSHUA LOWE   1828
New York until 1833.

LOWELL & SENTER   1830
Portland, Me.

JOSEPH LOWER   1806
Philadelphia, Pa., at Dock Street until 1820; at 44 Tammany Street to 1831.

EDWARD LOWNES   1817
Philadelphia, Pa., at 10½ South Third Street. Died, 1834.

JOSEPH LOWNES   1780
Philadelphia, Pa. Son of John and Agnes Lownes. Married Esther Middleton, daughter of Abel and Mary Middleton of Crosswicks, N. J., January 12, 1786. Advertised, 1780, 1792, and 1798, at Front between Walnut and Spruce Streets. Listed in Directory in 1813 at 124 South Front Street, and other addresses until 1816. Of firms of Lownes & Erwin; J. & J. H. Lownes.

JOSIAH H. LOWNES 1816
Philadelphia, Pa., at 124 South Front Street. Died 1822.

LOWS, BALL & CO. 1840
Boston, Mass.

HENRY LUPP 1783
New Brunswick, N. J.

LOUIS LUPP 1800
New Brunswick, N. J. Son of Peter Lupp.

PETER LUPP 1787
New Brunswick, N. J.

S. V. LUPP 1815
New Brunswick, N. J.

JOHN LYNCH 1761-1848
Baltimore, Md., 1786. Census List for 1790. Located on Boundary Street in 1796; Franklin Street, 1801-1848. Married Naomi Willey, January 21, 1804.

THOMAS LYNDE 1748-1812
Worcester, Mass., 1771. Born in Malden, April 19. Married Sarah Greenleafe in 1774. Died in Leicester, 1812.

JOHN BURT LYNG 1759
New York. Married Magdalane Jardine, September 11, 1759. Freeman, March 31, 1761. Advertised, *New York Gazette*, January 5, 1764; ". . . at private Sale, the House wherein John Burt Lyng, Silver-Smith now lives, in Broad-Way. N.B. The Gold and Silver-Smith Business is carried on as usual, by the Public's very humble Servant, John Burt Lyng." Notice at Great-George-Street, May 12, 1774. Will dated, 1773, proved April 20, 1785. Leaves net profits to his wife and children, settled at auction year after death.

ADAM LYNN 1775-1836
Alexandria, Va., 1796, advertised in *Alexandria Gazette,* ". . . In King Street, makes Coffee Pots . . . Table Crosses . . .". Census List for 1791. Formed Adam Lynn & Company, 1810.

R. A. LYTLE 1825
Baltimore, Md.

M

JOHN McFARLANE 1796
Boston, Mass.

WILLIAM MANNERBACK 1825
Reading, Pa.

BENJAMIN MARBLE 1840
Albany, N. Y. until 1850.

SIMEON MARBLE 1777-1856
New Haven, Conn., 1800, at Chapel Street, later on State. Dissolved partnership with Clark Sibley in 1806.

JACOB MARIUSGROEN   1701
New York. Died 1750.

MARQUAND & CO.   1820
New York on Broadway until 1833. Succeeded by Ball, Tompkins & Black 1851
by Ball, Black & Company.

FREDERICK MARQUAND   1823
New York at 166 Broadway. In partnership with brother.

THOMAS K. MARSH   1830
Paris, Ky., until 1850.

MARSHALL & TEMPEST   1813
Philadelphia, Pa., until 1830 at 87 South Second Street.

THOMAS H. MARSHALL   1809-1852
Albany, N. Y., 1832-1836. Rochester, 1838-1852.

PETER MARTIN   1756
New York, admitted Freeman, August 4.

PETER MARTIN II   1825
New York.

VALENTINE MARTIN   1842
Boston, Mass., until 1846.

J. D. MASON   1830
Philadelphia, Pa.

MATHER & NORTH   1825
New York. William B. North retired in 1827.

AUGUSTUS MATHEY   1825
New York.

NEWELL MATSON   1817-1887
Owego, N. Y., 1845.

R. H. MAYNARD   1825
Buffalo, N. Y., until 1829.

HUGH McCONNELL   1813
Philadelphia, Pa., at Dock near Second Street.

THOMAS McCONNELL   1768-1825
Wilmington, Del., 1806 advertised removal to Market Street where located until
1817. Held public offices. Died in Richmond, Va.

JOHN C. McCLYMON   1805
New York, 28 and 40 Warren Street until 1808; at 15 Rose Street, 1811.

WILLIAM McCLYMON   1800
Schenectady, N. Y., until 1815.

WILLIAM McDOUGALL 1825
Meredith, N. H.

WILLIAM HANSE McDOWELL 1795-1842
Philadelphia, Pa., 1819, at 130 South Front Street. Son of George and Susannah
Hanse McDowell. Married (1) Mary Stanley; (2) Martha Tennent Austin.
Retired from business in 1840. Was related to Elias Boudinot and Peter
Vergereau.

J. B. McFADDEN 1840
Pittsburgh, Pa.

JOHN McFARLANE 1796
Boston, Mass.

McFEE & REEDER 1793
Philadelphia, Pa., listed at 38 North Front Street. Dissolved 1796 by John McFee
and Abner Reeder.

HENRY McKEEN 1823
Philadelphia, Pa.

HUGH A. McMASTERS 1839
Philadelphia, Pa., until 1850.

JOHN McMULLIN 1765-1843
Philadelphia, Pa., 1790 Census List. Located at 120 South Front Street, 1795.
Firm of M'Mullin & Black.

McMULLIN & BLACK 1811
Philadelphia, Pa. John M'Mullin and John Black at 120 South Front Street, dissolved, 1813.

E. McNEIL 1813
Binghampton, N. Y.

WILLIAM McPARLIN 1780-1850
Annapolis, Md., 1805. Married Cassandra Woodward, December 15, 1816. Took
over shop of Charles Faris on West Street, to whom he was probably apprenticed.
His account book, 1827-1850 shows dealings with Baltimore silversmiths, Kirk,
Gelston, Campbell, Webb and others.

MEAD & ADRIANCE 1831
Utica, N. Y. Edward Mead and Edwin Adriance until 1834.

EDMUND MEAD 1850
St. Louis, Mo.

MEADOWS & CO. 1831
Philadelphia, Pa.

GEORGE MECUM 1825
Boston, Mass., at South Russell Street, until 1846.

THOMAS J. MEGEAR 1830
Wilmington, Del.

CREAMERS

Josiah Austin
1740

Daniel C. Fueter
1755

Bancroft Woodcock
1760

Myer Myers
1775

Freeman Woods
1790

Samuel Richards
1800

Elias Pelletreau
1810

Charles A. Burnett
1825

CANDLESTICKS
SNUFFER STAND

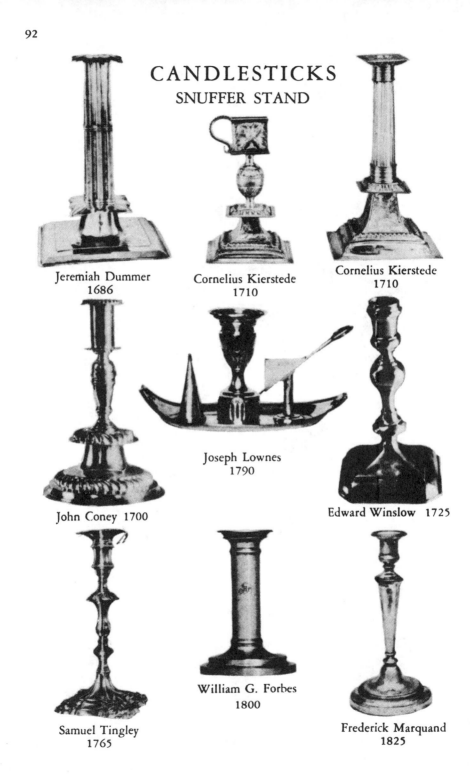

Jeremiah Dummer
1686

Cornelius Kierstede
1710

Cornelius Kierstede
1710

Joseph Lownes
1790

John Coney 1700

Edward Winslow 1725

Samuel Tingley
1765

William G. Forbes
1800

Frederick Marquand
1825

J. MERCHANT 1795
New York.

JOSEPH P. MEREDITH 1824
Baltimore, Md.

JOHN H. MERKLER 1780
New York at 93 Broadway. Died intestate. Wife, Elizabeth, was granted letter of administration, June 24, 1791.

MARCUS MERRIMAN 1762-1850
New Haven, Conn., 1787. Born in Cheshire, son of Silas, brother of Samuel. Partner of Zebul Bradley, later Bethuel Tuttle, 1802.

MARCUS MERRIMAN & CO. 1806
New Haven, Conn. After 1817 firm became Merriman & Bradley.

REUBEN MERRIMAN 1783-1866
Cheshire, Conn., 1810. Located in Litchfield in 1827 where he built shop.

SAMUEL MERRIMAN 1769-1805
New Haven, Conn., 1795. Born in Cheshire, son of Silas, where he learned trade. Removed and advertised on Chapel Street. Notice, June 1, 1796, *Connecticut Journal:* "Gold and Silversmithing. Having Workmen from Europe, last from New York, whose work will recommend itself in all branches of this line. Shop near the College." Fire destroyed shop in 1800 when he leased on Church Street.

MERRIMAN & BRADLEY 1817
New Haven, Conn.

JOHN MATHEW MIKSCH 1775
Bethlehem, Pa.

D. B. MILLER 1850
Boston, Mass.

JOHN DAVID MILLER 1780
Charleston, S. C.

I. R. MILLER 1810
Philadelphia, Pa.

L. H. MILLER & CO. 1840
Baltimore, Md.

MATHEW MILLER 1780-1840
Charleston, S. C., 1807. Married Rose Ann, May, 1805. Advertised as goldsmith at 40 Queen Street in 1807; 326 King Street, 1816.

PARDON MILLER 1810
Providence, R. I.

WILLIAM MILLER 1810
Philadelphia, Pa., at 85 Callowhill Street until 1847. Firm of Ward & Miller in 1822.

THOMAS MILLNER 1690-1745

Boston, Mass., 1715. Married Mary Reed. Received silversmith's tools in will of Richard Conyers in 1708.

EDMUND MILNE 1757

Philadelphia, Pa. Advertised, December 29, 1757. *Pennsylvania Gazette*: "Above named who has for these two years last past worked and carried on business for Mr. Charles Dutens, now begs leave to inform the public, that as Dutens has gone to the West Indies to reside, he has set up business for himself next door to the Indian King in Market Street in house with Mr. David Barnes, where all ladies and gentlemen who will honor him with their custom, may depend on being faithfully served in all branches." Second Street in 1767. Lost indentured servant in 1771. Made twelve cups for General Washington in 1777. Died in 1813.

THOMAS MILNE 1795

New York at 170 Fly Market until 1797.

SAMUEL MINOTT 1732-1803

Boston, Mass, 1764. Born in Concord. Married Elizabeth Davis. Partner of Josiah Austin, 1765-9. Later worked with William Simpkins. Advertised his shop opposite Williams Court, Cornhill, and also a shop North of the Draw Bridge, in 1772. He was arrested as a Tory in 1776 by order of the Common Council. Last address at Ann Street in 1789.

MINOTT & AUSTIN 1765

Boston, Mass. Samuel Minott and Josiah Austin, dissolved in 1769.

MINOTT & SIMPKINS 1769

Boston, Mass.

HENRY MITCHELL 1844

Philadelphia, Pa., until 1850.

WILLIAM MITCHELL 1820

Richmond, Va.

JOHN L. MOFFAT 1815

New York, at 203 Broadway.

MONELL & WILLIAMS 1825

New York. John J. Monell and Charles M. Williams at 25 Rhynder Street.

JAMES MONK 1800

Charleston, S. C., at 20 Broad Street. Married Jane Campbell, 1805. Last in Manchester, Vt.

JOHN & ROBERT MONTEITH 1814

Baltimore, Md., at 144 Baltimore Street until 1847.

ROBERT MONTEITH 1825

Baltimore, Md.

JOHN MOOD 1792-1864

Charleston, S. C., 1816. Son of Peter Mood. Married Catharine McFarlane. Was Methodist Preacher.

J. & P. MOOD 1834
Charleston, S. C. John and Peter, brothers advertised "At the Sign of the Cross Spoons." Wholesale and retail dealers until 1841.

PETER MOOD 1766-1821
Charleston, S. C., 1790, from Philadelphia. Married, Dorothy Sigwald. Became Member of the German Friendly Society in 1789. Continued in business with sons until he died.

CHARLES MOORE 1803
Philadelphia, Pa., at 8 Combes' Alley; North Front Street, 1806-7. Firm of Moore & Ferguson.

JARED L. MOORE 1835
New York at 294 Washington Street. In Brooklyn at Nassau and Stanton Streets in 1843.

JOHN C. MOORE 1835
New York at 51 Morton Street; 164 Broadway in 1844.

MOORE & BREWER 1835
New York.

MOORE & FERGUSON 1801
Philadelphia, Pa., at 42 North Front Street. Charles Moore and John Ferguson dissolved partnership in 1804.

ELIJAH MORGAN 1783-1857
Poughkeepsie, N. Y., 1807. Son of Elijah and Lavinia Morgan. Apprenticed to Andrew Billings. Married Nancy Smith, November 2, 1806. Of the firms, Sadd & Morgan; Morgan & Cook.

WILLIAM M. MORRELL 1828
New York.

SYLVESTER MORRIS 1745
New York. Married Maria Tevauw, October 25, 1741. Freeman, September 29, 1759. Grandson of Jacob Mariusgroen, silversmith.

J. H. MORSE 1795
Boston, Mass.

MOSES MORSE 1816
Boston, Mass., Brother of Hazen Morse. Apprenticed to Churchill & Treadwell. Apprentices, Obadiah Rich, H. Haddock, Charles West and J. Millar. Retired in 1830.

NATHANIEL MORSE 1685-1748
Boston, Mass., 1709. Apprenticed to John Coney. Married Sarah Draper. Estate appraised /by Samuel Edwards.

DAVID MOSELEY 1753-1812
Boston, Mass., 1775.

JACOB MOSES 1768
Birmingham, Ala. Advertised "From London, England", in partnership with William Sime. Later in Baltimore, Md.

J. S. MOTT 1790
New York.

JAMES S. MOTT 1830
New York.

W. & J. MOTT 1789
New York at 240 Water Street. This firm issued the first tradesman's tokens in the United States.

JOHN MOULINAR 1744
New York. Born in 1722, son of Rev. Jean Joseph Brumauld de Moulinars. Married to Elizabeth Bisset in 1743. Freeman in 1744. Lieutenant in expedition to Canada in 1746. Last record in Albany.

ABEL MOULTON 1784-1850
Newburyport, Mass., 1815, on State Street. Brother of William. Partner of John D. Davis in 1824.

EBENEZER MOULTON 1768-1824
Boston, Mass., 1795. Son of Joseph. Married Abigail Bourne, 1794. Located at 3 South Row, 1813.

EDWARD S. MOULTON 1778-1855
Rochester, N. H., 1800. Born in Portsmouth. Son of Joseph and Lydia Bickford Moulton.

ENOCH MOULTON 1780-1815
Portland, Me., 1805.

JOSEPH MOULTON 1744-1816
Newburyport, Mass., 1765. Son of William. Married Abigail Noyes.

JOSEPH MOULTON 1814-1903
Newburyport, Mass., 1835.

WILLIAM MOULTON 1720-1793
Newburyport, Mass., 1750. Married Lydia Greenleaf in 1742. Advertised in Marietta, Ohio, in 1788.

WILLIAM MOULTON 1772-1860
Newburyport, Mass., 1796. Son of Joseph W. Moulton. Shop on Merrimack Street. Married Judith Noyes.

MOULTON & DAVIS 1824
Newburyport, Mass. Abel Moulton and John W. Davis partnership dissolved in 1830.

MULFORD & WENDELL 1842
Albany, N. Y., at 480 Broadway until 1850. Successors of Boyd & Mulford.

H. MULLIGAN 1840
Philadelphia, Pa., at 414 Second Street.

HENRY B. MUMFORD 1813
Providence, R. I.

ASA MUNGER — 1778-1851
Herkimer, N. Y., 1810. Born in Granby, Mass., son of Joseph and Hannah Fiske Munger. Married Polly Chapin, in 1801. In Auburn, 1818. Firm of Munger & Benedict.

A. MUNGER & SON — 1840
Auburn, N. Y.

JAMES MUNROE — 1784-1879
Barnstable, 1806, and New Bedford, Mass.

NATHANIEL MUNROE — 1777-1861
Baltimore, Md., 1815 at East Baltimore Street until 1840.

JOHN MURDOCK — 1779
Philadelphia, Pa. Listed in 1785 at Front between Walnut and Spruce Streets.

JOHN MURDOCK & CO. — 1826
Utica, N. Y., until 1838.

MURDOCK & ANDREWS — 1822
Utica, N. Y., until 1849.

JAMES MURPHY — 1803
Boston, Mass., directory until 1816. Philadelphia Pa., listed 1828-1846.

JAMES MUSGRAVE — 1795
Philadelphia, Pa., at Chestnut and Third Streets. In 1796, advertised at 42 South Second Street, and 31 Cable Lane. Listed as "The late goldsmith" of Spruce Street in 1813. Firm of Parry & Musgrave.

H. B. MYER — 1818
Newburgh, N. Y. Buffalo in 1836.

JOHN MYERS — 1785
Philadelphia, Pa., to 1804 at North Second Street. Apprenticed to Richard Humphreys.

MYER MYERS — 1723-1795
New York, 1745, Freeman. Married Joyce Mears, March 18, 1767. Advertised, *New York Gazette*, 1753-4, 1767, 1771-3 "Removal of Shop from King Street to the Meal-Market. . . ." President of the New York Silversmiths Society, 1786. Located at Greenwich Street in 1786, Princess Street in 1788, 303 Water Street in 1802. Prominent Master Mason. Firms of Myers & Halsted, Hays & Myers.

DAVID MYGATT — 1777-1822
Danbury, Conn., 1800. Son of Eli from whom he learned his trade. Worked with brother Comfort Starr Mygatt. In South East N. Y. in 1811.

N

DANIEL NEALL — 1784-1846
Milford, Del., 1814.

WILLIAM NEEDLES   1807
Easton, Md. Advertised in *Republican Star*, July 28, "Opened Silver-Smith's Shop
near the Market-House." Firm of Bowdle & Needles. No record after 1818 when
Stephen Hussey took over the shop of William Needles. Second Door above the
Post-Office.

JOHN NELSON   1780
Portsmouth, N. H.

H. K. NEWCOMB   1821
Watertown, N. Y., until 1850.

JAN VAN NIEU KIRKE   1716
New York.

TIMOTHY H. NEWMAN   1778-1812
Groton, Mass., 1800.

BASSET NICHOLS   1815
Providence, R. I.

WILLIAM S. NICHOLS   1785-1871
Newport, R. I., 1808. Born in Providence. Apprenticed to Thomas Arnold. Advertised at 155 Thames Street in 1842.

RICHARD NIXON   1820
Philadelphia, Pa., at 240 South Seventh Street until 1831.

NEHEMIAH NORCROSS   1765-1804
Boston, Mass., 1796, directory until 1800.

W. B. NORTH & CO.   1823
New York. William B. North formed by company succeeded by Mather & North.

WILLIAM B. NORTH   1787-1838
New Haven, Conn., 1810, where he was born. Advertised in New York at 217
Broadway. Firm of Mather & North.

DAVID I. NORTHEE   1770
Salem, Mass. Died 1778.

ANDREW NORTON   1765-1838
Goshen, Conn., 1787 at his Inn House.

BENJAMIN R. NORTON   1845
Syracuse, N. Y.

C. C. NORTON   1820
Hartford, Conn. Partner of William Pitkin.

THOMAS NORTON   1733-1834
Farmington, Conn., 1796, advertised until 1806. Died in Albion, N. Y.

NORTON & PITKIN   1825
Hartford, Conn. C. C. Norton and William Pitkin.

NORTON & SEYMOUR   1850
Syracuse, N. Y.

MARTIN NOXON   1780-1814
Edenton, N. C., 1800. Son of Pasco and Anna Harris Noxon of Oswego, N. Y. Married Hannah Carpenter, 1804.

JOHN NOYES   1674-1749
Boston, Mass., 1699, advertised "Tankard Stolen". Notices dated February 10, 1706, March 15, 1707. Married Susanna Edwards. Member of the Artillery Company, 1699-1707. Died in Boston.

FREDERICK NUSZ   1819
Frederick, Md.

JOHANNIS NYS   1671-1734
Philadelphia, Pa., 1695. Married Grietse Ketteltas, who was related to Henricus Boelen. "Jan Neuss, Menonite and Silversmith", received the "Right of Citizenship of Germantown" in 1698. After serving apprenticeship in New York he removed to Bohemia Manor for religious reasons. Served in Albany Militia, 1689-1690, for which he received an award in 1717. William Penn purchased six tea spoons from him in 1704, which he presented to the children of Isaac Norris. Died in Kent County, Delaware, in 1734.

O

FREDERICK OAKES   1810
Hartford, Conn., advertised North of Marshall's Tavern. In 1814 firm of Oakes & Spencer. Listed in 1825.

OAKES & SPENCER   1814
Hartford, Conn.

JOHN OGILVIE   1764
New York. Born about 1732, son of Alexander and Jannette Schuyler Ogilvie. Married Anna Atkins, June 13, 1764, in Trinity Church.

ANDREW OLIVER   1750
Boston, Mass. Clerk of the Market, 1753.

DANIEL OLIVER   1805
Philadelphia, Pa.

PETER OLIVIER   1790
Philadelphia, Pa., at 6 Strawberry Street, until 1797. Died intestate in 1798 when notice appears in *Aurora*, April 30, by order of French Consulate, advertising for settlement of estate claims.

PETER OLIVER   1682-1712
Boston, Mass, 1705. Married (1) Jerusha Mather; (2) Hopestill Wensley in Charlestown, in 1709.

NATHANIEL OLMSTED   1785-1860
Farmington, Conn., 1808. Born in East Hartford. Apprenticed to Daniel Burnap of East Windsor. Advertised in New Haven, 1826. Freeman, September 6, 1698. Married Phideila Burnap.

GERRIT ONCKELBAG 1670-1732

New York, 1691. (Daughter Neeltse, Baptized, July 7, 1691, married Johannes Van Gelder, January 3, 1713, youngest son Gerritt was willed his grandfather's tankard and tools.) Step-son of Ahasuerus Hendricks to whom he was probably apprenticed. Married Elizabeth Van Schaick, first cousin of Johannis Nys. Elected Assistant Alderman, 1700-1703. Located in New Jersey to escape accusations but later returned. Witnessed Baptisms of grandchildren, 1713 and 1728.

WILLIAM OSBORN 1840

Providence, R. I.

JOHN OSGOOD, JR. 1817

Boston, Mass. Directory and Almanac, 1850.

ANDREW OSTHOFF 1810

Baltimore, Md., at Pearl Street; 27 Lexington Street in 1812. Advertised in Pittsburgh in 1815.

JONATHAN OTIS 1723-1791

Newport, R. I., 1750. Born in Sandwich, Mass. Nephew of Moody Russell. Major of Militia in 1778. Removed to Middletown, Conn., during the British Invasion.

GEORGE OTT 1806

Norfolk, Va.

JESSE OWEN 1794

Philadelphia, Pa., at Priest's Alley, Silversmith, Turner and Refiner until 1848.

JOHN OWEN 1804

Philadelphia, Pa., at 11 North Second Street and other addresses until 1831.

P

PALMER & BACHELDER 1850

Boston, Mass.

SAMUEL PANCOAST 1785

Philadelphia, Pa., at Front Street between Walnut and Spruce Streets until 1794. Advertised, 1795.

PANGBORN & BRINSMAID 1833

Burlington, Vt.

WILLIAM PARHAM 1785

Philadelphia, Pa., advertised as goldsmith at Front Street between Walnut and Spruce Streets; at 104 Swanson Street, 1791-1795.

OTTO PAUL DE PARISEN 1763

New York, advertised, *New York Gazette*, March 14; "Goldsmith, from Berlin, makes all Sorts of Platework, both plain and chased, in the neatest and most expeditious Manner; likewise undertakes chasing any piece of old Plate, at his House, the lower End of Batto Street." Notices, 1765, 1769. In 1774 "Silversmith in the Fly, in this City, took Fire By Means of his Furnace," Located in Dock Street. Admitted Freeman, January 31, 1764. Worked at 60 Queen Street, 1787-1789. In business with son Otto W. Commissioned by Corporation of the City to make a Gold Box, L 32/18/16.

SUGAR BOWLS

Jacob Hurd
1740

Jacob Hurd
1725

John LeRoux
1750

William Gilbert
1770

Jacob Boelen II
1765

Paul Revere
1775

Daniel Dupuy
1790

John Leacock
1760

Isaac Hutton
1800

TEA CADDIES

Christian Wiltberger
1790

Thauvet Besley
1730

Nathaniel Vernon
1820

PUNCH STRAINERS

Jonathan Clarke
1765

Paul Revere
1765

Bartholomew LeRoux
1740

ALLEN PARKER   1817
New York until 1819.

DANIEL PARKER   1726-1785
Boston, Mass., 1750, December, advertised in Boston Post. Born, November 20, 1726, son of Isaac. Married Margaret Jarvis, September 1, 1760. In Union Street, near "The Golden Ball," 1758. Continued until 1775, when he advertised in Salem. Died, December 31, 1785.

GEORGE PARKER   1804
Baltimore, Md., at Ross Street until 1823; Biddle Street to 1831.

ISAAC PARKER   1780
Deerfield, Mass. Merchant in directory, 1789.

CHARLES PARKMAN   1790
Boston, Mass. Advertised English Imported Goods in 1821.

JOHN PARKMAN   1738
Boston, Mass.

THOMAS PARKMAN   1793
Boston, Mass.

SAMUEL PARMELEE   1737-1803
Guilford, Conn., 1760, until revolutionary War, serving as Captain.

T. PARROTT   1775
Boston, Mass.

MARTIN PARRY   1756-1802
Portsmouth, N. H., 1780. Later Kittery, Me.

PARRY & MUSGRAVE   1793
Philadelphia, Pa., at 42 South Second Street, advertised until 1795, "elegant assortment". *Federal Gazette,* November 10, "Jewellers, The Partnership of Parry & Musgrave is this day dissolved; all persons indebted to, or to whom have any demands on said firm, will please apply to James Musgrave, at the old stand, 42, south Second street, or to Rowland Parry, 36 Chestnut Street."

ROWLAND PARRY   1790
Philadelphia, Pa., at 36 South Second Street, advertised after partnership of Parry & Musgrave, at South Chestnut Street, 1795. Notice of death, November 15, 1796.

JOHN PARSONS   1780
Boston, Mass.

JOHN PATTERSON   1751
Annapolis, Md.

JOHN PEABODY   1799
Enfield, Conn.

EDWARD PEAR   1830
Boston, Mass. Apprenticed to Lewis Cary. Advertised at 15 Pleasant Street. In partnership with Thomas Bacall in 1850.

W. PEARCE   1820
Norfolk, Va.

JOHN PEARSON   1791
New York at 13 Crown Street; Pearl Street until 1805.

EMMET T. PELL   1825
New York.

PELLETREAU, BENNET & COOKE   1815
New York.

ELIAS PELLETREAU   1726-1810
Southampton, N. Y., 1750. Born in Southampton, May 31, 1726, son of Francis
and Jane Osborn Pelletreau. His father left him in his will, dated March 11, 1736,
all of his houses and lands, his gold watch, sword, gun and one half of his personal
estate. At the age of thirteen he was sent to the boarding school of Mr. John
Proctor, a noted school master of New York, for one year. On November 19, 1741,
he was duly apprenticed to Simeon Soumaine, goldsmith of New York, for a term
of seven years, "To be taught the Art and Mystery of a Goldsmith." Admitted a
freeman of the City of New York, August 31, 1750. Removed to Southampton,
where he established himself as a silversmith and conducted a large farm. Married
Sarah Gelston, December 29, 1748. (2) Sarah Conkling, June 28, 1786. Commissioned as Lieutenant in the Southampton Company, 1761, and May 22, 1765,
as Captain. He died, November 2, 1810.

MALTBY PELLETREAU   1813
New York at 12 Rose Street; 170 Broadway, 1825; 26 Franklyn Street in 1835.

WILLIAM SMITH PELLETREAU   1786-1842
Southhampton, N. Y. 1810. Son of John Pelletreau and Mary Smith Pelletreau, born
June 8. Continued in the trade of his father and grandfather. Married (1) Nancy
Mackie, May 23, 1810. Appointed Purchasing Agent in War of 1812. Married
(2) Elizabeth Welles, June 26, 1834. Died, March 15, 1842.

PELLETREAU & RICHARDS   1825
New York. W. S. Pelletreau and Thomas Richards.

PELLETREAU & UPSON   1818
New York. Imported wares from Sheffield, England, 1818-1824, amounted to
£ 2,568-10-3.

PELLETREAU & VAN WYCK   1815
New York. Partnership of William S. Pelletreau and S. Van Wyck.

HENRY J. PEPPER   1814
Wilmington, Del., at 60 Market Street. Married Keziah Moore, June 7, 1817.
Removed to Philadelphia, Pa., at 46 Kunckle Street, 1828-1850.

HENRY J. PEPPER & SON   1846
Philadelphia, Pa., until 1850.

JACOB PERKINS   1766-1849
Newburyport, Mass., 1787, engaged to make dies for Massachusetts Mint. Born July
9. When fifteen years old his master, Davis, died, willing him the business. An
inventive genius, he was honored in London by Society of Liberal Arts. Invented
machine to manufacture wire into nails. During the War of 1812 he supervised
the restoring of old guns for the Government. Invented steam-gun to fire 100
balls a minute. In London in 1819 where he died, July 13, 1849.

JOSEPH PERKINS   1749-1789
Little Rest, R. I., 1770. Son of Edward and Elizabeth Brenton Perkins, born September 24. Purchased land for house in 1774. Married Mary Gardiner, 1776. Active in Revolution as Town Agent. Died, September 6.

HOUGHTON PERKINS   1735-1778
Boston, Mass., 1756. Apprenticed to Jacob Hurd. Later Taunton, Mass.

T. PERKINS   1810
Boston, Mass.

PETER PERREAU   1797
Philadelphia, Pa., at 220 North Front Street.

JAMES PETERS   1821
Philadelphia, Pa., at 90 South Second Street.

J. PETERS & CO.   1830
Philadelphia, Pa.

HENRY PETERSON   1783
Philadelphia, Pa.

MATTHEW PETIT   1811
New York at Provost Street.

ALEXANDER PETRIE   1748
Charleston, S. C. Advertised, *South Carolina Gazette*, August 30, as Goldsmith. Married Elizabeth Holland. Offers imported goods in 1756. Located "at his shop on the Bay," in 1761. Died, 1768.

CHARLES H. PHELPS   1825
Bainbridge, N. Y.

JAMES D. PHILIPS   1829
Cincinnati, Ohio, at "David Ross."

SAMUEL PHILLIPS   1658-1721
Salem, Mass., 1680. Born March 23. Married Mary Emerson of Gloucester.

JOHN PIERCE   1810
Boston, Mass.

O. PIERCE   1824
Boston, Mass.

BENJAMIN PIERPONT   1730-1797
Boston, Mass., 1756. Married Elizabeth Shepard, 1758. Shop at Newbury Street, 1760-1790. Advertised, *Boston News Letter*. October 31, 1771; "Lost four silver spoons, two London made, marked crest, a Spread Eagle; two no mark, Maker's Name, B. Pierpont. If offered for sale, it is desired they may be stopped."

HENRY PITKIN   1834
East Hartford, Conn. Brother of three silversmiths. Taught business to Nelson P. Stratten of Waltham Watch Company. Later Troy, N. Y.

JOHN O. PITKIN
1803-1891

East Hartford, Conn., 1837. Worked with Walter Pitkin from 1826. Retired 1840.

J. O. & W. PITKIN
1826

East Hartford, Conn., partnership dissolved in 1837.

WALTER PITKIN
1808-1885

East Hartford, Conn., 1830. Employed as many as forty workmen. In partnership with John O. Pitkin, later C. C. Norton. Fire destroyed factory in 1880.

WILLIAM J. PITKIN
1820

East Hartford, Conn.

WILLIAM L. PITKIN
1820

East Hartford, Conn.

PITKIN & NORTON
1825

Hartford, Conn. Walter Pitkin and C. C. Norton in partnership.

BENJAMIN PITMAN
1820

Providence, R. I.

I. PITMAN
1785

Baltimore, Md.

SAUNDERS PITMAN
1732-1808

Providence, R. I., 1775 at North corner of Main and Otis Streets to 1770. Married Mary Kinnicutt, June 29, 1760. Advertised in, *Providence Gazette*, April 2, 1796; "Takes this Method to acquaint his old Customers and the Public, that he makes and sells, at his Shop, a few Doors North of the State-House, Gold and Silversmith's Ware . . Wanted, as an Apprentice to the above Business, an honest industrious Lad, about 14 Years of age." Firms of Pitman & Dorrance, Pitman & Dodge.

WILLIAM R. PITMAN
1835

New Bedford, Mass.

RICHARD PITTS
1744

Philadelphia, Pa. Advertised as silversmith on Front Street, 1744. In Charleston, S. C., in 1746.

PLATT & BROTHER
1825

New York. Partnership of George W. and N. C. Platt.

G. W. & N. C. PLATT
1820

New York.

WILLIAM POLLARD
1687-1746

Boston, Mass., 1715.

LEWIS J. PONCET
1800

Baltimore, Md., until 1822.

THOMAS PONS
1757-1817

Boston, Mass., 1789 at Newbury Street. Directory until 1805.

WILLIAM POOLE 1764-1846

Wilmington, Del., 1790. Son of William and Elizabeth Canby Poole. Married May 5, 1791, Sarah Sharpless. Apprenticed to Bancroft Woodcock.

F. W. PORTER 1820

New York.

HENRY C. PORTER & CO. 1830

New York at 183 Division Street.

JOSEPH S. PORTER 1783-1862

Utica, N. Y., 1805.

FREDERICK J. POSEY 1820

Hagerstown, Md.

J. O. & J. R. POTTER 1810

Providence, R. I., at 15 North Main Street until 1824.

JOHN POTWINE 1698-1792

Boston, Mass., 1721 to 1737. Son of John and Sarah Hill Potwine. Joined Brattle Street Church, 1715. Married (1) Sarah Jackson, 1721. Located on Newbury Street. Appointed Clerk of the Market in 1734. Removed to Hartford, Conn., 1737-1753. Lated advertised in Coventry and East Windsor. Married (2) Elizabeth Moseley, widow of Capt. Abner Moseley, 1771. His account book, 1752-3 records transactions. Partner of Charles Whiting 1761-2, in Hartford, Conn. Died in Scantic, May 16, 1792, where for many years he was Pastor of Congregational Church.

ABRAHAM POUTREAU 1726

New York. Baptized in French Church, April 5, 1701, son of Daniel and Martha Couson Poutreau. Married Maria Vreeland October 23, 1726. Robert Lyell, son of David Lyell, silversmith, was apprenticed to him.

HENRY PRATT 1708-1749

Philadelphia, Pa., 1730. Born, April 30, 1708, son of Henry and . . . Hobart Pratt. Married Rebecca Claypool, May 1, 1729, in Christ Church. Advertised shop at corner Taylor's Alley, between Walnut and Chestnut Streets. His son Matthew Pratt was the noted painter. Died in Philadelphia, January 31, 1749.

NATHAN PRATT 1772-1842

Essex, Conn., 1792. Born in Lyme. Son of Phineas.

HENRY PRESCOT 1828

Keeseville, N. Y., until 1831.

STEPHEN L. PRESTON 1850

Newburgh, N. Y. Firm of Curry & Preston.

JOB PRINCE 1680-1703

Milford, Conn., 1703. Born in Hull, Mass. Died in Milford.

WILLIAM PURSE 1760-1844

Charleston, S. C., 1798 at 112 Broad Street until 1803. Married Elizabeth Hammett, May 1, 1793. Lieutenant in 1809.

EDWARD PUTNAM   1825
Boston, Mass., until 1830.

PUTNAM & LOW   1822
Boston, Mass.

REUBEN H. PUTNEY   1816
Sackets Harbor, N. Y. In Watertown, 1821-1828.

Q

PETER QUINTARD   1699-1762
New York, 1731, registered as Freeman. Son of Isaac and Jeanne Fune Quintard, of Bristol, England, born June 14, 1699. Baptized in French Church of New York. Married (1) Jean O'Dart Ballereau, May 8, 1731. (2) Deborah Knapp of Stamford. Advertised, *New York Gazette,* "Goldsmith, living near the New Dutch Church." 1735. Notice, *New York Mercury,* September, 1764, "Stolen, out of the House of Daniel Dunscomb, of this City, a Silver Tankard, marked on the Bottom thus M
                                   D D, containing a Wine Quart. It had a large bruise on the side, the hinge pretty much wore, the Maker's Stamp PQ near the Handle." Removed to Norwalk, Conn., in 1737 where he died in 1762.

R

ROBERT RAIT   1830
New York at 45 Ann Street. Commissioned by City Council to design badges for New York Police Department.

W. D. RAPP   1828
Philadelphia, Pa.

ANTHONY RASCH   1807
Philadelphia, Pa., in High Street until 1819. Firms of Rasch & Willig, Chaudron & Rasch. Later in New Orleans, La.

ANTHONY RASCH & CO.   1820
Philadelphia, Pa., on High Street.

W. A. RASCH   1830
New Orleans, La.

FREDERICK RATH   1830
New York.

JOSEPH RAYNES   1835
Lowell, Mass.

CLAUDIUS REDON   1828
New York.

ISAAC REED & SON   1830
Philadelphia, Pa., until 1830.

OSMON REED   1831
Philadelphia, Pa., at 176 North Second Street, until 1841.

O. REED & CO. 1841
Philadelphia, Pa.

STEPHEN REED 1805
New York; in Philadelphia, Pa., at 147 South Twelfth Street, 1846-1850.

ABNER REEDER 1766-1841
Philadelphia, Pa., 1793. Born in Ewing, N. J., October 10, son of John and
Hannah Mershon Reeder. Married Hannah Wilkinson, May 22, 1796. Advertised at
38 South Front Street, 1793-1800. In partnership with John McFee. Later located
in Trenton, N. J., on State Street, where he was appointed Postmaster. Was President of State Bank. Died, October 25.

JOSEPH REEVE 1803
Newburgh, N. Y., until 1813. New York until 1828.

ENOS REEVES 1753-1807
Charleston, S. C., 1784. Served as Adjutant in Revolution. Reeves' Letter-Books
published, giving description of times. Member of the South Carolina Society of
Cincinnati.

J. F. REEVES 1835
Baltimore, Md.

STEPHENS REEVES 1767
Cohansey Bridge, Cumberland County, N. J. Later in Burlington. Also Black
Horse Alley and Second Street, Philadelphia, 1766. Advertised in, *New York
Gazette,* October 7, 1776, "Gold and Silversmith, Living near the corner of
Burling's Slip, in Queen Street. Takes this method to inform his friends and customers, and the public in general, that he now carries on his business as usual,
such as making and mending all kinds of gold and silver ware, mounting and
mending swords, and making all sorts of jeweler's work, &c. &c. He returns his sincere thanks for all past favors and he hopes for a continuance of the same, as he
flatters himself of giving general satisfaction to all who may be pleased to employ
him. N. B. Ready money for old gold and silver."

PAUL REVERE 1702-1754
Boston, Mass., 1725. Born in Riancaud, France, Apollos Rivoire (Paul Revere),
was Apprenticed to John Coney of Boston, 1715. Rivoire did not serve his full apprenticeship, for the administrator of Coney's estate received £ 40, "Cash for Paul
Rivoire's time." At the age of twenty-one, 1723, he revisited Guernsey for a short
time. On his return, he established himself as a gold and silversmith and
changed his name to Paul Revere. Married Deborah Hitchborn, 1729. His third
child and eldest son Paul, was born January 1, 1735. Member of the New Brick
Church. Died in Boston, January, 1754.

PAUL REVERE 1735-1818
Boston, Mass., 1757. Born January 1, son of Apollos Rivoire (Paul Revere).
Educated at Master Tillston's School. Trained in father's shop. Participated in
expedition to capture Crown Point in 1756. On his return, married (1) Sarah
Orne, (2) Rachael Walker. Opened a shop as a goldsmith and engraver.
Advertised completion of the "Rescinders Bowl," *Boston Gazette,* August 8, 1768.
Engraved plates for the earliest paper money of Massachusetts. Became one of
thirty North-end Mechanics to patrol Boston Streets. He made his famous ride,
April 19, 1775. Became Lieut. Col. of Artillery. In the Penobscot Expedition in
1779. After the Revolution, continued his trade at 50 Cornhill Street. Established
a large copper-rolling mill in Canton, Mass., in 1801. Was first President of the
Massachusetts Charitable Mechanics Association. The town, Revere, Mass., was
named in his honor.

THOMAS REVERE   1739-1817
Boston, Mass., 1789, at Newbury Street. Directory until 1803. Brother of Paul, the patriot.

JOHN REYNOLDS   1770-1832
Hagerstown, Md., 1790.

HENRY P. RICE   1815
Albany, N. Y. In Saratoga Springs, N. Y., 1827-1830.

JOSEPH RICE   1784
Baltimore, Md. Firm of Rice & Barry.

JOSEPH T. RICE   1813
Albany, N. Y., at 5 Pearl Street. Continued until 1850.

OBADIAH RICH   1830
Boston, Mass. Apprenticed to Moses Morse. Located at 69 Washington Street, 1830; 7 Chapman Place, 1850. Member of the Massachusetts Charitable Mechanics Association, 1836. Firm of Ward & Rich.

SAMUEL R. RICHARDS, JR.   1793
Philadelphia, Pa., at 136 South Front Street until 1818. Partner of Samuel Williamson.

STEPHEN RICHARDS   1815
New York, at 153 Broadway until 1822.

THOMAS RICHARDS   1815
New York, until 1829.

RICHARDS & PELLETREAU   1825
New York, Stephen Richards and William S. Pelletreau.

RICHARDS & WILLIAMSON   1797
Philadelphia, Pa. Samuel R. Richards, Jr., and Samuel Williamson, until 1800.

FRANCIS RICHARDSON   1681-1729
Philadelphia, Pa., 1710. Born, November 25, 1681, in New York. Removed to Philadelphia, 1690, where he married Elizabeth Growden, daughter of Joseph Growden. Records of Minutes of City Common Council, "Goldsmith, Francis Richardson, Goldsmith, on May 20th, 1717, was admitted Freeman of Philadelphia, and paid 5 s., 6 d." Died in 1729.

FRANCIS RICHARDSON, JR.   1729
Philadelphia, Pa. Born, 1708, son of Francis and Elizabeth Growden Richardson. Married, Mary Fitzwater, September 26, 1742. Advertised, *Pennsylvania Gazette*, 1734, "Reward for runaway apprentice, Isaac Marceloe, formerly with William Heurtin, Goldsmith of New York." Located in Market Street, 1736-7. Advertised, February 15, 1738, "Lately imported and to be sold by Francis Richardson at the house of Joseph Richardson, Goldsmith, in Front Street, China, Cambricks Etc."

JOSEPH RICHARDSON   1711-1784
Philadelphia, Pa., 1732. Son of Francis, I. Married, (1) Hannah Worrell; (2) Mary Allen, 1748. Advertised until 1784. Was joined by his sons, Joseph, Jr., and Nathaniel.

CASTERS–MUFFINEERS

William Jones
1725

Peter Van Dyke
1725

Jacobus Vander Spiegel
1690

Peter Van Dyke
1710

Philip Goelet
1735

Adrian Bancker
1725

Philip Syng
1750

Daniel Henchman
1760

SALT DISHES
MUSTARD POTS

Simeon Soumaine
1725

Jacob G. Lansing
1700

Jacob Hurd
1730

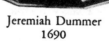

Jeremiah Dummer
1690

Peter Van Dyke
1710

Joseph Shoemaker
1790

Daniel Van Voorhis
1790

Philip Syng
1750

Lewis Fueter
1775

JOSEPH RICHARDSON, JR.   1752-1831

Philadelphia, Pa., 1773. Married, Ruth Hoskins, at Burlington, N. J., June 15, 1780. In partnership with brother Nathaniel, continuing father's business on Front Street, until 1791. Was appointed Assayer to the Mint by George Washington in 1810, when he sold his business to James Howell.

JOSEPH & NATHANIEL RICHARDSON   1771

Philadelphia, Pa., at Front Street below Walnut Street until dissolved in 1791. Nathaniel became an ironmonger.

FRANKLIN RICHMOND   1815

Providence, R. I., at 17 Market Street; 14 High Street in 1820.

JOHN RIDGEWAY   1780-1851

Boston, Mass., 1813 at Cambridge Street.

GEORGE RIDOUT   1745

New York. From London, registered in Goldsmith's Hall, "Geo. Ridout, Lombard St., 17 Oct., 1743." Admitted freeman in New York, February 18, 1745. Advertised, "Goldsmith, Near Ferry-Stairs . . ." *New York Gazette,* June 10, 1751. Also, Rydout.

BENJAMIN McKENNY RIGGS   1799-1839

Paris, Ky., 1820.

GEORGE W. RIGGS   1777-1864

Baltimore, Md., 1810. Firm of Riggs & Griffith.

RICHARD RIGGS   1810

Philadelphia, Pa. Church records death in 1819.

RIGGS & GRIFFITH   1816

Baltimore, Md.

PETER RIKER   1797

New York, at 378 Pearl Street; 151 Cherry Street in 1814. Firms of Clapp & Riker; Riker & Alexander.

CHRISTOPHER ROBERT   1708-1783

New York, 1731, Freeman, May 4th. Apprenticed to John Hastier, from May 8th, 1723, for seven years.

ROBERTS & LEE   1772

Boston, Mass. Advertised, *Boston News Letter,* November 19; "Jewellers, Opposite the Old Brick Meeting-house, Cornhill. . . . Town and Country may be supplied with every article usually imported in that way, on very advantageous terms. . . ."

ANTHONY W. ROBINSON   1798

Philadelphia, Pa., at 23 Strawberry Street. Advertised, *Federal Gazette,* at 36 South Second Street, 1800-1803.

HANNAH ROBINSON   1845

Wilmington, Del., at 91 Market Street. Born, February 2, 1803.

JOHN F. ROBINSON   1812-1867

Wilmington, Del., 1844 at 91 Market Street. Son of Joseph and Susanna Foulk Robinson.

O. ROBINSON   1800
New Haven, Conn.

EDWARD ROCKWELL   1807
New York, advertised, *New York Weekly Museum,* August 29, "Jewellery and
Silverware of his own manufacture at the shop at 4 Park Place." Located at 200
Broadway, 1811-1822.

S. D. ROCKWELL   1830
New York.

THOMAS ROCKWELL   1775
Norwalk, Conn. Inventory of estate dated 1795, lists tools for manufacture of
silverware and watches.

JAMES ROE   1770
Kingston, N. Y. Son of William and Eleanor . . . Roe, of Phillipse Patent,
Dutchess County.

WILLIAM ROE   1795
Kingston, N. Y. Brother of James.

W. ROE & STOLLENWERCK   1800
New York.

DANIEL ROGERS   1753-1792
Newport, R. I., 1774. Brother of Joseph with whom he served apprenticeship to
John Tanner. Died in 1792.

JOSEPH ROGERS   1760
Newport, R. I. Apprenticed to John Tanner with Brother Daniel. Advertised in
Hartford, Conn., 1808, at corner of Trumbull and Pratt Streets.

WILLIAM ROGERS   1801-1873
Hartford, Conn., 1822. Apprenticed to Joseph Church who admitted him to business. Advertised, 1822-1843. Founded the William Rogers Manufacturing Company of 1847.

WILLIAM ROGERS & SON   1850
Hartford, Conn.

JOHN A. ROHR   1807
Philadelphia, Pa., until 1813.

NICHOLAS ROOSEVELT   1715-1771
New York. Freeman, March 20, 1738-9. Married Catharina Confert, June 5, 1737.
Received a commission from City for two gold boxes, £ 38-8. Advertised, *New
York Gazette,* January 30, 1769; "To be Let, and enter'd upon the 1st of May next,
The house in which Nicholas Roosevelt now lives, at the lower end of Thames
Street, on the wharf fronting the North-River: The conveniency and commodious-
ness of the situation excells any on the river; it fronts two slips, one of which
is near 100 feet broad, and the greatest part of the year is fill'd with boats and
crafts, from the Jersies and North-River. Is a roomy and convenient house, with
seven fire-places; a large yard, in which is a pump and cistern, and a garden and
grass plot. Likewise a silver-smith's shop to be let, and the tools of the trade to
be sold. Also to be sold by said Roosevelt, a parcel of ready made silver, large and

small, Viz. Silver tea-pots and tea spoons, silver hilted swords, sauce-boats, salts and shovels, soup-spoons both scollep'd and plain, table spoons, tea-tongs, punch ladles and strainers, milk-pots, snuff-boxes, and sundry other small articles, both gold and silver, as buckles, clasps, buttons, broaches, rings, and lockets, both plain and set with paste moco, &c. &c. which he will sell very reasonable, as he intends declining business, and to move in the Country in the Spring."

CHARLES BOUDINOT ROOT   1818-1903
Raleigh, N. C., 1843. Son of Elihu and Sophia Gunn Root of Montague, Mass. Apprenticed to Barnard Dupuy. Prominent citizen and died in Raleigh, May 7, 1903.

L. M. & A. C. ROOT   1830
Pittsfield, Mass.

W. M. ROOT   1840
Pittsfield, Mass.

W. N. ROOT & BROTHER   1850
New Haven, Conn.

JOHN ROSS   1756-1798
Baltimore, Md., 1790.

ROBERT ROSS   1789
Frederica, Del., advertised, *Delaware Gazette,* April 2, 1791; Gold and Silver-Smith, opposite to the store of William Berry, Frederica, respectfully informs the public, and his friends in particular, that he continues to carry on the gold and silversmith business in its various branches, at the above place. Work done in the best manner and on as reasonable terms as in the City of Philadelphia."

BARTHOLOMEW ROSWELL   1805
Hartford, Conn.

NELSON ROTH   1837
Utica, N. Y., until 1850.

WILLIAM MADISON ROUSE   1812-1888
Charleston, S. C., 1835, at King and Vanderhorst Streets. Apprenticed to John Ewing for four years. Married Sarah Lord.

WILLIAM ROUSE   1639-1704
Boston, Mass., 1660. Mentioned, *Boston News Letter,* January 20, 1704; "William Rowse, goldsmith, died in Boston." Appraisal of estate by John Coney amounted to £ 575. 11s.6d.

J. RUDD & CO.   1831
New York.

DANIEL RUSSELL   1735
Newport, R. I. Advertised "Working Goldsmith."

JOHN H. RUSSEL   1792
New York, at 3 Broad Street and 1 New Street, 1794-1798.

JONATHAN RUSSELL   1804
Ashford, Conn., Born, 1770.

MOODY RUSSELL   1694-1761
Barnstable, Mass., 1715. Born August 30. Son of Jonathan and Martha Russell. Apprenticed to Edward Winslow. His uncle, Eleaser Russell of Boston was a silversmith, 1663-1691. Deacon of the East Church, 1740. His sister Abigail married Nathaniel Otis, son was Major Jonathan Otis. Died July 3, 1761.

RICHARD RUTTER   1790
Baltimore, Md.

LOU RYERSON   1760
York, Penna.

S

HARVEY SADD   1776-1840
New Hartford, Conn., 1810. Born in New Windsor, in 1829. Moved to Austinburg, Ohio.

PHILIP B. SADTLER   1771-1860
Baltimore, Md., 1800 at 166 Baltimore Street. Firm of Sadtler & Pfaltz until 1803.

P. B. SADTLER & SON   1850
Baltimore, Md.

HENRY SAFFORD   1800
Gallipolis, Marrietta, 1810; Zanesville, Ohio, 1812.

HENRY SALISBURY   1831
New York.

SALISBURY & CO.   1835
New York.

A. SANBORN   1850
Lowell, Mass.

EDWARD SANDELL   1816
Baltimore, Md., at 115 Baltimore Street. Died 1822.

BENJAMIN SANDERSON   1649-1678
Boston, Mass., 1675.

ROBERT SANDERSON   1608-1693
Boston, Mass., 1638. Born in England where he learned his trade. With first wife Lydia, was among earliest settlers in Hampton in 1638. In Watertown, 1642 when he married (2) Mary Cross, widow of John. Freeman, September 7, 1639. Removed to Boston in 1652 and joined John Hull in minting Pine Tree Shillings. Died, October 7, 1693. Son, Robert continued business.

F. S. SANFORD   1828
Nantucket, Mass.

WILLIAM SANFORD   1817
New York, at 36 William Street; Water Street, 1818.

ENSIGN SARGEANT   1820
Boston, Mass., at May Street until 1823.

H. SARGEANT   1825
Hartford, Conn.

JACOB SARGEANT   1761-1843
Hartford, Conn., 1785. "Shop 10 rods south of State House." Born in Mansfield.
Married Olive Payne. At 229 Main Street, 1796-1843.

THOMAS SARGEANT   1816
Springfield, Mass.

MOREAU SARRAZIN   1710-1761
Charleston, S. C., 1734, advertised as jeweller. Joined the South Carolina Society,
1737. Ensign in Militia. Partner of William Wright. Died, February 4, 1761.

JOHN Y. SAVAGE   1820
Raleigh, N. C. Of firm Savage & Stedman, 1819-1820. Advertised in Richmond,
Virginia, 1829.

THOMAS SAVAGE   1664-1749
Boston, Mass., 1689, March 22, admitted freeman. Married (1) Mabel Harwood,
February 5, 1690; (2) Elizabeth . . . prior to 1717. Became a Captain, 1705.
Returned from Bermuda to Boston, October 30, 1714. Appointed Sealer of
Weights, June 4, 1725-1736. Removed to Newbury in 1737 where he died August
23, 1749.

WILLIAM M. SAVAGE   1805
Glasgow, Ky.

SILAS W. SAWIN   1825
New York, at 106 Reade Street, until 1838.

H. I. SAWYER   1840
New York.

JOEL SAYRE   1778-1818
New York, 1799. Born in Southhampton, November 2, son of Mathew and
Mehitable Herrick Sayre. Brother of John. Married, Sarah Brown, of Newark, N. J.
January 25, 1808. In New York, in 1802 at 437 Pearl Street; Maiden Lane, 1805-
1811. Died in Cario, N. Y. September 28, 1818.

JOHN SAYRE   1771-1852
New York, 1792. Born in Southhampton, June 13. Brother of Joel. Married
Elizabeth Downer of Westfield, N. J., April 10, 1816. In New York, 1796 at 281
Pearl Street until 1801. Partner of Thomas Richards, 1802-11. He published first
Bible commentary and other religious works. Removed to Cohoes, N. Y., to be-
come director of cotton factory in 1824. Died in Plainfield, N. J., November 26,
1852.

PAUL SAYRE   1785
Southhampton, N. Y.

SAYRE & RICHARDS   1802
New York. John Sayre and Thomas Richards dissolved partnership in 1811.

BARTHOLOMEW SCHAATS 1670-1758

New York, 1695. Freeman, May 22, 1708. Married (1) Christina Kermer, November 28, 1706. Daughter Antse, baptised, April 27, 1715. (2) Jacoba Kierstede, widow, April 21, 1734. In, Abstracts of New York Wills; "Bartholomew Skaats of New York, Goldsmith, being weak in body, I leave to my son, Rynier, my negro man Caesar. I leave to my grandson, Bartholomew Skaats, ℔ 10. I leave to my wife, Jacoba, and my son, all the rest of my real and personal estate." Dated, July 14, 1758; proved September 4, 1758.

GARRET SCHANCK 1791

New York, at 25 Fair Street; 133 Water Street in 1795. Partner of Daniel Van-Voorhis, dissolved, 1792. His wife Sarah and brother John were granted letters of administration, November 12, 1795.

JOHN A. SCHANCK 1795

New York. Advertised, *The Time Piece,* March 31, 1797, at 133 Water Street, "Where he carries on business in all its branches, with elegance and dispatch." John administered brother Garret's estate in 1795.

I. SCOTT 1750

Albany, N. Y.

JEHU SCOTT 1806

Raleigh, N. C. Advertised, *Raleigh Register,* until 1819 when he died, "an industrious and worthy citizen."
Hartford, Conn., at 20 Windsor Street. Firm of Seymour and Hollister.

JOHN B. SCOTT 1820

New York.

SCOVIL & KINSEY 1830

Cincinnati, Ohio.

WILLIAM SEAL 1816

Philadelphia, Pa., at 118 South Fourth Street to 1820. Firm of Browne & Seal.

JOSEPH SEYMOUR & CO. 1850

Syracuse, N. Y.

OLIVER D. SEYMOUR 1843

Hartford, Conn., at 20 Windsor Street. Firm of Seymour & Hollister.

SEYMOUR & HOLLISTER 1845

Hartford, Conn.

W. & G. SHARP 1848

Philadelphia, Pa.

J. S. SHARRARD 1850

Shelbyville, Ky.

SHAW & DUNLEVY 1833

Philadelphia, Pa., at 7 Lodge Road.

JOHN A. SHAW 1819

Newport, R. I.

ROBERT SHEPHERD 1805
Albany, N. Y. Partner of William Boyd in 1810.

SHEPHERD & BOYD 1810
Albany, N. Y., at 136 Market Street. Robert Shepherd and William Boyd, succeeded by Boyd & Hoyt.

SHETHAR & THOMPSON 1801
Litchfield, Conn., Samuel Shethar and Isaac Thompson dissolved partnership in 1805.

CALEB SHIELDS 1773
Baltimore, Md., advertised at his house in Gay Street, June 21. Notice of settlement of accounts requested, *Maryland Journal,* July 30, 1782. Brother of Thomas Shields.

THOMAS SHIELDS 1765
Philadelphia, Pa. "Opened Shop in Front Street, the Third Door above the Drawbridge. . . " *Penna. Gazette,* July 14, 1765. "At the sign of the Golden Cup and Crown." 1771. Listed in directory, 1785-1791 at 126 South Front Street, Brother of Caleb.

NATHANIEL SHIPMAN 1764-1853
Norwich, Conn., 1790. Apprenticed to Thomas Harland. Represented town in General Assembly. Appointed Judge of the County and Probate Courts.

SHIPP & COLLINS 1850
Cincinnati, Ohio.

GODFREY SHIVING 1779
Philadelphia, Pa. Advertised, *Penna. Packet;* "Goldsmith and Jeweller. Takes this method to acquaint the Public, and his Friends in Particular, that he is removed from Second Street, to the South Side of the King of Prussia, where he carries on the Goldsmith and Jewellery business, in its different branches as usual." Different spellings, Schriving, Schwing.

JOSEPH SHOEMAKER 1793
Philadelphia, Pa., at 12 North Front Street; 24 Pewter Platter Alley until 1798; 38 North Front Street, 1802-1816. Listed until 1839.

CLARK SIBLEY 1778-1808
New Haven, Conn., 1800. Born in New Haven. Advertised until 1806. Partner of Simeon Marble.

JOHN SIBLEY 1810
New Haven, Conn.

SIBLEY & MARBLE 1801
New Haven, Conn., on Church Street, next North of Trinity Church. Clark Sibley and Simeon Marble dissolved partnership in 1806.

H. SILL 1840
New York.

H. & R. W. SILL 1840
New York.

HEZEKIAH SILLIMAN 1739-1804
New Haven, Conn., 1767. Firm of Cutler, Silliman, Ward & Co., 1768.

WILLIAM SIMES 1773-1834
Portsmouth, N. H., 1800.

ANTHONY SIMMONS 1797
Philadelphia, Pa., at 13 North Second Street; 27 Sassafras Street until 1808.
Firm of Simmons & Alexander: Simmons & Williamson.

JAMES SIMMONS 1815
New York, at 46 Cliff Street. Firm of J. & A. Simmons.

J. & A. SIMMONS 1805
New York, at 275 Pearl Street.

S. SIMMONS 1797
Philadelphia, Pa.

SIMMONS & ALEXANDER 1800
Philadelphia, Pa., at 44 South High Street. Anthony Simmons and Samuel Alexander continued at this address until 1804.

SIMMONS & WILLIAMSON 1797
Philadelphia, Pa., at 13 North Second Street, dissolved following year by Anthony Simmons and Samuel Williamson.

THOMAS BARTON SIMPKINS 1728-1804
Boston, Mass., 1750, at Fish Street until 1789; Ann Street in 1796.

WILLIAM SIMPKINS 1704-1780
Boston, Mass., 1730. Born, March 20th. Married Eliza Symmes, May 14, 1726. Served as Sergeant of Artillery Company, 1743. Ensign, 1757. Advertised, "Goldsmith, near the Drawbridge, the library of the late Rev. Robert Stanton of Salem." June 20, 1728. Notice, "Loss of a piece of silver three inches broad, 1/4 inch thick and weighing fourteen ounces." *Boston Evening Post,* January 27, 1746.

ABRAHAM SKINNER 1756
New York. Freeman, May 18. Notice, *New York Gazette,* June 7, 1762, "Silversmith, on the New-Dock between the Ferry Stairs and Rotten Row." Married, Catharine Foster, August 27, 1773.

MATT SKINNER 1752
Philadelphia, Pa.

THOMAS SKINNER 1712-1761
Marblehead, Mass., 1740.

JOSHUA SLIDELL 1765
New York. Freeman, October 1. Married Jane Ashford, April 30, 1764.

DAVID SMITH 1787
Lansingburgh, N. Y., until 1793. Born in London. Immigrated to Virginia, March 4, 1774.

FLOYD SMITH 1815
New York.

SUGAR BOXES

Edward Winslow
1702

John Coney
1700

INK STANDS

John Coney
1700

Philip Syng
1752

TRAYS

Thomas Savage
1700

Henry Pratt
1725

Adrian Bancker
1725

Charles LeRoux
1740

Elias Boudinot
1760

JOHN SMITH   1814
Baltimore, Md.

JOHN LEONARD SMITH   1850
Syracuse, N. Y.

JOSEPH SMITH   1742-1789
Boston, Mass., 1765 at 48 Newbury Street, 1789.

RICHARD E. SMITH   1827
Louisville, Ky. Firm of Smith & Grant.

WILLIAM SMITH   1770
New York, advertised as "Gold and Silver-smith in Chapel-Street." November 5,
1770, *New York Gazette.*

ZEBULON SMITH   1786-1865
Maine, 1820.

SMITH & GRANT   1827
Louisville, Ky., until 1831.

JEREMIAH SNOW, JR.   1808
Williamsburg, Mass. Opened shop and advertised for apprentice.

SAMUEL SOUMAINE   1718-1765
Annapolis, Md., 1740-1754. Married Susanna Minskie, September 7, 1742. Advertised, *Maryland Gazette,* March 21, 1763; "Goldsmith and Jeweller, from Philadelphia, opened Shop in South-east Street, Near St. Ann's Church, where he makes
all sorts of Gold and Silver Work, such as Tureens, Tea Kettles, Bread Baskets,
Chaffing Dishes, Coffee Pots, Butter Boats, large and small Waiters, holding from
one glass to 18, fluted soup ladles, Tankards of all sizes, Sugar-dishes, Punch
Bowles, Tea Pots." Returned to Philadelphia in 1754 where he died, 1765.

SIMEON SOUMAINE   1685-1750
New York, 1706. Born in London, son of Simeon and Jean Piaud Soumaine. In
New York, 1690. Married about 1705 Mary Burt, daughter of Samuel Burt, promi-
nent merchant. Vestryman in Trinity Church, 1712-1750. William Anderson, 1710,
Elias Boudinot, 1722, and Elias Pelletreau, 1741, served as his apprentices at
his shop near Old Slip Market. Notice, April 3, 1727, "Gold Work, wrought by
Simeon Soumain of New York, Goldsmith, all of the newest Fashion. The highest
prize consists of an Eight square Tea-Pot, six Tea-Spoons, Skimmer and Tongs,
Valued, at 18 £ 3 s. 6d."

THOMAS SPARROW   1764
Annapolis, Md.

ISAAC SPEAR   1836
Boston, Mass., near Manchester Street. In Newark, N. J., 1837.

G. SPENCE   1830
Newark, N. J.

S. P. SQUIRE   1835
New York.

SQUIRE & BROTHER   1846
New York.

SQUIRE & LANDER   1840
New York.

PHILEMON STACY, JR.   1819
Boston, Mass. Born in Gloucester, Mass., March 1, 1798, son of Philemon and
Polly Bray Stacy, March 1, 1798. Apprenticed to Jesse Churchill of 88 Newberry
Street. Young Stacy had a shop in rear of 26 Marlboro (Washington Street).
Died, July 13, 1829.

JOHN STANIFORD   1737-1811
Windham, Conn., 1789. Firm of Elderkin & Staniford.

DANIEL STANTON   1755-1781
Stonington, Conn., 1776. Son of Phineas and Elizabeth Stanton. Brother of Enoch
and Zebulon. Served in Revolutionary War at Fort Griswold, Groton, where
he was killed.

ENOCH STANTON   1745-1781
Stonington, Conn., 1766. Killed with brother Daniel at Fort Griswold.

WILLIAM P. & H. STANTON   1826
Rochester, N. Y.

ZEBULON STANTON   1753-1828
Stonington, Conn., 1775. Son of Phineas and Elizabeth Stanton. Brother of Enoch.
Married Esther Gray. The shop he erected with help of his brothers is still standing
on Main Street. Died July 18, 1828.

HENRY B. STANWOOD   1818-1869
Boston, Mass., 1840.

J. E. STANWOOD   1850
Philadelphia, Pa.

JOHN J. STAPLES, JR.   1788
New York.

RICHARD STARR   1807
Boston, Mass., at Franklin Street.

THOMAS E. STEBBINS   1830
New York.

THOMAS E. STEBBINS & CO.   1835
New York.

STEBBINS & HOWE   1832
New York.

T. S. STEELE   1800
Hartford, Conn.

T. STEELE & CO.   1815
Hartford, Conn.

GEORGE STEPHENS 1791
New York, at White Hall Slip to 1793; 25 Rose Street in 1795. Probably Gothelf
Stephens or Godfrey Shiving of Philadelphia.

THOMAS STEPHENSON 1835
Buffalo, N. Y., until 1848.

STEVENS & LAKEMAN 1825
Salem, Mass.

C. W. STEWART 1850
Lexington, Ky.

JOHN STEWART 1791
New York, at 32 Duke Street. In Baltimore, Md., after 1810.

JOHNATHAN STICKNEY, JR. 1796
Newburyport, Mass. Advertised. *Newburyport Herald,*; "Silversmith and jeweler,
has removed from Water Street to Middle Street." Ordained Minister in Maine,
1800.

M. P. STICKNEY 1820
Newburyport, Mass.

E. STILLMAN 1825
Stonington, Conn.

RICHARD STILLMAN 1805
Philadelphia, Pa.

JACOB STOCKMAN 1828
Philadelphia, Pa., until 1850, at 46 Chestnut Street.

STOCKMAN & PEPPER 1828
Philadelphia, Pa., 1845.

JONATHAN STODDER, JR. 1825
New York.

STODDER & FROBISHER 1816
Boston, Mass. Directory until 1825.

STOLLENWERCK & BROTHERS 1805
New York.

STOLLENWERCK & CO. 1800
New York, at 137 William Street; later Stollenwerck & Brother.

ADAM STONE 1804
Baltimore, Md., at Saint's Lane; Baltimore Street, 1812.

ABRAHAM G. STORM 1779-1836
Poughkeepsie, N. Y., 1800. Born in Hopewell, March 28, son of Goris Storm
and Maria Conklin Storm. Married Mary Adriance. Firm of Storm & Wilson.
Secretary of Mechanics Society. Trustee of Village.

A. G. STORM & SON   1823
Poughkeepsie, N. Y., to 1826.

E. C. STORM   1815
Rochester, N. Y.

STORM & WILSON   1802
Poughkeepsie, N. Y. James Wilson and Abraham G. Storm, dissolved partnership in 1818.

S. N. STORY   1845
Worcester, Mass.

NATHAN STORRS   1768-1839
Northampton, Mass., 1792, from New York. Born in Mansfield, Conn., August 7, son of Amariah and Mary Gilbert Storrs. Apprenticed to Jacob Sargeant.

STORRS & COOK   1827
Northampton, Mass. Partnership of Nathan Storrs and Benjamin Cook until 1833.

STORRS & COOLEY   1827
Utica, N. Y.

J. D. STOUT   1817
New York.

LUCAS STOUTENBURGH   1691-1743
Charleston, S. C., 1718. Born in New York, son of Tobias and Anna Van Roologom Stoutenburgh. Captain of Militia in 1721, and in "Command of the Watch." Married Sarah Beating. Will, recorded, October 25, 1743, mentioned brother, Tobias, silversmith.

TOBIAS STOUTENBURGH   1700-1759
New York. Brother of Lucas. Freeman, May 25, 1731. Married Maria Ten Brock, April 29, 1733. Petitioned against the election of Adolph Phillipse in 1737, with fellow silversmiths, Peter Van Dyke, Charles Le Roux and Philip Goelet. Advertised, "Houses for sale, all belonging to the Estate of Tobias Stoutenburgh (father of goldsmith), late deceased. Inquire of Tobias Stoutenburgh, Gold-Smith, near the Spring Garden." *New York Weekly Post Boy,* October 22, 1744.

JOHN STOW   1748-1802
Wilmington, Del., 1772. Son of Charles and Lydia Stow. Born March 18. Married, 1777: (2) Mrs. Sarah Smith. Contributed to organization of the First Baptist Church. Advertised, *Penna. Packet,* Nov. 30, 1772; "Begs leave to inform the public, that he has opened a shop in Market-Street, next door below Mr. Gabriel Springer where he intends to carry on his business in all its branches; having had peculiar advantages in the large way, such as making coffee-pots, tea-pots, tankards, canns &c., he will undertake any piece of plate that may be wanted." Died, April 9, 1802.

GEORGE W. STRIKER   1825
New York.

JOHN STUART   1720
Providence, R. I. Died December 11, 1737. Mentioned as jeweller in will.

C. D. SULLIVAN 1850
St. Louis, Mo.

D. SULLIVAN & CO. 1820
New York.

ROBERT SWAN 1795
Andover, Mass. Philadelphia, Pa., at 77 South Second Street, 1799-1831. Spelled Swaine, 1802.

WILLIAM SWAN 1715-1774
Boston, Mass., 1740. Diary and letter of Benjamin Pickman, "Swan, Silversmith of Worcester, made a two handled cup having Pickman arms engraved on one side and on the other, the inscription "The Gift of the Province of Massachusetts to Benjamin Pickman, Esq. 1749." Advertised in *Boston News-Letter,* May 27, 1773. Died in Worcester about April 14, 1774.

JOHN SWEENEY 1816
Geneva, N. Y., until 1827.

JOHN SYMMES 1767
Boston, Mass. Advertised, "Goldsmith, near the Golden Ball. . . ." *Boston Gazette,* May 4, 1767.

DANIEL SYNG 1713-1745
Lancaster, Pa., 1734. Born in Ireland, 1713. Married Mary Gray, August 10, 1733, Christ Church, Philadelphia. One of the original vestrymen of St. James Church of Lancaster. Will, dated and proved, 1745 and 1746.

JOHN SYNG 1734
Philadelphia, Pa. *Penna. Gazette,* June 27, "All sorts of Gold and Silver Work made and mended, also Gold and Silver bought, by John Syng, Goldsmith, in Market Street over against the Market House, next Door but one to the Crown."

PHILIP SYNG 1676-1739
Philadelphia, Pa., 1715. Born in Ireland, one of nine sons, of Richard and Alicia Syng. From Bristol, England, arrived in Philadelphia, July 14, 1714, with his first wife, Abigail Murdock, and their three sons, Philip, Daniel and John. Mentioned as a Gentleman and Goldsmith. Philip Syng & Co., acquired land in Maryland, May, 1722, which was later taken away by court order. Married, second wife, Hannah Leaming, May 24, 1724; third, Susannah Price, February 26, 1733. Advertised, *American Mercury,* May 19, 1720; "Goldsmith, near the Market Place." Removed to Annapolis, Md., where he died, May 18, 1739. His eldest son, Philip, received one half of his estate, second son, Daniel, one quarter, and his grandson, Philip Syng, the remaining quarter.

PHILIP SYNG, JR. 1703-1789
Philadelphia, Pa., 1726. Born in Ireland, September 29, eldest son of Philip and Abigail Murdock Syng. Came to America with parents in 1714. Returned to Philadelphia after a trip to England in 1726. Married Elizabeth Warner, February 5, 1729. Became acquainted with Benjamin Franklin about this time. Grand Master, Masonic Grand Lodge (Modern) in 1741; Director of the Library Company, 1731. Advertised, *Penna. Gazette,* September 14, 1738; "Silversmith, on Front Street." The electrical machine used by Franklin in 1747 was a contrivance of Syng's. An original trustee of Academy of Philadelphia, later to become the University of Pennsylvania. He made the inkstand purchased for the Provincial Assembly for £ 25-16 s., in 1752, used at the signing of the Declaration of Independence, and the Constitution of the United States, which is now on exhibi-

tion in Independence Hall. Elected Manager of the House for Employment of the Poor, May 15, 1766. Announced retirement from business in notice, which appeared, September 23, 1772, appointing Richard Humphreys, a former apprentice, his successor to his goldsmith's business. Died May 8, 1789. Buried in Christ's Church Burying Ground, Philadelphia. Estate was shared by his eighteen children.

T

JOHN TANGUY   1801
Philadelphia, Pa., at 33 North Third Street, until 1818. Brother of Peter.

JOHN TANNER   1713-1785
Newport, R. I., 1740. Taught trade to Joseph and Daniel Rogers.

PERRY G. TANNER   1842
Utica, N. Y. In Cooperstown, until 1850.

TANNER & ROGERS   1750
Newport, R. I. In partnership with apprentices, Joseph and Daniel Rogers.

JOHN TARGEE   1797
New York, at 24 Gold Street; 192 Water Street, 1805-1815.

JOHN & PETER TARGEE   1811
New York, at 192 Water Street.

N. TAYLOR & CO.   1825
New York.

WILLIAM TAYLOR   1775
Philadelphia, Pa. Advertised, *Penna. Evening Post,* October 23, 1777; "Goldsmith, In Front Street, near the Drawbridge. Makes and Repairs all kinds of Swords and Hangers, and has for sale a variety of Jewellery, gold, and silver articles."

TAYLOR & HINSDALE   1807
New York from Newark, N. J. Located at 146 Broadway. Succeeded by Taylor & Baldwin.

TAYLOR & LAWRIE   1837
Philadelphia, Pa., at 114 Arch Street.

BARENT TEN EYCK   1714-1795
Albany, N. Y., 1735. Son of Koenraet. Baptized, October 3, 1714. Married Effie . . . who died, 1791. Elected Assistant Alderman in the Second Ward, 1746. In 1794 he subscribed £ 40 toward establishment of Union College. Died February 27, 1795.

JACOB C. TEN EYCK   1705-1793
Albany, N. Y., 1725. Baptized, April 29, 1705. Son of Koenraet and Geertje Van Schaick Ten Eyck. Apprenticed to Cornelius Kierstede, August 10, 1718, for seven years of which he served nine months to complete term with Charles LeRoux. Married Catharyna Cuyler, August 17, 1736. Worked until 1770. Held important public offices, becoming Mayor of Albany. Died September 9, 1793.

KOENRAET TEN EYCK   1678-1753
Albany, N. Y., 1703. Baptized April 9. Married Geertje Van Schaick, October 15, 1704. In New York where he became a Freeman, May 8, 1716. Returned to Albany. Held numerous appointed offices. Representative to Colonial Assembly, 1747-1750. Died January 23, 1753, in Albany.

WILLIAM I. TENNEY   1840
New York.

GEER TERRY   1775-1858
Enfield, Conn., 1800. Appointed Postmaster. Removed to Worcester, Mass. Returned to Enfield, 1814.

WILBERT TERRY   1785
Enfield, Conn.

JOSEPH B. THAXTER   1791-1863
Hingham, Mass., 1815. Born, October 15. Married Sally Gill, November 12, 1815. Died May 8, 1863.

FRANCIS & FELIX THIBAULT   1807
Philadelphia, Pa., at 172 South Second Street.

THIBAULT & BROTHERS   1810
Philadelphia, Pa., at 66 South Second Street, until 1835.

WALTER THOMAS   1769
New York. Freeman, February 10, and March 21.

D. B. THOMPSON   1825
Litchfield, Conn.

WILLIAM THOMPSON   1795
Baltimore, Md. Advertised at Gay Street; Market Street, 1814; Pratt Street in 1824.

ISAAC THOMSON   1801

JAMES THOMSON   1834
New York, at 129 William Street; later in Brooklyn.

WILLIAM THOMSON   1810
New York, at 399 Broadway; William Street, 1811-1825. Commissioned to make presentation silver service by the City for Captain Samuel Reid for gallant bravery at the Battle of Fayal.
Litchfield, Conn. Partner of S. Shether until 1805.

JAMES TILEY   1740-1792
Hartford, Conn., 1765. Member of St. John's Lodge of Free Masons, 1763. Advertised, 1765-1784, at King Street and later on Front Street where he was injured in a gunpowder explosion. Notice, May 11, 1784; "Offers articles in the silversmith's and Jeweller's line in exchange for white pine boards, shingles, and window sash stuffs." Tiley received enough building material to erect a house suitable for entertainment, which he opened in 1786. Member of the Governor's Guard in 1771. Served as Captain in the Revolutionary War. In the South after 1790.

F. TINKHAM & CO.   1850
New York.

SAMUEL TINGLEY   1754
New York. "Removed from his Shop in the Fly, to the Rotten-Row, where he continues his Business, in 1767. The Shop he left is to Let." *New York Mercury,* May 11. Married Susannah Clem, November 6, 1767. Removed to Philadelphia in 1796.

B. H. TISDALE   1824
Providence, R. I., at 148 North Main Street.

FRANCIS TITCOMB   1790-1832
Newburyport, Mass., 1813, on Merrimack Street, May 11, advertisement.

JAMES TITUS   1833
Philadelphia, Pa.

JOHN TOUZELL   1726-1785
Salem, Mass., 1756. Grandson of Philip English. Advertised, *Boston News-Letter*, November 5, 1767; "The Subscriber's Shop in Salem was Broke Open the first of this Instant, in the Night, and the following Articles were Stolen from him, viz: 1½ Dozen Tea-Spoons marked I:T, one large Spoon, Maker's Name J. Towzell. Any Person that will discover the Thief or the Goods, that the Owner may recover them again, shall have Ten Dollars Reward and all necessary Charges paid by me. John Towzell, Goldsmith."

IRA S. TOWN   1825
Montpelier, Vt.

THOMAS TOWNSEND   1701-1777
Boston, Mass., 1725.

OBADIAH W. TOWSON   1813
Baltimore, Md., 1813-1819; Philadelphia, Pa., at 73 St. John Street; 1819-1824. Apprenticed to Charles L. Boehme.

ISAAC N. TOY   1771-1834
Abingdon, Md., 1790. Eldest son of Joseph Toy.

JOSEPH TOY   1748-1826
Abingdon, Md., 1776. Married Frances Dallam May 20, 1770. Was Professor of Mathematics and English, in Cokesbury College, in 1788, as well as a silversmith. In Baltimore after 1796. Worked with William Wilson about 1790.

TOY & WILSON   1790
Abingdon, Md. Joseph Toy and William Wilson.

GORDON TRACY   1767-1792
Norwich, Conn., 1787. Brother of Erastus. Advertised in New London, 1791.

JOHN PROCTOR TROTT   1769-1852
New London, Conn., 1792. Born in Boston, son of Jonathan from whom he learned trade. On State Street in 1799. Firms of Trott & Cleveland; Trott & Brooks.

JONATHAN TROTT   1730-1815
Boston, Mass., 1758-1771, advertised, "At his Shop between the White Horse and Lamb Tavern, South End." Removed to Norwich, Conn., 1772, and New London, 1784, where he became an innkeeper of Peck's Tavern.

JONATHAN TROTT, Jr.   1771-1813
New London, Conn., 1795. Born in Boston. Brother John Proctor. Advertised on Beach Street in 1800.

J. P. TROTT & SON   1820
New London, Conn.

SAUCE DISHES

Charles LeRoux
1715

Paul Revere
1745

Gerrit Onckelbag & Jesse Kip
1695

Joseph Richardson
1760

John & Tunis Denise
1800

Joseph Anthony
1785

DISHES–TUREENS

John Coburn
1764

William Cowell
1716

Joseph Richardson
1775

William Gale
1825

John W. Forbes
1830

Charles L. Boehme
1800

TROTT & BROOKS   1798
New London, Conn., on State Street for one year.

TROTT & CLEVELAND   1792
New London, Conn. John Proctor Trott and William Cleveland dissolved partnership in 1794.

HENRY R. TRUAX   1760-1834
Albany, N. Y., 1815 at 25 Steuben Street until 1819.

JAMES TURNER   1744
Boston, Mass. Advertised in Cornhill, 1748. Died in Philadelphia, 1759.

ANDREW TYLER   1692-1741
Boston, Mass., 1715. Married Mary Pepperell. Served on Town Board, 1720-1732.
Listed as subscriber to *Prince's Chronology*, 1728-1736. Died August 12, 1741.

DAVID TYLER   1760-1804
Boston, Mass., 1781.

D. M. TYLER   1810
Boston, Mass.

GEORGE TYLER   1740-1785
Boston, Mass., 1765.

JOHN H. TYLER & CO.   1840
Boston, Mass.

U

UFFORD & BURDICK   1812
New Haven, Conn. William S. Burdick advertised dissolution in 1814.

ANDREW UNDERHILL   1780
New York.

THOMAS UNDERHILL   1779
New York. Married Elizabeth Thorne, November 25, 1779. Admitted as Freeman, August 20, 1787. Firm of Underhill & Vernon.

UNDERHILL & VERNON   1787
New York. John Vernon and Thomas Underhill advertised at 41 Water Street.

V

JOHN VANALL   1752
Charleston, S. C. Married Elizabeth Bonneau, June 26, 1747. Advertised in *South Carolina Gazetter*, until 1767.

PETER VAN BEUREN   1795
New York, at 52 Maiden Lane; 272 Pearl Street in 1798.

WILLIAM VAN BEUREN   1790
New York, at Cortlandt Street; 22 Maiden Lane in 1794.

CORNELIUS VANDER BURGH 1652-1699

New York, 1675. Son of Lucas and Annetse Cornelius Vander Burgh. Married Levyntie Leumen, January 7, 1673. On Tax List in 1677 as owner of two houses, one on High Street, the other in the Fort, "where ye Silversmith liv'd." Appointed High Constable in 1689. "Recommended with Jacob Boelen for Office for Regulation of Weights and Scales, Curr'y, Gold, and Silver," in 1694. Made the Gold Cup presented to Governor Fletcher in 1693.

JACOBUS VANDER SPIEGEL 1668-1708

New York, 1689. Son of Laurens Vander Spiegel. Married Ann Sanders. Daughter, Sarah, baptized, February 7, 1694. Captain in the Army, 1691. Constable in 1698. Freeman, February 24, 1701.

PETER VAN DYKE 1684-1751

New York, 1705. Married Rachael LeRoux, October 27, 1711, daughter of Bartholomew LeRoux to whom he was apprenticed. Later married Cornelia Van Varick. Appointed Constable of the East Ward in 1708. Mentioned as appraiser of lottery in 1727. Assessor of City, 1730. Will, dated August 1st, 1750, proved January 5, 1751.

RICHARD VAN DYKE 1717-1770

New York, 1750. Son of Peter and Rachael Le Roux Van Dyke. Married Elizabeth Strang of Rye. Advertised at Hanover Square, 1750-1756.

PETER VAN INBURGH 1689-1740

New York, 1710.

JAN VAN NIEU KIRKE 1716

New York.

VAN NESS & WATERMAN 1835

New York, at 9 City Hall Place.

NICHOLAS VAN RENSSELAER 1765

New York and Albany, N. Y.

TUNIS VAN RIPER 1813

New York, at 69 Division Street, until 1816.

VANSANT & CO. 1850

Philadelphia, Pa.

G. VAN SCHAICK 1800

Albany, N. Y.

JOHN VAN STEENBERG, Jr. 1775

Kingston, N. Y.

HENRY VAN VEGHTEN 1760

Albany, N. Y. Died intestate in 1787.

DANIEL VAN VOORHIS 1751-1824

Philadelphia, 1782. Born in Oyster Bay, August 30, son of Cornelius and Neeltje Hoagland Van Voorhis. Married Catherine Richards in 1775. Advertised, *Penna. Gazette,* May 6, 1782; "Front Street, Philadelphia." *New Jersey Gazette,* Febry. 5,

1783; "Removal to Princeton." Located in New York, 1785, and in partnership with William Coley. Working at 72 Hanover Square, 1787; Queen Street in 1789. Firm of Van Voorhis & Schanck, 1791-2. At various addresses until 1798, when he admitted his son into business. Appointed as Weigher in Custom House in 1805, after death of his son. Died in Brooklyn, June 10, 1824.

VAN VOORHIS, SCHANCK & McCALL 1800
Albany, N. Y.

VAN VOORHIS & COLEY 1786
New York, Hanover Square, Daniel Van Voorhis and William Coley.

VAN VOORHIS & SCHANCK 1791
New York, at Queen Street. Daniel Van Voorhis and his cousin, Garret Schanck, dissolved partnership in 1792.

STEPHEN VAN WYCK 1805
New York.

PETER VERGEREAU 1720
New York. Freeman, July 11. Born 1700. Advertised on Queen Street, commonly known as Smith's Valley. Married Susanna Boudinot, sister of Elias Boudinot, silversmith, October 24, 1737. Will, dated, November 29, 1753, "indisposed and weak." His wife, daughter and son, Peter, shared his estate, proved, January 23, 1756.

JOHN VERNON 1787
New York. Advertised at 41 Water Street, 1793; 93 John Street, 1794-5; 75 Gold Street, 1815. Firm of Underhill & Vernon.

NATHANIEL VERNON 1777-1843
Charleston, S. C., 1802, at 136 Broad Street. Married Ann Eliza Russel, 1814. Continued in business until 1835. Died October 4, 1843, buried in Christ Church Parish.

N. VERNON & CO. 1803
Charleston, S. C., at 140 Broad Street. Vernon & Co., 1806-1807.

SAMUEL VERNON 1683-1737
Newport, R. I., 1705. Son of Daniel and Ann Dyer Vernon, born in Newport, December 6. Married April 10, 1707; again, January 12, 1725. Registered as Freeman in 1714. Appointed by Assembly to settle land controversy, 1726, when he also assisted Governor in investigating health conditions of the Colony.

WILLIAM VILANT 1725
Philadelphia, Pa. Advertised in *American Mercury*, August 12-19, as "Goldsmith."

R. H. L. VILLARD 1833
Georgetown, D. C., at Bridge Street.

RICHARD VINCENT 1799
Baltimore, Md.

DAVID VINTON 1790
Providence, R. I. Advertised, *United States Chronicle*, January 24, 1793; "Goldsmith and Jeweller from Boston, Informs the Ladies and Gentlemen of Providence

and its Vicinity, that he has for sale at his Shop, the North End Corner of Market Parade and nearly opposite, His Excellency, Governor Fenner, a complete assortment of gold and silversmith's wares. N.B. All kinds of Gold and Silverware made and repaired in the neatest manner and on the shortest notice."

JOHN VOGLER 1783-1881

Salem, N. C., 1802. Son of George and Anna Kunzel Vogler. Married Christina Spack in 1820. Was active in the Moravian Church. Died in Salem, June 15, 1881.

W

ISAIAH WAGSTER 1780

Baltimore, Md. Advertised as goldsmith in *Maryland Journal*, "at Market, near Calvert Street."

JOHN WAITE 1742-1817

South Kingstown, R. I., 1763. Son of Benjamin and Abigail Waite. Married Margaret Sheffield, 1767. Apprenticed to Samuel Casey. Colonel in Revolutionary War. Held public offices.

WILLIAM WAITE 1730-1826

Wickford, R. I., 1760. Brother of John. Purchased land in Little Rest. Removed to Cambridge, N. Y.

D. WALDRON 1789

New York, at Greenwich Road.

GEORGE WALKER 1797

Philadelphia, Pa., at 19 North Third Street until 1814.

HANNAH WALKER 1816

Philadelphia, Pa., at 19 North Third Street where she worked with brother George.

L. WALKER 1825

Boston, Mass. (I. Walker).

WILLIAM WALKER 1793

Philadelphia, Pa., at 2 Quarry Street; at Second Street, 1802-1816.

JOHN WALLEN 1763

Philadelphia, Pa.

JOHN WALRAVEN 1771-1814

Baltimore, Md., 1792, at 4 Bridge Street; Baltimore Street, 1796-1814.

JACOB WALTER 1782-1865

Baltimore, Md., 1815.

JOSEPH M. WALTER 1835

Baltimore, Md.

AMBROSE WARD 1735-1808

New Haven, Conn., 1767. Firm of Hezekiah Silliman & Ambrose Ward & Co.

BILIOUS WARD 1729-1777

Middletown, Conn., 1750. Born in Guilford, son of William. Died in Wallingford.

JAMES WARD   1768-1856
Hartford, Conn., 1798. Born in Guilford. Apprenticed to Col. Miles Beach, with
whom he joined in partnership, 1789-1798. Advertised shop located "North of the
Bridge, at the Sign of the Golden Tea Kettle." Firms of Ward & Bartholomew;
Ward, Bartholomew & Brainard.

JEHU & W. L. WARD   1837
Philadelphia, Pa.

JOHN WARD   1805
Middletown, Conn.

WILLIAM WARD   1736-1826
Litchfield, Conn., 1757. Born in New Haven.

WARD & BARTHOLOMEW   1804
Hartford, Conn., at Front Street, until 1809. Charles Brainard, an apprentice, became partner.

ABIJAH B. WARDEN   1842
Philadelphia, Pa., until 1845.

JOSEPH WARFORD   1810
Albany, N. Y.

ANDREW ELLICOTT WARNER   1786-1870
Baltimore, Md., 1805. In partnership with eldest brother Thomas until 1812.
Captain in the War of 1812. Advertised at Gay Street.

CALEB WARNER   1784-1861
Salem, Mass., 1805. Born in Portsmouth, N. H., where he advertised. Firm of
Warner & Fellows.

C. & J. WARNER   1825
Salem, Mass.

D. WARNER   1820
Ipswich, later Salem, Mass.

JOSEPH WARNER   1742-1800
Wilmington, Del., 1775. Son of William and Mary Warner. Advertised as gold
and silversmith at the Sign of the Golden Cann at Market Street.

JOSEPH P. WARNER   1811-1862
Baltimore, Md., 1830. Son of Thomas and Mary Ann Meigs Warner. Colonel of the
Fourth Maryland Regiment. Appointed City Assayer, 1844-1852. Died September
30, 1862.

SAMUEL WARNER   1797
Philadelphia, Pa., at Pewter Platter Alley. Advertised in Baltimore, Md., in 1812.

THOMAS H. WARNER   1805
Baltimore, Md. Brother of Andrew. Appointed Assayer for the City of Baltimore,
1814. Advertised shop at 9 East Street, in 1819.

THOMAS & A. E. WARNER   1805
Baltimore, Md., at 5 North Gay Street until partnership was dissolved in 1812.

SAMUEL WATERS 1803
Boston, Mass. Inherited Benjamin Burt's tools.

EDWARD E. WATSON 1821
Boston, Mass. Died 1839.

JAMES WATSON 1830
Philadelphia, Pa., at 72 High Street.

WATSON & BROWN 1830
Philadelphia, Pa.

EMMOR T. WEAVER 1808
Philadelphia, Pa., at 17 Elfreth's Alley; Lox Legs Court in 1820.

JOSHUA WEAVER 1815
West Chester, Penna.

NICHOLAS N. WEAVER 1791-1853
Utica, N. Y., 1815.

BARNABAS WEBB 1756
Boston, Mass. Advertised, *Boston Gazette,* January 19, "Goldsmith, near the Market." Notice that he was burnt out and has opened a shop in Back Street, 1761. In Ann Street, 1762-1789.

EDWARD WEBB 1705
Boston, Mass. Notice appears, *Boston News-Letter,* November 24, 1718. "Goldsmith, of Boston, died October 21, 1718, and 'having no poor friends in England that wanted, and getting his money here, he bequeathed Two Hundred Pounds . . . for the use of the poor of Boston.'; Silver spoons with maker's marks WEBB and COWELL were advertised as stolen", 1739.

GEORGE W. WEBB 1812-1890
Baltimore, Md., 1835.

JAMES WEBB 1788-1844
Baltimore, Md., 1810, at 13 Chatham Street.

HENRY L. WEBSTER 1831
Providence, R. I.; firm of Gorham & Webster.

HENRY L. WEBSTER & CO. 1842
Providence, R. I.

SIMON WEDGE 1774-1823
Baltimore, Md., 1798. Married Anna Steine. Advertised shop at 13 Light Street, 1800; Baltimore Street until 1823.

ALFRED WELLES 1783-1860
Hebron, Conn., 1804. Worked with brother George. Served as General in War of 1812.

ALFRED & GEORGE WELLES 1807
Boston, Mass. Directory until 1810.

GEORGE WELLES   1784-1823
Boston, Mass., 1805. Member of the Charitable Mechanic Association, 1822.
Brother of Alfred.

WELLES & CO.   1816
Boston, Mass., George Welles and Hugh Gelston in Directory until 1821.

WELLES & GELSTON   1840
Boston, Mass.

LEMUEL WELLS   1790
New York on Broadway; 2 Queen Street, 1791-2. Firm of Wells & Co.; Lemuel
& Horace Wells.

LEMUEL WELLS & CO.   1794
New York.

LEMUEL & HORACE WELLS   1794
New York, at 158 Pearl Street.

JOHN WENDOVER   1694
New York. Alderman in 1698. Will, dated, July 21, 1716. Died in 1727.

BARNARD WENMAN   1789
New York, at Fly Market; Partition and William Streets until 1805.

JASON WENTWORTH   1846
Boston, Mass.

WENTWORTH & CO.   1850
New York.

B. WEST   1830
Boston, Mass. Advertised, "1½ metres from South Bridge."

JOHN L. WESTERVELT   1845
Newburgh, N. Y.

CHARLES WILLIAM WESTPHAL   1802
Philadelphia, Pa., at 118 Sassafras Street; 209 Callow Hill in 1811.

THOMAS WHARTENBY   1811
Philadelphia, Pa., at 47 Shippen Street. Firm of Whartenby & Bunn.

CALVIN WHEATON   1790
Providence, R. I. Advertised, *United States Chronicle:* "At the Sign of the Clock,
opposite Friends Meeting House." Located on Main Street, 1798.

WHEELER & BROOKS   1830
Livonia, N. Y.

WILLIAM WHETCROFT   1735-1799
Annapolis, Md., 1766, "near the Town-gate." In Baltimore at Gay Street, 1767.
Returned to Annapolis, where he married Frances Cudmore Knapp.

AMOS WHITE   1745-1825
East Haddam, Conn., 1766. Known as Silversmith and Sea Captain. Served in
Revolution. Located later in Maryland.

C. WHITE 1830
Mobile, Ala.

EDWARD WHITE 1757
Ulster County, N. Y. Will dated 1767.

PEREGRINE WHITE 1747-1834
Woodstock, Conn., 1774.

SILAS WHITE 1754-1798
New York, 1791, at Great Dock Street; 43 Roosevelt Street, 1792-1794. Died
September 23, 1798.

WILLIAM WILSON WHITE 1805
Philadelphia, Pa., at 111 North Second Street. In New York, at 70½ Bowery Lane
until 1841.

B. WHITING 1765
Norwich, Conn.

CHARLES WHITING 1725-1765
Norwich, Conn., 1750. Married Honor Goodwich, of Wethersfield, in 1749. Land
purchased in 1755 sold to Jacob Perkins in 1760.

THOMAS B. WHITLOCK 1805
New York, at 102 Pearl Street.

WILLIAM H. WHITLOCK 1805
New York, at 32 Ross Street. Directory until 1827.

AMOS WHITNEY 1800
New York, until 1805.

EBEN WHITNEY 1805
New York, at 20 Chambers Street; 3 Franklin Square, 1822. Directory until 1828.

M. F. WHITNEY 1823
New York and Schenectady, N. Y.

WHITNEY & HOYT 1828
New York.

EZRA WHITON 1813-1879
Boston, Mass., 1835, at 87 Washington Street; at 6 Court Avenue, 1850. Died 1879.

WILLIAM WHITTEMORE 1710-1770
Portsmouth, N. H., 1735.

ALANSON D. WILCOX 1843
Troy, N. Y., until 1850.

CYPRIAN WILCOX 1795-1875
New Haven, Conn., 1816. Born in Berlin. Brother of Alvan. Was First Selectman;
Judge of Probate, 1855-1857. Died in Ithaca, N. Y.

A. WILLARD 1810
Utica, N. Y.

BOXES

William Jones
1730

Garret Forbes
1810

Philip Syng
1725

Jacob Hurd
1730

John Ewan
1825

CLASPS AND KNITTING
NEEDLE HOLDERS

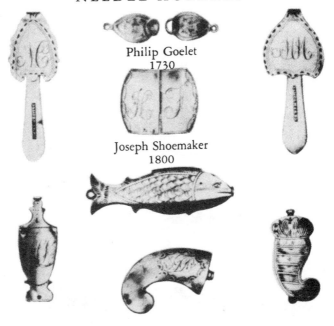

Philip Goelet
1730

Joseph Shoemaker
1800

FLATWARE

1665   1678   1690   1702   1725

1730   1767   1793   1806   1825   1825

1750   1725

1790   1825

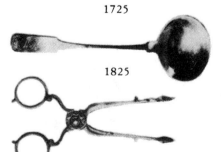

1790   1750

JAMES WILLARD   1815
East Windsor, Conn.

JOHN WILLIAMS   1793
Philadelphia, Pa., at 91 North Front Street.

STEPHEN WILLIAMS   1799
Providence, R. I.

WILLIAM A. WILLIAMS   1787-1846
Alexandria, Va., 1809. At Pennsylvania Avenue, Washington, D. C., in 1829.

SAMUEL WILLIAMSON   1794
Philadelphia, Pa., advertised at 13 North Second Street; 118 South Front Street
until 1813. Firm of Richards & Williamson.

ANDREW WILLIS   1842
Boston, Mass.

STILLMAN WILLIS   1813
Boston, Mass., at Union Street. Directory until 1825.

WILLIAM S. WILLIS   1830
Boston, Mass.

SAMUEL WILMOT   1777-1846
New Haven, Conn., 1800. Removed to Georgetown, S. C., 1825-1843.

SAMUEL & THOMAS T. WILMOT   1837
Charleston, S. C., listed on King Street after his store burned in the Great Fire.

THOMAS T. WILMOT   1840
Charleston, S. C.

HOSEA WILSON   1812
Philadelphia, Pa., at Second Street; Baltimore, Md., in 1819 at 126 Baltimore Street.

ROBERT WILSON   1805
New York, at 25 Dey Street. In Philadelphia in 1816 at 80 North 5th Street.
Firm of R. & W. Wilson, 1831.

R. & W. WILSON   1831
Philadelphia, Pa.

S. & S. WILSON   1805
Philadelphia, Pa.

WILLIAM WILSON   1755-1829
Abingdon, Md., 1785. Surveyor and Silversmith. Mentioned in land records from
1782-1807. Died in Harford County, Md., 1829.

WILSON & TOY   1790
Abingdon, Md. William Wilson and Joseph Toy worked in partnership.

CHRISTIAN WILTBERGER   1766-1851
Philadelphia, Pa., 1793. Married Ann Warner, in Christ Church, March or May
26, 1791. Advertised, *Federal Gazette,* April 29, 1799; as "Silversmith and Jeweller, Informs his Friends and the Public, that he has removed from 33 South-Second
Street to No. 13 North Second Street, nearly opposite Christ Church, where he

continues to carry on the business in all its branches as usual. A considerable quantity of silver wares manufactured immediately under his own inspection, which he means to sell on most reasonable terms." Listed in Directory until 1819. Died October, 1851. Of Firm of Wiltberger & Alexander.

MOSES WING 1785
Windsor, Conn.,and Worcester, Mass., 1809.

EDWARD WINSLOW 1669-1753
Boston, Mass., 1695. Born November 1, 1669. Son of Edward and Elizabeth Hutchinson Winslow. Married (1) Hannah Moody, daughter of Rev. Joshua Moody of First Church of Boston, (2) Elizabeth Dixie. Appointed Constable in 1699. Freeman, 1702. Advertised in 1711. Captain of Artillery Company in 1714. Sheriff of Suffolk County, 1728-1743. Colonel in Boston Regiment, 1733. Judge of Inferior Court of Common Pleas. Died in Boston.

HUGH WISHART 1784
New York, at two shops, 62 Wall, and 98 Market Street; 319 Pearl Street, 1797. Last at 66 Maiden Lane in 1810.

CHARLES & FREDERICK WITTICH 1805
Charleston, S. C., at 25 Broad Street. Charles and Frederick continued until 1807.

WOLCOTT & GELSTON 1820
Boston, Mass. Directory until 1830.

FRANCIS H. WOLFE 1829
Philadelphia, Pa., 9 Norris Alley.

GENERAL JAMES WOLF 1800
Wilmington, Del., at Market and High Streets until 1814. Active in Army with rank of Major. In Philadelphia, G. James Wolff, 1828-1833.

JAMES G. WOLF 1830
In Philadelphia, Pa., 1830, at 125 North Second Street.

WOLFE & WRIGGINS 1837
Philadelphia, Pa., at Chestnut and Fifth Streets.

BENJAMIN B. WOOD 1805
New York, at 47 Beaver Street until 1811; 96 Reade Street, 1815. Directory until 1846.

J. E. WOOD 1845
New York.

JOHN WOOD 1770
New York. Advertised, *New York Gazette,* April 30: ". . . Situated in the lower end of Maiden-lane, near the upper end of the Fly-Market, where he intends to carry on the gold and silver's work, in its various branches. . . ." In Schenectady, N. Y., 1780-1792.

A. & W. WOOD 1850
New York, at 55 Thompson Street.

WOOD & HUGHES 1846
New York, at 142 Fulton Street.

BANCROFT WOODCOCK 1732-1817

Wilmington, Del., 1754. Married Ruth Andrews, June 28, 1759. Advertised, *Penna. Gazette*, July 4, 1754; "Goldsmith. Hereby informs the publick, that he has set up his business in Wilmington, near the upper Market house, where all persons that please to favor him with their custom, may be supplied with all sorts of Gold and Silver work, after the neatest and newest fashions. N.B. Said Woodcock gives full value for old gold and silver." Continued at same address in 1772. Died 1817, and buried in Friends Meeting Yard. Firm of Woodcock & Byrnes.

ISAAC WOODCOCK 1787

Wilmington, Del.

WOODCOCK & BYRNES 1793

Wilmington, Del. Bancroft Woodcock and his nephew and apprentice, Thomas Byrnes, in partnership.

FREEMAN WOODS 1791

New York, at 11 Smith Street until 1793. Last record in North Carolina.

ANTIPAS WOODWARD 1763-1812

Middletown, Conn., 1791. Born in Waterbury in 1763. "Under the Printing Office. Located in 1792, North of the Coffee-house, where he continues to carry on his business."

WOODWARD & GROSJEAN 1847

Boston, Mass., at 13 Court Square, until dissolved in 1850.

JEREMIAH WARD WOOL 1791

New York. Freeman, June 24. Married Deborah Bratt, July 28, 1760. Listed as a Member of the General Society of Mechanics and Tradesmen.

JOSEPH WYATT 1797

Philadelphia, Pa., at Callowhill Street and Cable Lane.

ELEAZER WYER, JR. 1786-1848

Portland, Me., 1820, at 1 Prebles Road. Son of Eleazer Wyer, Silversmith of Boston. Firms of, Wyer & Farley; Wyer & Noble.

WYER & FARLEY 1828

Portland, Me., Eleazer Wyer and Charles Farley in partnership until 1832.

BENJAMIN WYNKOOP 1675-1728

New York, 1698. Son of Cornelius of Kingston, N. Y. Married Femmetje Van Der Heul, October 21, 1697. Freeman, August 9, 1698. Collector and Assessor of Taxes, 1703-1722. Son Cornelius continued business.

BENJAMIN WYNKOOP, JR. 1730

Fairfield, Conn. Baptized, May 23, 1705; married, Eunice Burr, November 22, 1730, daughter of Judge Peter Burr.

CORNELIUS WYNKOOP 1724

New York. Born 1701, son of Benjamin. Married Elizabeth Vander Spiegel, sister of Jacobus Vander Spiegel, silversmith. May 9, 1724. Freeman, 1726. Continued business of father in South Ward in 1727. Retired in 1740.

JACOBUS WYNKOOP 1765

Kingston, N. Y.

CHRISTOPHER WYNN 1795-1883

Baltimore, Md., 1820. Born in Centerville. Apprenticed to Simon Wedge. Listed at 44 South Charles Street, 1822.

Y

S. YATES 1810

Albany, N. Y.

DANIEL YOU 1743

Charleston, S. C. Advertised, *South Carolina Gazette,* 1744 at Broad Street; 1747; 1752, "Stolen, out of the Printer's House, Four Silver Table Spoons, weighing about 2 Ounces and a half each, one of them marked I.G, and pretty old; the other three with maker's name twice stamp'd near the bowl, thus: D.You. Who ever will discover the thief so that he may be convicted, or will restore the spoons to me shall have a reward of Five Pounds." Member of South Carolina Society in 1749. Died 1750.

THOMAS YOU 1753

Charleston, S. C. Son of Daniel You. Advertised at the sign of the Golden Cup on King Street. *South Carolina Gazette,* to January 30, 1775; "Spoons of all Sorts. Punch Bowls, Slop Ditto, Sugar Dishes, Pint Mugs, Strainers, Ladles, Pepper Boxes, Salt Cellars, Rings, Buttons, Buckles, and many other Articles. And, as his Dependence is entirely on the working part, he will endeavor to merit the Favor of those who will be kind enough to employ him." Married Elizabeth Clifford, 1783. Member of South Carolina Society in 1756. Died 1786.

ALEXANDER YOUNG 1784-1856

Camden, S. C., 1807, from Baltimore, Md. Born in Scotland. Firm of A. Young & Co.

EBENEZER YOUNG 1778

Hebron, Conn. Born 1756.

S. E. YOUNG 1840

Laconia, N. H.

WILLIAM YOUNG 1761

Philadelphia, Pa. Advertised, *Penna. Gazette,* Sept. 24; "In Second Street three doors above Arch Street . . . makes and sell all sorts of Goldsmith's Work; Where may be had, at most reasonable Rates, Chased and plain Tea-pots, Sugar-dishes, Cream-pots, Castors and Salts. Silver Handle Knives and Forks, with Cases of different sizes, and sundry other Things too tedious to mention." Notice, 1768; "Said, Young would take an Apprentice of a reputable Family, and an Ingenious Turn, if any should apply within three weeks, to serve not less than five years." Mentioned as a witness to a will in Philadelphia County in 1778.

Z

G. M. ZAHM 1840

Lancaster, Pa.

ZAHM & JACKSON 1830

New York.

ISAAC ZANE 1795

Zanesfield, Ohio.

JESSE SHENTON ZANE 1796

Wilmington, Del. Son of Joel and Esther Zane. Married September 18, 1794, Susannah Hanson, of Wilmington. Advertised, *The Delaware Gazette,* July 5, 1796: "The corner of Third and Market-street (Opposite Patrick O'Flinn's Tavern) the subscriber carries on the silversmith's Business in its various Branches, and gives The highest price for old silver."

NINETEENTH CENTURY

Wood & Hughes
1845

William Gale
1845

Gale & Hayden
1845

Chapter II

MARKS OF EARLY AMERICAN SILVERSMITHS
1650-1850

THE HISTORY of the makers' marks is of broad interest and a matter for special study. A mark essentially is a sign of a merchant or shopkeeper, although its implied significance is to identify an artist-craftsman. Careful attention to the details of a mark is necessary for accurate comparison, identification and attribution. For easy reference and for clarity of presentation the letters of the initials and names of the silversmiths have been listed alphabetically. These early American makers' marks found on various places of pieces of silver fashioned by these skillful craftsmen are as a rule enclosed in rectangles, ovals, shaped shields, and sometimes in the earlier marks, accompanied in combination with symbols such as a cross, crescent, bird, animal, crown, etc.

This system of marking with the silversmith's stamp is not new. In the Old World the master craftsman, when too distant from the Guild-Hall, used his private mark without the hall-marks of the town, city or country. The silversmith of good reputation was responsible for standard of quality of silver and fine workmanship and the patron accepted the pieces of silver in confidence and appreciation. This practice of marking silver in the New World without controls dates from 1650 until the present day, with only one exception.

Later at the close of the eighteenth century and the early part of the nineteenth century we find additional marks of eagles, eagles' heads, sheaves of wheat, stars, and other stamps with pseudo English hall-marks. They were probably used to distinguish silversmiths' work and possibly to compete with English imported silver. In 1814 the State of Maryland passed a law requiring all silver fashioned in Baltimore to be stamped with three marks, Arms of Baltimore, a date-letter, and the Head of Liberty, in addition to the maker's mark. This law was not too popular and was not enforced after 1830 when the practice was discontinued.

In conjunction with marks of similar makers' initials the identification of a piece of early American silver may sometimes be established by tracing the engraved arms or cyphers of the original owner. Genealogical and historical research is very important in proving conclusively the authenticity of a piece of silver.

A·ARMSTRONG	A. Armstrong	Philadelphia	1806
AB AB	Adrian Bancker	New York	1725
AB	Andrew Billings	Poughkeepsie, N. Y.	1773
AB	Abel Buel	New Haven, Conn.	1777
A·BEACH A BEACH	A. Beach	Hartford, Conn.	1823
ABHALL	Abraham B. Hall	Geneva, N. Y.	1806
A·BILLINGS	Andrew Billings	Poughkeepsie, N. Y.	1773
ABLANCHARD	Asa Blanchard	Lexington, Ky.	1808
ABRADLEY	Abner Bradley	Watertown, Conn.	1778
A.BRASIER	Anable Brasier	New York	1790
ABRINDSMAID	Abraham Brinsmaid	Burlington, Vt.	1815
AC	Alexander Cameron	Albany, N. Y.	1813
AC	Abraham Carlisle	Philadelphia	1791
AC	Aaron Cleveland	Norwich, Conn.	1820
AC AC	Arnold Collins	Newport, R. I.	1690
🔶 ◇ 🔶	Albert Cole	New York	1844
ACarlisle	Abraham Carlisle	Philadelphia	1791

A·C.BENEDICT	A. C. Benedict	New York	1840
A&C.BRANDT	A. & C. Brandt	Philadelphia	1800
A·C.BURR	Albert Chapin Burr	Rochester, N. Y.	1826
A·CLEVELAND	Aaron Cleveland	Norwich, Conn.	1820
A·CUTLER	A. Cutler	Boston	1842
AD	Amos Doolittle	New Haven, Conn.	1780
AD	Abraham Dubois	Philadelphia	1777
A·DIKEMAN	Aaron Dikeman	New York	1824
A·DUBOIS ADubois	Abraham Dubois	Philadelphia	1777
A·D.WILCOX	Alanson D. Wilcox	Troy, N. Y.	1843
A·E	Alfred Elderkin	Windham, Conn.	1792
AE	John Aaron Elliott	Sharon, Conn.	1815
AEW A·E·W	Andrew E. Warner	Baltimore, Md.	1805
A·E·WARNER 11²	Andrew E. Warner	Baltimore, Md.	1805
AF	Abraham G. Forbes	New York	1769
A.F.B. BOSTON	A. F. Burbank	Worcester, Mass.	1845
A.F.BURBANK	A. F. Burbank	Worcester, Mass.	1845
AGF NYORK	Abraham G. Forbes	New York	1769
A.G.STORM	A. G. Storm	Poughkeepsie, N. Y.	1800

Mark	Name	Place	Date
	A. & G. Welles	Boston	1807
	A. & G. Welles	Boston	1807
	Ahasuerus Hendricks	New York	1678
	A. A. Henderson	Philadelphia	1837
	Abraham Hews, Jr.	Boston	1823
	Adrian B. Holmes	New York	1801
	George Aiken	Baltimore, Md.	1787
	A. Jackson	Norwalk, Conn.	1840
	Abel Jacobs S.M.	Philadelphia	1816
	A. J. Jacobs & Co. S.M.	Philadelphia	1820
	A. Johnston	Philadelphia	1830
	Aaron Lane	Elizabeth, N. J.	1784
	Adam Lynn	Alexandria, Va.	1796
	A. L. Clapp	New York	1802
	Allen Leonard	New York	1830
	Allcock & Allen	New York	1820
	A. L. Lincoln	St. Louis, Mo.	1850
	Alfred Lockwood	New York	1817
	Adam Logan	New York	1803
	Adam Lynn	Alexandria, Va.	1796

Mark	Name	Place	Date
A MATHEY	Augustus Mathey	New York	1825
A·MOULTON	Abel Moulton	Newburyport, Mass.	1815
A.MUNGER	Asa Munger P.M.	Herkimer, N. Y.	1810
A.MUNGER & SON	A. Munger & Son	Auburn, N. Y.	1840
ANDRAS	William Andras S.M.	New York	1795
ANDRAS & CO	Andras & Co. S.M.	New York	1800
Andrew Willis	Andrew Willis	Boston	1842
ANDᵂE·WARNER	Andrew E. Warner B.M.	Baltimore, Md.	1805
A·NORTON	Andrew Norton	Goshen, Conn.	1787
ANTYRASCH	Anthony Rasch	Philadelphia	1807
AO	Andrew Oliver	Boston	1750
A·OSTHOFF ❶	Andrew Osthoff	Baltimore, Md.	1810
AP	Alexander Petrie	Charleston, S. C.	1748
AP AP	Abraham Poutreau	New York	1726
APARKER	Allen Parker	New York	1817
APPLETON	George B. Appleton	Salem, Mass.	1850
A·R PHIA	Anthony Rasch	Philadelphia	1807
A&R	Alexander & Riker	New York	1797
A RASCH & CO	Anthony Rasch & Co.	Philadelphia	1820
A·RASCH	Anthony Rasch	Philadelphia	1807

A·REEDER	Abner Reeder	Philadelphia	1793
A&RIKER	Alexander & Riker	New York	1797
ARNOLD ARNOLD	Thomas Arnold	Newport, R. I.	1760
A·ROBINSON	Anthony W. Robinson	Philadelphia	1798
AS	Anthony Simmons	Philadelphia	1797
AS AS	Abraham Skinner	New York	1756
AS	Adam Stone	Baltimore, Md.	1804
ASANBORN LOWELL	A. Sanborn P.M.	Lowell, Mass.	1850
ASIMMONS	Anthony Simmons	Philadelphia	1797
A Skinner	Abraham Skinner	New York	1756
AT AT AT	Andrew Tyler	Boston	1715
A·T·BATTLE	A. T. Battle	Utica, N. Y.	1847
ATYLER	Andrew Tyler	Boston	1715
AU	Andrew Underhill	New York	1780
A·UNDERHILL	Andrew Underhill	New York	1780
Austin	Ebenezer J. Austin	Charlestown, Mass.	1760
Austin	Nathaniel Austin	Boston	1760
AW	Antipas Woodward	Middletown, Conn.	1791
AW	Ambrose Ward	New Haven, Conn.	1767
A Welles	Alfred Welles	Hebron, Conn.	1804

AWHITE	Amos White	East Haddam, Conn.	1766
A·WHITNEY	Amos Whitney	New York	1800
A·WILLARD	A. Willard	Utica, N. Y.	1810
A & W·WOOD	A. & W. Wood S.M.	New York	1850
A·YOUNG	Alexander Young	Camden, S. C.	1807
⊛ Ⓑ ◉	Theophilus Bradbury	Newburyport, Mass.	1815
Babcok	Samuel Babcock	Middletown, Conn.	1812
BACHMAN	A. Bachman S.M.	New York	1848
BAILEY&CO ⊠◉	Bailey & Co.	Philadelphia	1848
BAILEY & KITCHEN	Bailey & Kitchen	Philadelphia	1833
BALDWIN BALDWIN	Ebenezer Baldwin	Hartford, Conn.	1810
BALDWIN &CO	Baldwin & Co.	Newark, N. J.	1830
BALDWIN &JONES	Baldwin & Jones	Boston	1813
BALL	William Ball	Philadelphia	1759
BALLBLACK&CO	Ball, Black & Co. S.M.	New York	1850
BALL &HEALD	Ball & Heald	Baltimore, Md.	1812
BALLTOMPKINS&BLACK	Ball, Tompkins & Black S.M.	New York	1839
BARD∞LAMONT	Bard & Lamont	Philadelphia	1841
BARKER & MUMFORD	Barker & Mumford	Newport, R. I.	1825
Barry BARRY №92 ◉	Standish Barry B.M.	Baltimore, Md.	1784

BASSETT	Francis Bassett	New York	1774
BASSETT& WARFORD	Bassett & Warford	Albany, N. Y.	1806
BAYEUX	Henry Bayeux	Troy, N. Y.	1801
BAYLEY	Simeon A. Bayley	New York	1789
BB	Barzillai Benjamin	New York	1825
BB	Benjamin Brenton	Newport, R. I.	1717
BB	Benjamin Bunker	Nantucket, Mass.	1780
BB	Benjamin Bussey	Dedham, Mass.	1778
B.BEMENT	B. Bement	Pittsfield, Mass.	1810
B BENJAMIN	Barzillai Benjamin	New York	1825
B.B.WOOD	Benjamin B. Wood	New York	1805
B·B URT	Benjamin Burt	Boston	1750
BC	Benjamin Cleveland	Newark, N. J.	1800
B.C.Frobisher	Benjamin C. Frobisher	Boston	1836
BCG	Benjamin Clark Gilman	Exeter, N. H.	1784
B·Cleveland B·CLEVELAD	Benjamin Cleveland	Newark, N. J.	1800
B.COLEMAN	Benjamin Coleman	Burlington, N. J.	1795
B&D	Barrington & Davenport	Philadelphia	1806
BDROWNE	Benjamin Drowne	Portsmouth, N. H.	1780
B·DUPUY	Barnard Dupuy	Raleigh, N. C.	1828

BEACH BEACH	Miles Beach	Hartford, Conn.	1775
BEAL	Caleb Beal	Hingham, Mass.	1796
B E COOK NORTHAMPTON	Benjamin E. Cook	Northampton, Mass.	1825
BEEBE	William Beebe S.M.	New York	1850
BENEDICT & SQUIRE	Benedict & Squire	New York	1839
BENJAMIN BURT	Benjamin Burt	Boston	1750
BENTLEY	Thomas Bentley	Boston	1789
B·G	Baldwin Gardiner S.M.	Philadelphia	1814
B·GARDINER	Baldwin Gardiner S.M.	Philadelphia	1814
B.GARDINER & CO	B. Gardiner & Co.	New York	1836
B G & CO	B. Gardiner & Co.	New York	1836
B.Goodwin B GOODWIN	Benjamin Goodwin	Boston	1756
B:GREEN	Benjamin Green	Boston	1733
BH	Benjamin Hiller	Boston	1711
B·H	Benjamin Hurd	Boston	1760
B.H.Tisdale B H TISDALE	B. H. Tisdale	Providence, R. I.	1824
B&H	Brinsmaid & Hildreth	Burlington, Vt.	1830
B·Hurd	Benjamin Hurd	Boston	1760
BIGELOW BROS	Bigelow Brothers	Boston	1840
B & J	Boyce & Jones	New York	1825

Mark	Name	Place	Date
B&J N.YORK	Boyce & Jones	New York	1825
B&J. COOPER	B. & J. Cooper	New York	1810
B&K	Bailey & Kitchen S.M.	Philadelphia	1833
BL	Benjamin Lemar	Philadelphia	1775
BLACKMAN	John Clark Blackman	Bridgeport, Conn.	1827
BLEASOM&REED	Bleasom & Reed	Portsmouth, N. H.	1830
B·LORD	Benjamin Lord	Pittsfield, Mass.	1796
Blowers Blowers	John Blowers	Boston	1738
BR	Bartholomew Le Roux	New York	1738
B&M	Bradley & Merriman	New Haven, Conn.	1826
BMBAILEY	B. M. Bailey	Ludlow, Vt.	1848
B.M.RIGGS	Benjamin McK. Riggs	Paris, Ky.	1820
BOSWORTH	Samuel Bosworth	Buffalo, N. Y.	1816
BOUDO	Louis Boudo	Charleston, S. C.	1810
BOWER	C. Bower	Philadelphia	1828
BOYCE&JONES	Boyce & Jones	New York	1825
BOYD&MULFORD	Boyd & Mulford	Albany, N. Y.	1832
Boyer BOYER	Daniel Boyer	Boston	1750
B·P B·P	Benjamin Pierpont	Boston	1756
B·PIERPONT B·PIERPONT	Benjamin Pierpont	Boston	1756

B PITMAN Pure Coin	Benjamin Pitman	Providence, R. I.	1820
BR	Bartholomew Le Roux	New York	1787
B & R	Brower & Rusher	New York	1834
B~R	Burnet & Ryder	Philadelphia	1795
BRADBURY 1825	Theophilus Bradbury S.M.	Newburyport, Mass.	1815
BRADY	E. Brady	New York	1825
BRASHER N YORK	Ephraim Brasher	New York	1766
BREWSTER	Abel Brewster	Norwich, Conn.	1797
BRIDGE BRIDGE	John Bridge	Boston	1751
Brigden	Zachariah Brigden	Boston	1760
BRINSMAID	Abraham Brinsmaid	Burlington, Vt.	1815
B.R.NORTON	Benjamin R. Norton	Syracuse, N. Y.	1845
BROOKS	Samuel Brooks	Philadelphia	1793
BROWN & KIRBY	Brown & Kirby	New Haven, Conn.	1850
BROWNE	Liberty Browne	Philadelphia	1801
BROWNE & SEAL	Browne & Seal	Philadelphia	1810
BRYAN	Phillip Bryan	Philadelphia	1802
BS	Bartholomew Schaats	New York	1695
BS	Benjamin Sanderson	Boston	1675
B & S	Beach & Sandford	Hartford, Conn.	1785

BT&B	Ball, Tompkins & Black	New York	1839
B·E B·E	Barent Ten Eyck	Albany, N. Y.	1735
BUCKLEY	J. B. Buckley	Philadelphia	1807
BUEL BUEL	Abel Buel	New Haven, Conn.	1770
BULLES & CHILDS HARTFORD	Bulles & Childs	Hartford, Conn.	1840
BUMM & SHEPPER	Bumm & Shepper	Philadelphia	1819
Burger Burger B B	John Burger	New York	1780
BURT	Benjamin Burt	Boston	1750
BUTLER & M'CARTY	Butler & M'Carty	Philadelphia	1850
BW	Bilious Ward	Middletown, Conn.	1750
BW	Barnabas Webb	Boston	1756
BW NYORK BW	Barnard Wenman	New York	1789
B·W B·W	Bancroft Woodcock	Wilmington, Del.	1754
BW	Benjamin Wynkoop, Jr.	Fairfield, Conn.	1730
BW&Cº	Butler, Wise & Co.	Philadelphia	1842
B&W	Beach & Ward S.M.	Hartford, Conn.	1789
B.WENMAN	Barnard Wenman	New York	1789
B.WEST	B. West	Boston	1830
B:WHITING	B. Whiting	Norwich, Conn.	1765
B.WOOD	Benjamin B. Wood	New York	1805

B·WOODCOCK	Bancroft Woodcock	Wilmington, Del.	1754
WK B / WK B	Benjamin Wynkoop	New York	1698
C·A·B	Charles A. Burnett	Alexandria, Va.	1793
C·A·BURNETT	Charles A. Burnett	Alexandria, Va.	1793
C·A·BURR	Cornelius A. Burr	Rochester, N. Y.	1838
C·AL·DIS	Charles Aldis	New York	1814
C·ALLEN	Charles Allen	Boston	1760
CAMPBELL	Christopher Campbell	New York	1808
CAMPBELL 10.15	Robert Campbell B.M.	Baltimore, Md.	1819
CANFIELD	Samuel Canfield	Middletown, Conn.	1780
CANFIELD & HALL	Canfield & Hall	Middletown, Conn.	1800
CAPELLE ST.LOUIS	J. Capelle	St. Louis, Mo.	1850
CARLETON	George Carleton	New York	1810
CARRELL	John & Daniel Carrell	Philadelphia	1785
Carson & Hall	Carson & Hall	Albany, N. Y.	1810
C·B	Caleb Beal	Hingham, Mass.	1796
CB	Clement Beecher	Berlin, Conn.	1801
CB	Caleb Beal	Hingham, Mass.	1796
C·BABBITT	C. Babbitt	Taunton, Mass.	1815
C·BARD 205ARCH ST	Conrad Bard	Philadelphia	1825

Mark	Name	Location	Date
CBEAL	Caleb Beal	Hingham, Mass.	1796
C·BILLON	Charles Billon	St. Louis, Mo.	1821
C.Boehme ✠	Charles L. Boehme	Baltimore	1799
C.BREWER C.Brewer	Charles Brewer	Middletown, Conn.	1810
C·BREWER & Cº	C. Brewer & Co.	Middletown, Conn.	1815
C.B ROOT	Charles Boudinot Root	Raleigh, N. C.	1843
C·BURR	Christopher A. Burr	Providence, R. I.	1810
CC	Charles Candell	New York	1795
CC	Charles Carpenter	Norwich, Conn.	1790
CC	Christian Cornelius	Philadelphia	1810
C&C ✪ ✪ ✪	Colton & Collins S.M.	New York	1825
C.C.COLEMAN	C. C. Coleman	Burlington, N. J.	1835
✪ C.C.&D ✪	Charters, Cann & Dunn	New York	1850
C.C NORTON	C. C. Norton	Hartford, Conn.	1820
CC.NORTON & W.PITKIN	Norton & Pitkin	Hartford, Conn.	1825
C.COEN & CO	C. Coen & Co.	New York	1810
C.CORNELIUS C.Cornelius	Christian Cornelius	Philadelphia	1810
CC.& S	Curtis, Candee & Stiles	Woodbury, Conn.	1831
C.DAVISON	Charles Davison	Norwich, Conn.	1805
C D SULLIVAN	C. D. Sullivan	St. Louis, Mo.	1850

Mark	Name	Location	Date
C·DUNN	Cary Dunn	New York	1765
C FARLEY	Charles Farley	Portland, Me.	1812
C·FORBES	Colin V. G. Forbes S.M.	New York	1816
C F WITTICH	Charles & Frederick Wittich	Charlestown, S. C.	1805
CG ★ CG	Caesar Ghiselin	Philadelphia	1700
C.Giffing NY	Christopher Giffing	New York	1815
C·H	Charles Hall	Lancaster, Pa.	1765
C·H	Charles Hequembourgh, Jr.	New Haven, Conn.	1810
C H	Christopher Hughes	Baltimore, Md.	1771
C·Hall	Charles Hall	Lancaster, Pa.	1765
CHANDLER	Stephen Chandler	New York	1812
Charles O Bruff	Charles Oliver Bruff	New York	1763
Chas Faris	Charles Faris	Annapolis, Md.	1793
CHAUDRON	Chaudron & Co.	Philadelphia	1807
CHAUDRON&RASCH	Chaudron & Rasch	Philadelphia	1812
CHEDELL	John H. Chedell	Auburn, N. Y.	1827
C.HEQUEMBOURGH JR	Chas. Hequembourgh, Jr. S.M.	New Haven, Conn.	1810
C.HPHELPS	Charles H. Phelps	Bainbridge, N. Y.	1825
CHURCH & ROGERS	Church & Rogers	Hartford, Conn.	1825
CHURCHILL	Jesse Churchill	Boston	1795

CHURCHILL & TREADWELL	Churchill & Treadwell	Boston	1805
C&JWFORBES	Colin & J. W. Forbes	New York	1825
C & J.WARNER	C. & J. Warner	Salem, Mass.	1825
C JOHNSON	Chauncey Johnson	Albany, N. Y.	1825
CK CK	Cornelius Kierstede	New York	1696
C.KENDALL	Charles Kendall	New York	1787
CL	Charles Le Roux	New York	1710
CL	Charles Leach	Boston	1789
CLARK	I. Clark	Boston	1754
CLARK NORWALK	Levi Clark	Norwalk, Conn.	1825
CLARK & ANTHONY	Clark & Anthony	New York	1790
CLARK & BRO	Clark & Brother	Norwalk, Conn.	1825
C.L.B	Charles L. Boehme	Baltimore, Md.	1799
CLBOEHME	Charles L. Boehme	Baltimore, Md.	1799
CLEVELAND	William Cleveland	Norwich, Conn.	1791
C.LINDSLEY	Clark Lindsley	Hartford, Conn.	1850
CLR CLR	Charles Le Roux	New York	1710
C & M	Coit & Mansfield	Norwich, Conn.	1816
C.MOORE	Charles Moore	Philadelphia	1803
C.O.B C.O.BRUFF	Charles Oliver Bruff	New York	1763

Charles Oliver Bruff	New York	1763
Coe & Upton	New York	1840
John Cook	New York	1795
Oliver B. Cooley	Utica, N. Y.	1828
Joseph Coolidge, Jr.	Boston	1770
Cooper & Fisher	New York	1850
Walter Cornell	Providence, R. I.	1780
Ralph Cowles	Cleveland, Ohio	1840
Clark & Pelletreau	New York	1819
Cleveland & Post	Norwich, Conn.	1815
Curry & Preston	Philadelphia	1831
Charles Parkman	Boston	1790
Charles P. Butler	Charleston, S. C.	1790
Clark, Pelletreau & Upson	Charleston, S. C.	1823
Christopher Robert	New York	1731
Claudius Redon P.M.	New York	1828
Caleb Shields	Baltimore, Md.	1773
Charles Faris	Annapolis, Md.	1793
Currier & Trott	Boston	1836
Curry & Preston	Philadelphia	1831

CURTISS CANDEE& STILES	Curtiss, Candee & Stiles	Woodbury, Conn.	1831
CURTISS &-DUNNING	Curtiss & Dunning	Woodbury, Conn.	1828
CURTISS&STILES	Curtiss & Stiles	Woodbury, Conn.	1835
AB CV	Cornelius Vanderburgh	New York	1675
C·V·GF	Colin V. G. Forbes	New York	1816
CW	Charles Whiting	Norwich, Conn.	1750
C·W	Christian Wiltberger	Philadelphia	1793
CWARNER	Caleb Warner	Salem, Mass.	1805
CWESTPHAL	Charles William Westphal	Philadelphia	1802
CWHEATON	Calvin Wheaton	Providence, R. I.	1790
CWHITE MOBILE	C. White	Mobile, Ala.	1830
C.WLCOX	Cyprian Wilcox	New Haven, Conn.	1816
CWiltberger	Christian Wiltberger	Philadelphia	1793
C.W.STEWART	C. W. Stewart	Lexington, Ky.	1850
WK	Cornelius Wynkoop	New York	1724
CWYNN	Christopher Wynn	Baltimore, Md.	1820
DARBY	John Darby	Charlestown, S. C.	1801
DARROW	John F. Darrow S.M.	Catskill, N. Y.	1818
DAVID KINSEY	David I. Kinsey	Cincinnati, Ohio	1845
DAVIS	Samuel Davis	Plymouth, Mass.	1801

DAVIS PALMER & CO	Davis Palmer & Co.	Boston	1842
DAVIS & BROWN	Davis & Brown	Boston	1809
DAVIS WATSON & CO	Davis, Watson & Co.	Boston	1820
DB	Duncan Beard	Appoquimink, Del.	1765
DB	Daniel Boyer	Boston	1750
D & B	Downing & Baldwin	New York	1832
DBACKUS	Delucine Backus	New York	1792
DB & AD	Bayley & Douglas	New York	1798
D.BARRIERE	David Barriere	Baltimore, Md.	1806
D.B.H & Cº	D. B. Hindman & Co.	Philadelphia	1833
D.Billings	Daniel Billings	Preston, Conn.	1795
D.B.MILLER	D. B. Miller	Boston	1850
D.BROWN	D. Brown	Philadelphia	1811
DBThompson	D. B. Thompson	Litchfield, Conn.	1825
D·C	Daniel Bloom Coen	New York	1787
DCF YORK	Daniel C. Fueter	New York	1754
D & Cº	DeForest & Co.	New York	1827
D.COEN	Daniel Bloom Coen	New York	1787
D.COLTON Jʀ	Demas Colton, Jr.	New York	1826
DD	Daniel Deshon	New London, Conn.	1730

Daniel Dupuy	Philadelphia	1745
Dupuy & Sons	Philadelphia	1784
John DeLarue	New Orleans, La.	1822
Andrew Demilt	New York	1805
Dennis & Fitch	New York	1836
John Deverell	Boston	1785
Daniel Dupuy, Jr.	Philadelphia	1785
D. Duyckinck	New York	1798
David Greenleaf, Jr.	Hartford, Conn.	1788
D. Goddard & Co.	Worcester, Mass.	1850
D. Goddard & Son	Worcester, Mass.	1845
David Greenleaf	Norwich, Conn.	1763
David Griffeth	Portsmouth, N. H.	1768
David Hall	Philadelphia	1765
Daniel Henchman	Boston	1753
David Hall	Philadelphia	1765
David Hotchkiss	Syracuse, N. Y.	1848
Daniel Jackson	New York	1782
David Jesse	Boston	1695
David I. Burger	New York	1805

D·I·NORTHEE	David I. Northee	Salem, Mass.	1770
DJACKSON	Daniel Jackson	New York	1782
D.KINSEY	David I. Kinsey	Cincinnati, Ohio	1845
DM	David Moseley	Boston	1775
DM	David Mygatt	Danbury, Conn.	1800
DMFITCH	Dennis M. Fitch	Troy, N. Y.	1840
D.Moseley DMoseley	David Moseley	Boston	1775
D.M.TYLER	D. M. Tyler	Boston	1810
D.MYGATT DMYGATT	David Mygatt	Danbury, Conn.	1800
D·N	Daniel Neall	Milford, Del.	1814
DN	David I. Northee	Salem, Mass.	1770
D·N·DOLE	D. N. Dole	Newburyport, Mass.	1810
D.NEALL	Daniel Neall	Milford, Del.	1814
DOANE DOANE	Joshua Doane	Providence, R. I.	1740
D.OLIVER	Daniel Oliver	Philadelphia	1805
DOWNING & PHELPS	Downing & Phelps	Newark, N. J.	1810
D:P	Daniel Parker	Boston	1750
D&P NEWARK	Downing & Phelps	Newark, N. J.	1810
D:PARKER	Daniel Parker	Boston	1750
DR	Daniel Russell	Newport, R. I.	1735

DR DR	Daniel Rogers	Newport, R. I.	1774
D.ROGERS	Daniel Rogers	Newport, R. I.	1774
DS	David Smith	Lansingburgh, N. Y.	1787
DS	Daniel Syng	Lancaster, Pa.	1734
DSMITH	David Smith	Lansingburgh, N. Y.	1787
D Stanton	Daniel Stanton	Stonington, Conn.	1776
D.SULLIVAN & CO	D. Sullivan & Co.	New York	1820
DSYNG	Daniel Syng	Lancaster, Pa.	1734
DT DT DT	David Tyler	Boston	1781
D.T.G	D. T. Goodhue	Boston	1840
D.T.GoodHUe	D. T. Goodhue	Boston	1840
DUHME	Duhme & Co.	Cincinnati, Ohio	1839
DUMOUTET	John Baptiste Dumoutet	Philadelphia	1793
DUNBAR&BANGS	Dunbar & Bangs	Worcester, Mass.	1850
D.V DV D.V	Daniel Van Voorhis	Philadelphia	1782
DV	David Vinton	Providence, R. I.	1790
DVV D.V.V	Daniel Van Voorhis	Philadelphia	1782
D.V.VOORHIS	Daniel Van Voorhis	Philadelphia	1782
D&W	Davis & Watson	Boston	1815
DWALDRON	D. Waldron	New York	1789

Mark	Name	Place	Date
D.WARNER	D. Warner	Ipswich, Mass.	1820
DY	Daniel You	Charleston, S. C.	1743
EA	Ebenezer J. Austin	Charlestown, Mass.	1760
E.A.BEAUVAIS	E. A. Beauvais	St. Louis, Mo.	1840
E.ADRIANCE STLOUIS	Edwin Adriance	St. Louis, Mo.	1835
EASTON & SANFORD	Easton & Sanford	Nantucket, Mass.	1830
EAYRES	Thomas S. Eayres	Boston	1785
EB	Eleazer Baker	Ashford, Conn.	1785
EB EB	Ephraim Brasher	New York	1766
EB	Everadus Bogardus	New York	1698
EB	Elias Boudinot	Philadelphia	1730
EB EB	Ezekiel Burr	Providence, R. I.	1793
E.BAKER	Eleazer Baker	Ashford, Conn.	1785
E.BALCH	Ebenezer Balch	Hartford, Conn.	1750
E.B.BOOTH	Ezra B. Booth	Rochester, N. Y.	1838
EB & Cº	E. Benjamin & Co.	New Haven, Conn.	1830
E.B.&CO	Erastus Barton & Co.	New York	1822
E.BENJAMIN	Everard Benjamin	New Haven, Conn.	1830
E BENJAMIN&CO	Everard Benjamin & Co.	New Haven, Conn.	1830
E.BERARD	E. Berard	Philadelphia	1800

E.BORHEK STANDARD	E. Borhek	Philadelphia	1835
E.BOWMAN	Elias Bowman	Rochester, N. Y.	1834
E.BRADY	E. Brady	New York	1825
E.BURNAP	Ela Burnap	Boston	1810
E.BURR E.Burr	Ezekiel Burr	Providence, R. I.	1793
E.C	Elias Camp	Bridgeport, Conn.	1825
E.C E.C E.CHITTENDEN	Ebenezer Chittenden	New Haven, Conn.	1765
E.C	Ephraim Cobb	Plymouth, Mass.	1735
E.Chittenden	Ebenezer Chittenden	New Haven, Conn.	1765
E.Cobb	Ephraim Cobb	Plymouth, Mass.	1735
E.COIT PURE.COIN	E. Coit	Norwich, Conn.	1825
E.COLE	Ebenezer Cole	New York	1818
E.COOK	Erastus Cook	Rochester, N. Y.	1815
E.C.STORM	E. C. Storm	Rochester, N. Y.	1815
E.CURRIER	Edmund M. Currier	Salem, Mass.	1830
E.CUTLER	Eben Cutler	Boston	1846
E.D	Edward Davis	Newburyport, Mass.	1775
E.DAVIS E.Davis	Edward Davis	Newburyport, Mass.	1775
E.&D.KINSEY	E. & D. Kinsey	Cincinnati, Ohio	1845
E.DODGE E.Dodge	Ezekiel Dodge	New York	1792

E·E·BAILEY	E. E. Bailey	Portland, Me.	1825
EE&SC BAILEY	E. E. & S. C. Bailey	Portland, Me.	1830
EG	Eliakim Garretson	Wilmington, Del.	1785
E.GARRETSON	Eliakim Garretson	Wilmington, Del.	1785
E.Gifford	E. Gifford	Fall River, Mass.	1825
E GUNN	Enos Gunn	Waterbury, Conn.	1792
EH	Eliphaz Hart	Norwich, Conn.	1810
E·H EH	Eliakim Hitchcock	New Haven, Conn.	1757
E HART	Eliphaz Hart	Norwich, Conn.	1810
E&H	Eoff & Howell	New York	1805
E·HOLSEY	E. Holsey	Philadelphia	1820
E HUGHES	Edmund Hughes	Middletown, Conn.	1804
E.J.AUSTIN	Ebenezer J. Austin	Charlestown, Mass.	1760
E.JEFFERIS	Emmor Jefferis	Wilmington, Del.	1827
E JEFFERSON	Ephraim Jefferson	Smyrna, Del.	1815
E.JONES	Elisha Jones	New York	1827
E K LAKEMAN	E. K. Lakeman	Salem, Mass.	1830
EL	Edward Lang	Salem, Mass.	1763
E L BAILEY & CO	E. L. Bailey & Co.	Claremont, N. H.	1835
E LESCURE	Edward P. Lescure	Philadelphia	1822

Elias Davis	Elias Davis	Boston	1805
E. Lincoln	Elijah Lincoln	Hingham, Mass.	1815
ELLISTON	Peter Elliston	New York	1791
E. Loring	Elijah Loring	Barnstable, Mass.	1765
E. LOWNES	Edward Lownes	Philadelphia	1817
EM EM	Edmund Milne	Philadelphia	1757
E. McNEIL	E. McNeil	Binghamton, N. Y.	1813
E.ME	Edgar M. Eoff	New York	1850
E.MEAD	Edmund Mead	St. Louis, Mo.	1850
Emery	Stephen Emery	Boston	1775
E. MILNE	Edmund Milne	Philadelphia	1757
E. MORGAN	Elijah Morgan	Poughkeepsie, N. Y.	1807
E. MOULTON	Enoch Moulton	Portland, Me.	1805
ENOS GUNN	Enos Gunn	Waterbury, Conn.	1792
E. OFF & HOWELL	Eoff & Howell	New York	1805
EOLLES & DAY	Eolles & Day	Hartford, Conn.	1825
EP	Edward Pear	Boston	1830
EP	Elias Pelletreau	Southampton, N. Y.	1750
E.P	Edward Putman	Boston	1825
E & P	Eoff & Phyfe	New York	1844

Mark	Name	Place	Date
EPL EPL	Edward P. Lescure	Philadelphia	1822
ER	Enos Reeves	Charleston, S. C.	1784
E·S ⊕ C ⊠	Edward Sandell B.M.	Baltimore, Md.	1816
E·S	Enoch Stanton	Stonington, Conn.	1766
E&S	Eoff & Shepherd P.M.	New York	1825
E.SARGEANT	Ensign Sargeant	Boston	1820
E.SM ESM	Edward S. Moulton	Rochester, N. H.	1800
E·S MOULTON	Edward S. Moulton	Rochester, N. H.	1800
E.STEBBINS & CO	E. Stebbins & Co.	New York	1825
E.Stillman	E. Stillman	Stonington, Conn.	1825
E.T PELL	Emmet T. Pell	New York	1825
E.T.W	Emmor T. Weaver	Philadelphia	1808
EVANS EVANS	Robert Evans	Boston	1798
EW	Edward Webb	Boston	1705
EW EW EW	Edward Winslow	Boston	1695
E.Watson E.WATSON	Edward E. Watson	Boston	1821
E.WHITE	Edward White	Ulster County, N. Y.	1757
E.WHITNEY	Eben Whitney	New York	1805
E.Whiton Boston	Ezra Whiton	Boston	1835
E.WYER	Eleazer Wyer, Jr.	Portland, Me.	1820

Mark	Name	Location	Year
F. ACKLEY	Francis M. Ackley	New York	1797
FARLEY	Charles Farley	Portland, Me.	1812
FARNAM & WARD	Farnam & Ward	Boston	1816
FARRINGTON & HUNNEWELL	Farrington & Hunnewell	Boston	1830
F. BICKNELL	Francis Bicknell	Rome, N. Y.	1818
FELLOWS	Abraham Fellows S.M.	Troy, N. Y.	1809
FELLOWS & STORM	Fellows & Storm	Albany, N. Y.	1839
FENNO & HALE	Fenno & Hale	Bangor, Me.	1840
F & F THIBAULT	Francis & Felix Thibault	Philadelphia	1807
F & G PHILAD^A	Fletcher & Gardiner S.M.	Boston	1809
F & H	Farrington & Hunnewell	Boston	1837
F. H. CLARK & C°	F. H. Clark & Co.	Memphis, Tenn.	1850
F. H. WOLFE	Francis H. Wolfe S.M.	Philadelphia	1829
F. J. POSEY	Frederick J. Posey	Hagerstown, Md.	1820
F. LOCKWOOD	Frederick Lockwood	New York	1828
FLOYD SMITH	Floyd Smith	New York	1815
F.M C ☒ ℓ	Frederick Marquand	New York	1823
F & M	Frost & Mumford	Providence, R. I.	1815
FMA	Francis M. Ackley	New York	1797
F. MARQUAND	Frederick Marquand S.M.	New York	1823

F NUSZ	Frederick Nusz	Frederick, Md.	1819
FORCE	Jabez W. Force	New York	1819
FORBES	William Forbes	New York	1830
FORBES & SON	C. V. G. Forbes & Son	New York	1835
FOSTER **FOSTER**	Joseph Foster	Boston	1785
Fourniquet	Louis Fourniquet	New York	1795
FR	Francis Richardson	Philadelphia	1710
F·R	Francis Richardson	Philadelphia	1729
FRANCIS **FRANCIS**	Nathaniel Francis	New York	1804
F·RATH	Frederick Rath	New York	1830
FREEMAN & WALLIN	Freeman & Wallin	Philadelphia	1850
F.RICHMOND	Franklin Richmond	Providence, R. I.	1815
F ROBISHER	Benjamin C. Frobisher	Boston	1836
F.S.B & Co	Frederick S. Blackman & Co.	Danbury, Conn.	1840
F.S.BLACKMAN	Frederick Starr Blackman	Danbury, Conn.	1830
F S.Sandford	F. S. Sanford	Nantucket, Mass.	1828
F.TINKHAM & Cc	F. Tinkham & Co.	New York	1850
F.TITCOMB	Francis Titcomb	Newburyport, Mass.	1813
FUETER **FUETER**	Lewis Fueter	New York	1770
FW	Freeman Woods S.M.	New York	1791

FWC NY	Francis W. Cooper S.M.	New York	1846
F.W.COOPER	Francis W. Cooper	New York	1846
F.W.PORTER	F. W. Porter	New York	1820
G.A GA GA	George Aiken	Baltimore, Md.	1787
G.Aiken GAIKEN	George Aiken	Baltimore, Md.	1787
GALE & WILLIS	Gale & Willis	New York	1840
G.B	George Bardick	Philadelphia	1790
G.B NY	Geradus Boyce	New York	1814
G.BAKER	George Baker	Providence, R. I.	1825
G.B.BOTSFORD	Gideon B. Botsford	Woodbury, Conn.	1797
GBO	Gerrit Onckelbag	New York	1691
G.BOYCE NYORK	Geradus Boyce	New York	1814
G.BOYCE E JONES	Boyce & Jones	New York	1825
GC	George Cannon	Warwick, R. I.	1800
G.C	Gideon Casey	Warwick, R. I.	1763
G.CANNON	George Cannon	Warwick, R. I.	1800
G-CASEY	Gideon Casey	Warwick, R. I.	1763
GCCLARK	George C. Clark	Providence, R. I.	1824
G.D GD	George Christopher Dowig	Baltimore, Md.	1765
G&D	Goodwin & Dodd	Hartford, Conn.	1812

Mark	Name	Place	Date
GDCLARK IO.15	Gabriel D. Clark B.M.	Baltimore, Md.	1830
GE.DISBROW N.W	G. E. Disbrow	New York	1825
GEE	Joseph Gee	Philadelphia	1785
GEFFROY	Nicholas Geffroy	Newport, R. I.	1795
G.ELLIOTT	George Elliott	Wilmington, Del.	1835
GELSTON	George S. Gelston S.M.	New York	1833
GELSTON & CO.	Gelston & Co. S.M.	New York	1837
GELSTON LADD & CO	Gelston, Ladd & Co. S.M.	New York	1836
GELSTON & TREADWELL	Gelston & Treadwell S.M.	New York	1836
GEO B.HOYT Coin	George B. Hoyt	Albany, N. Y.	1830
GEO.C HOWE & Cº	George C. Howe & Co. P.M.	New York	1837
G.EOFF	Garret Eoff	New York	1806
G.EOFF J.C MOORE	Eoff & Moore	New York	1835
George Baker	George Baker	Providence, R. I.	1825
GEORGE B.FOSTER	George B. Foster	Salem, Mass.	1838
GEORGE C.HOWE	George C. Howe	New York	1825
GEO W.WEBB	George W. Webb	Baltimore, Md.	1835
Germon Phila	John D. Germon	Philadelphia	1782
GERRISH	Timothy Gerrish	Portsmouth, N. H.	1775
Gerrish & Pearson	Gerrish & Pearson	New York	1800

George Fielding	New York	1731
Garret Forbes	New York	1808
George Franciscus	Baltimore, Md.	1776
Greenbury Gaither	Washington, D. C.	1822
George Gordon	Newburgh, N. Y.	1800
G. Gray	Portsmouth, N. H.	1839
George Hanners	Boston	1720
Gale & Hayden	Charleston, S. C.	1846
George Hanners	Boston	1720
William Ghiselin	Philadelphia	1751
William Gibson	Philadelphia	1845
William W. Gilbert	New York	1767
Caleb Gill	Hingham, Mass.	1798
George Jacob	Baltimore, Md.	1802
General James Wolf	Wilmington, Del.	1800
George K. Childs	Philadelphia	1828
George Kippen	Bridgeport, Conn.	1815
Gabriel Lewyn	Baltimore, Md.	1770
G. Lenhart	Bowling Green, Ky.	1845
G. Loomis & Co.	Erie, Pa.	1850

Mark	Name	Place	Date
G&M 🜚 🜚	Gale & Mosely	New York	1830
G.MECUM	George Mecum	Boston	1825
G.MZAHM	G. M. Zahm	Lancaster, Pa.	1840
⦿	Gerrit Onckelbag	New York	1691
GOODING	Henry Gooding	Boston	1820
GOODWIN	H. & A. Goodwin	Hartford, Conn.	1811
GORDON _Gordon_	Alexander S. Gordon	New York	1795
Gorham & Thurber	Gorham & Thurber	Providence, R. I.	1850
Gorham & Webster	Gorham & Webster	Providence, R. I.	1831
Gorham Webster & Price	Gorham, Webster & Price	Providence, R. I.	1835
G.Ott	George Ott	Norfolk, Va.	1806
GOULD&WARD	Gould & Ward	Baltimore, Md.	1850
G.PARKER	George Parker B.M.	Baltimore, Md.	1804
GR	George Ridout	New York	1745
GR	George W. Riggs	Baltimore, Md.	1810
GRAY	Samuel Gray	New London, Conn.	1710
GRD N·YORK	G. R. Downing	New York	1810
GREGG.HAYDEN&CO	Gregg, Hayden & Co.	Charleston, S. C.	1846
GREENLEAF	David Greenleaf	Norwich, Conn.	1763
GRIFFEN & HOYT	Griffen & Hoyt S.M.	New York	1830

GRIFFEN & SON	Griffen & Son S.M.	New York	1832
Grigg Grigg	William Grigg	New York	1765
GS	Godfrey Shiving	Philadelphia	1779
GS	George Stephens P.M.	New York	1791
G.&S	Gale & Stickler	New York	1823
GSCHANCK m	Garret Schanck	New York	1791
G.S.GELSTON	George S. Gelston	New York	1833
GSPENCE NEWARK NJ.	G. Spence	Newark, N. J.	1830
GT	George Tyler	Boston	1765
G.TERRY	Geer Terry	Enfield, Conn.	1800
G.TRACY	Gordon Tracy	Norwich, Conn.	1787
GUINAUD	Frederick E. Guinaud B.M.	Baltimore, Md.	1814
GURNEE	Benjamin Gurnee	New York	1820
GUTHRE& JEEFERIS	Guthre & Jefferis	Wilmington, Del.	1840
G.V.ⁿ Schaick	G. Van Schaick	Albany, N. Y.	1800
G.Walker	George Walker	Philadelphia	1797
G.W.BULL	G. W. Bull	Farmington, Conn.	1840
G.W.&H	Gale, Wood & Hughes P.M.	New York	1830
G.W.&N.C.PLATT	G. W. & N. C. Platt	New York	1820
G.W.STRIKER	George W. Striker	New York	1825

G.W.WEBB 10·15	George W. Webb	Baltimore, Md.	1835
HA	Henry Andrews	Philadelphia	1800
HADDOCK LINCOLN & FOSS	Haddock, Lincoln & Foss	Boston	1850
H & ADRIANCE	Hayes & Adriance	Poughkeepsie, N. Y.	1816
HADWEN ★	William Hadwen	Nantucket, Mass.	1820
Halsted HALSTED	Benjamin Halsted	New York	1764
HALL & ELTON	Hall & Elton	Geneva, N. Y.	1841
HAMLIN	William Hamlin	Providence	1795
H.A.M.MASTERS	Hugh A. McMasters	Philadelphia	1839
HARDY	Stephen Hardy	Portsmouth, N. H.	1805
HARLAND	Thomas Harland	Norwich, Conn.	1775
HARRIS & STANWOOD	Harris & Stanwood	Boston	1842
HARRIS & WILCOX	Harris & Wilcox	Boston	1844
HART & SMITH	Hart & Smith B.M.	Baltimore, Md.	1815
HARVEY LEWIS	Harvey Lewis	Philadelphia	1811
HASCY	Alexander R. Hascy	Albany, N. Y.	1835
HASTINGS	B. B. Hastings	Cleveland, Ohio	1835
H.A.Seymour	Holister A. Seymour	Hartford, Conn.	1845
HAYDEN & GREGG	Hayden & Gregg	Charleston, S. C.	1838
HAYES & ADRIANCE	Hayes & Adriance	Poughkeepsie, N. Y.	1816

HB	Henry Bailey S.M.	Boston	1800
HB	Henry Biershing	Hagerstown, Md.	1815
HB HB	Henricus Boelen	New York	1718
H&B	Hart & Brewer	Middletown, Conn.	1800
HBMyer	H. B. Myer	Newburgh, N. Y.	1818
H.BOUDO	Heloise Boudo S.M.	Charleston, S. C.	1827
H.COGSWELL	Henry Cogswell	Salem, Mass.	1846
HEAD G ✪ D	Joseph Head	Philadelphia	1798
H.E.BALDWIN&CO	H. E. Baldwin & Co.	New Orleans, La.	1825
Helme	Nathaniel Helme	Little Rest, R. I.	1782
Henchman	Daniel Henchman	Boston	1753
HENDERSON	A. A. Henderson	Philadelphia	1837
Henry B. Stanwood	Henry B. Stanwood S.M.	Boston	1840
HENRY EVANS	Henry Evans S.M.	New York	1820
HENRY HOYT	Henry E. Hoyt	New York	1820
HEDGES	Daniel Hedges, Jr.	East Hampton, N. Y.	1810
H.E.HOYT	Henry E. Hoyt	New York	1820
HEQUEMBOURGH.	Charles Hequembourgh, Jr. S.M.	New Haven, Conn.	1810
H.ERWIN	Henry Erwin	Philadelphia	1817
HF	Henry Farnam	Boston	1799

H·FARNAM	Henry Farnam	Boston	1799
HH HH	Henry Hurst	Boston	1690
H&H	Hall & Hewson	Albany, N. Y.	1828
H·HASTINGS	H. Hastings	Ohio	1815
HH&B	Hall, Hewson & Brower	Albany, N. Y.	1850
HHYMAN	Henry Hyman	Lexington, Ky.	1799
H&I	Heydorn & Imley	Hartford, Conn.	1810
HIGBIE & CROSBY	Higbie & Crosby	Boston	1820
HINSDALE	Horace Hinsdale	New York	1805
HINSDALE & ATKIN	Hinsdale & Atkin	New York	1836
HJPEPPER	Henry J. Pepper	Wilmington, Del.	1814
H I SAWYER	H. I. Sawyer	New York	1840
H·J·PEPPER	Henry J. Pepper	Wilmington, Del.	1814
HJPEPPER&SON	Henry J. Pepper & Son	Philadelphia	1846
H·JUDSON	Hiram Judson	Syracuse, N. Y.	1824
H·K·NEWCOMB	H. K. Newcomb	Watertown, N. Y.	1821
H·L	Harvey Lewis	Philadelphia	1811
H·L	Henry Loring	Boston	1800
H·LEWIS	Harvey Lewis	Philadelphia	1811
H·Longley	Henry Longley	New York	1810

	Henry Lupp	New Brunswick, N. J.	1783
	Henry L. Webster & Co.	Providence, R. I.	1842
	Henry L. Webster	Providence, R. I.	1831
	Hall & Merriman	New Haven, Conn.	1825
	Hayes & Meyers	New York	1770
	Henry McKeen	Philadelphia	1823
	H. Mulligan	Philadelphia	1840
	Hyde & Nevins S.M.	New York	1815
	Houlton, Otto & Folk	Philadelphia	1797
	Nathan Hobbs S.M.	Boston	1815
	Littleton Holland B.M.	Baltimore, Md.	1800
	Robert Holloway	Baltimore, Md.	1822
	Edward Holyoke	Boston	1817
	Hood & Tobey	Albany, N. Y.	1849
	William Homes	Boston	1739
	Joseph W. Hopkins	Waterbury, Conn.	1760
	Harley Hosford	New York	1820
	Houlton & Browne	Baltimore, Md.	1799
	James Howell	Philadelphia	1802
	Houghton Perkins	Boston	1756

HP.	Henry Peterson	Philadelphia	1783
HP	Henry Pitkin	East Hartford, Conn.	1834
HP	Henry Pratt	Philadelphia	1730
HPORTER&CO	Henry C. Porter & Co.	New York	1830
H·PRESCOT	Henry Prescot	Keeseville, N. Y.	1828
H·PRICE	Henry P. Rice P.M.	Albany, N. Y.	1815
H.ROBINSON	Hannah Robinson	Wilmington, Del.	1845
HRT	Henry R. Traux	Albany, N. Y.	1815
H&R.W.SILL	H. & R. W. Sill	New York	1840
HS	Hezekiah Silliman	New Haven, Conn.	1767
H&S	Hart & Smith B.M.	Baltimore, Md.	1815
H.SADD	Harvey Sadd	New Hartford, Conn.	1810
H.SAFFORD	Henry Safford	Gallipolis, Ohio	1800
H.Sargeant	H. Sargeant	Hartford, Conn.	1825
H.SILL	H. Sill	New York	1840
HU.GELSTON	Hugh Gelston B.M.	Baltimore, Md.	1816
Huntington HUNTINGTON	Richard Huntington	Utica, N. Y.	1823
Hurd HURD Hurd Hurd	Jacob Hurd	Boston	1723
HUTCHINS	Jacob Hutchins	New York	1774
HUTTON 🏛 ALBANY 🦅 Isaac Hutton		Albany, N. Y.	1790

Mark	Name	Place	Date
HUYLER	George Huyler	New York	1819
HVV	Henry Van Veghten	Albany, N. Y.	1760
H&W	Hart & Wilcox	Norwich, Conn.	1805
HWALKER	Hannah Walker	Philadelphia	1816
H.WILSON	Hosea Wilson	Philadelphia	1812
HWISHART	Hugh Wishart S.M.	New York	1784
HYDE & GOODRICH	Hyde & Goodrich	New Orleans, La.	1830
Hyde & NEVINS	Hyde & Nevins S.M.	New York	1815
JA	John Adam, Jr.	Alexandria, Va.	1800
JA JA JA	John Allen	Boston	1695
JA JA	Isaac Anthony	Newport, R. I.	1715
JA	Joseph Anthony, Jr.	Philadelphia	1783
JA IA	Joseph Anthony, Jr.	Philadelphia	1783
IA IA	Josiah Austin	Charlestown, Mass.	1745
IA JA	John Avery	Preston, Conn.	1760
JA JE	Allen & Edwards	Boston	1700
IA BOYER	Boyer & Austin	Boston	1770
IA Minott	Minott & Austin	Boston	1765
JACKSON	John Jackson	New York	1731
IADAM JAdam JA	John Adam, Jr.	Alexandria, Va.	1800

J.Aitken AITKEN	John Aitken	Philadelphia	1785
I·ALEXANDER	Isaac Alexander	New York	1850
J.Alstyne	Jeronimus Alstyne	New York	1787
I·ANDREW	John Andrew	Salem, Mass.	1769
I·ANDREWS NORFOLK	Joseph Andrews	Norfolk, Va.	1800
J.Anthony	Joseph Anthony, Jr.	Philadelphia	1783
I·A·SHAW	John·A. Shaw	Newport, R. I.	1819
Jas Thomson	James Thomson	New York	1834
I Austin	Josiah Austin	Charlestown, Mass.	1745
I Austin BOYER	Austin & Boyer	Boston	1770
I Austin Minott	Minott & Austin	Boston	1765
I·AVERY	John Avery	Preston, Conn.	1760
IB IB IB N·YORK	John Bayly	Philadelphia	1755
JB	James Barret	New York	1805
IB IB	John Benjamin	Stratford, Conn.	1743
IB	Jurian Blanck	New York	1666
IB IB IB	Jacob Boelen III	New York	1785
IB	Jacob Boelen II	New York	1755
IB IB	Jacob Boelen	New York	1680
IB	Joseph Bruff	Easton, Md.	1755

I·B	John Burger	New York	1780
IB	John Burt	Boston	1712
IB	James Butler	Boston	1734
IBAYLY JBayly	John Bayly	Philadelphia	1755
I.BALDWIN	Jedediah Baldwin	Hanover, N. H.	1793
I·BALL	John Ball	Concord, Mass.	1763
I BARTLET	Israel Bartlet	Newbury, Mass.	1800
I.B.CURRAN	I. B. Curran	Ithaca, N. Y.	1835
JBedford	John Bedford	Fishkill, N. Y.	1782
IBELL	Joseph Bell	New York	1817
IBL NYORK	John Burt Lyng	New York	1759
IBLACK	James Black	Philadelphia	1795
IBLISS	Jonathan Bliss	Middletown, Conn.	1800
IBOONE	Jeremiah Boone	Philadelphia	1791
IBRIDGE	John Bridge	Boston	1751
IBROCK NEW YORK	John Brock	New York	1833
I·BRUFF	Joseph Bruff	Easton, Md.	1755
IBURT IBURT	John Burt	Boston	1712
IBV BV	John Brevoort	New York	1742
IC	John Carman	Philadelphia	1771

Joseph Carpenter	Norwich, Conn.	1775
James Chalmers	Annapolis, Md.	1749
James Chalmers	Annapolis, Md.	1749
John Champlin	New London, Conn.	1768
I. Clark	Boston	1754
Jonathan Clarke	Newport, R. I.	1734
John Cluet	Kingston, N. Y.	1725
John Coburn	Boston	1750
John Coddington	Newport, R. I.	1712
John Coney	Boston	1676
Joseph Cook	Philadelphia	1785
Jesse Churchill	Boston	1795
I. Clark	Boston	1754
Jonathan Clarke	Newport, R. I.	1734
John Cook	New York	1795
Jacques W. Cortelyou	New Brunswick, N. J.	1805
John Coverly	Boston	1766
John Crawford	New York	1815
John David	Philadelphia	1763
John Dixwell	Boston	1710

Jeremiah Dummer	Boston	1666
Jonathan Davenport	Baltimore, Md.	1789
Jonathan Davenport	Baltimore, Md.	1789
John David	Philadelphia	1763
Joshua G. Davis	Boston	1796
Isaac D. Cluster	St. Louis, Mo.	1850
Jabez Delano	New Bedford, Mass.	1843
Isaac Dixon	Philadelphia	1784
John D. Miller	Charleston, S. C.	1780
John D. Miller	Charleston, S. C.	1780
Joshua Doane	Providence, R. I.	1740
Joshua Dorsey	Philadelphia	1793
Jeremott W. Douglass	Philadelphia	1790
Joseph Dubois	New York	1790
James Duffel	Georgetown, S. C.	1790
John Edwards	Boston	1691
Joseph Edwards, Jr.	Boston	1758
Allen & Edwards	Boston	1700
Joseph Edwards, Jr.	Boston	1758
John Fite	Baltimore, Md.	1810

I·FOSTER	Joseph Foster	Boston	1785
IG	John Gardiner	New London, Conn.	1760
IG	James Geddes	Williamsburg, Va.	1760
I.G I·G	John D. Germon	Philadelphia	1782
IG	Joseph Goldthwaite	Boston	1731
I·G	John Gray	Boston	1713
IcL	Jacob Gerittse Lansing	Albany, N. Y.	1700
IcL IcL	Jacob G. Lansing	Albany, N. Y.	1765
IH IH	John Hastier	New York	1726
IH IH	John Hull	Boston	1645
IH	Jacob Hurd	Boston	1723
IH IH	John S. Hutton	New York	1720
IH RS	Hull & Sanderson	Boston	1652
JHall IHALL	Joseph Hall	Albany, N. Y.	1781
I·HALSEY	Jabez Halsey	New York	1789
JHart	Judah Hart	Middletown, Conn.	1799
I·HASELTON	Ira Haselton	Portsmouth, N. H.	1821
I·&H·CLARK	I. & H. Clark	Portsmouth, N. H.	1821
I&HJenkins	I. & H. Jenkins	Albany, N. Y.	1815
I·HEATH	John Heath	New York	1761

IHL	Josiah H. Lownes	Philadelphia	1816
IHM	John H. Merkler	New York	1780
JHowell	James Howell	Philadelphia	1802
JHowell&Co	J. Howell & Co.	Philadelphia	1810
IHR	John H. Russell	New York	1792
IHURD IHURD	Jacob Hurd	Boston	1725
II	John Inch	Annapolis, Md.	1745
I·I I·I	Jacob Jennings	Norwalk, Conn.	1763
J.Monell & C.M.Williams	Monell & Williams	New York	1825
I·J	John Jenkins	Philadelphia	1777
I·JENCKES	John C. Jenckes	Providence, R. I.	1798
I·K I·K	Joseph Keeler	Norwalk, Conn.	1810
I·K	James Kendall	Wilmington, Del.	1785
I·K	Jesse Kip	New York	1682
I·KETCHAM	James Ketcham	New York	1807
I·Kneeland	Joseph Kneeland	Boston	1720
I·KUCHER	Jacob Kucher	Philadelphia	1806
I·L I·L	Jeffery Lang	Salem, Mass.	1733
I·L I·L I·L	John Leacock	Philadelphia	1748
I·L I·L	John Le Roux	New York	1716

IL **I·L** ⊙	John Lynch	Baltimore, Md.	1786
I·L	John Burt Lyng	New York	1759
ILANG **ILANG**	Jeffery Lang	Salem, Mass.	1733
I·LEACOCK	John Leacock	Philadelphia	1748
ILent	John Lent	New York	1787
I·LeTeLier **ILeTelier**	John LeTelier	Philadelphia	1770
I·LEWIS **I·LEWIS**	Isaac Lewis	Huntington, Conn.	1796
ILG	John L. Gale	New York	1819
I·L·GALE	John L. Gale	New York	1819
I·Loring *I·Loring*	Joseph Loring	Boston	1775
I·Lownes	Joseph Lownes	Philadelphia	1780
ILOWE	Joshua Lowe P.M.	New York	1828
IR	John Le Roux	New York	1716
I·Lt	John Le Telier	Philadelphia	1770
I·LYNCH	John Lynch	Baltimore, Md.	1786
IM **I·M** ⊙	John McMullin	Philadelphia	1790
IM	Jacob Mariusgroen	New York	1701
IM	John Moulinar	New York	1744
I·M *IM*	Joseph Moulton	Newburyport, Mass.	1765
IM	James Murdock	Philadelphia	1779

McClymon	John C. McClymon	New York	1805
I.McMullin	John McMullin	Philadelphia	1790
IM·MIKSCH	John M. Miksch	Bethlehem, Pa.	1775
IMMULLIN	John McMullin	Philadelphia	1790
IMOOD	John Mood	Charleston, S. C.	1816
IMOULTON	Joseph Moulton	Newburyport, Mass.	1765
IMUNROE	James Munroe	Barnstable, Mass.	1806
Murdock	John Murdock	Philadelphia	1779
IMYERS *Myers*	John Myers	Philadelphia	1785
IN	John Nelson	Portsmouth, N. H.	1780
VK VK	Jan Van Nieu Kirke	New York	1716
IN IN	John Noyes	Boston	1699
IN IN IN IN	Johannis Nys	Philadelphia	1695
I·NR INR	J. & N. Richardson	Philadelphia	1771
INTOY	Isaac N. Toy	Abingdon, Md.	1790
IO IO IO	Jonathan Otis	Newport, R. I.	1750
I*OGILVIE	John Ogilvie	New York	1764
IOtis	Jonathan Otis	Newport, R. I.	1750
I·OWEN	John Owen	Philadelphia	1804
IP	John Patterson	Annapolis, Md.	1751

IP	John Pearson	New York	1791
IP IP	Jacob Perkins	Newburyport, Mass.	1787
IP IP	John Potwine	Boston	1721
IP	Job Prince	Milford, Conn.	1703
IPARKER	Isaac Parker	Deerfield, Mass.	1780
IPARSONS	John Parsons	Boston	1780
JPearson	John Pearson	New York	1791
JPitman	I. Pitman	Baltimore, Md.	1785
IPotwine	John Potwine	Boston	1721
JPT	John Proctor Trott	New London, Conn.	1792
IPT&SON	John P. Trott & Son	New London, Conn.	1820
I&PT	John & Peter Targee	New York	1811
I·PTARGEE	John & Peter Targee	New York	1811
JR	John Reynolds	Hagerstown, Md.	1790
IR	Joseph Richardson	Philadelphia	1732
IR IR IR	Joseph Richardson, Jr.	Philadelphia	1773
IR	Joseph Rice	Baltimore, Md.	1784
IR IR	Joseph Rogers	Newport, R. I.	1760
IR	John Ross	Baltimore, Md.	1790
JR	Johnson & Riley	Baltimore, Md.	1785

Mark	Name	Place	Date
IRA STOWN	Ira S. Town	Montpelier, Vt.	1825
IREED & SON	Isaac Reed & Son	Philadelphia	1830
J.Reeve	Joseph Reeve	Newburgh, N. Y.	1803
J.Rice I.RICE	Joseph Rice	Baltimore, Md.	1784
I.R.MILLER	I. R. Miller	Philadelphia	1810
I.ROE I.ROE	James Roe	Kingston, N. Y.	1770
I.ROHR	John A. Rohr	Philadelphia	1807
IR & S	Isaac Reed & Son	Philadelphia	1830
IS	John Stuart	Providence, R. I.	1720
IS	Joseph Smith	Boston	1765
IS	John Syng	Philadelphia	1734
I.SAYRE (S) SAYRE	John Sayre	New York	1792
J.Sayre J.Sayre	Joel Sayre	New York	1799
I.SCHANCK (S) m	John A. Schanck	New York	1795
J.Scott	Jehu Scot	Raleigh, N. C.	1806
I.SMITH I.SMITH	Joseph Smith	Boston	1765
I.SMITH	John Smith	Baltimore, Md.	1814
I.Snow	Jeremiah Snow, Jr.	Williamsburg, Mass.	1808
I.SPEAR	Isaac Spear P.M.	Boston	1836
I.S.Porter UTICA	Joseph S. Porter	Utica, N. Y.	1805

I·S·STICKNEY	Jonathan Stickney, Jr.	Newburyport, Mass.	1796
Stow	John Stow	Wilmington, Del.	1772
S·V·S	Jacobus VanDer Spiegel	New York	1689
J·Sweeney	John Sweeney	Geneva, N. Y.	1816
I·Symmes	John Symmes	Boston	1767
IT IT	John Tanner	Newport, R. I.	1740
IT ♥ ?	John Targee	New York	1797
IB IT	Jacob C. Ten Eyck	Albany, N. Y.	1725
IT	John Touzell	Salem, Mass.	1756
I·T	Joseph Toy	Abingdon, Md.	1776
IT WW	Toy & Wilson	Abingdon, Md.	1780
IT	Jonathan Trott, Jr.	New London, Conn.	1795
IT	James Turner	Boston	1744
I·TANGUY	John Tanguy	Philadelphia	1801
IE	Jacob C. Ten Eyck	Albany, N. Y.	1725
I·THOMSON	Isaac Thomson	Litchfield, Conn.	1801
I·Tiley I·TILEY	James Tiley	Hartford, Conn.	1765
I·TITUS	James Titus	Philadelphia	1833
I·TROTT	Jonathan Trott	Boston	1758
IV ▨ ▨	John Vernon	New York	1787
I·VANALL	John Vanall	Charleston, S. C.	1752

IVOGLER	John Vogler	Salem, N. C.	1802
VK	Jan Van Nieu Kirke	New York	1716
ISV	Jacobus VanDer Spiegel	New York	1689
IVS IVS	John Van Steenberg, Jr.	Kingston, N. Y.	1775
IW	Isaiah Wagster	Baltimore, Md.	1780
IW	Joseph Warner	Wilmington, Del.	1775
IW	Joshua Weaver	West Chester, Pa.	1815
IW	Jeremiah Ward Wool	New York	1791
IWAITE	John Waite	South Kingstown, R. I.	1763
JWalraven	John Walraven	Baltimore, Md.	1792
IWARNER	Joseph Warner	Wilmington, Del.	1775
IWF ⬤ ⬤ ⬤ ⬤	John W. Forbes P.M.	New York	1802
IWFORBES	John W. Forbes P.M.	New York	1802
IWG	John Ward Gilman	Exeter, N. H.	1792
JWGethen	John W. Gethen	Philadelphia	1811
IW & IK FELLOWS	I. W. & J. K. Fellows	Lowell, Mass.	1834
IWOLFF	James G. Wolf	Philadelphia	1830
IWOODCOCK	Isaac Woodcock	Wilmington, Del.	1787
IWood	John Wood	New York	1770
IY SAVAGE	John Y. Savage	Raleigh, N. C.	1820

IZANE	Isaac Zane	Zanesfield, Ohio	1795
JA	John Adam, Jr.	Alexandria, Va.	1800
JA JA	Jeronimus Alstyne	New York	1787
J·A	Joseph Anthony, Jr.	Philadelphia	1783
JA	John Avery	Preston, Conn.	1760
JA & IA	Joseph Anthony & Sons	Philadelphia	1810
JABBOTT	John W. Abbott	Portsmouth, N. H.	1839
JACCARD&CO	Jaccard & Co.	St. Louis, Mo.	1850
Jacob Hurd	Jacob Hurd	Boston	1723
JACKSON	John Jackson	New York	1731
J ADAM	John Adam, Jr.	Alexandria, Va.	1800
James Munroe	James Munroe	Barnstable, Mass.	1806
JAMES MURDOCK &CO	James Murdock & Co.	Utica, N. Y.	1826
J ANDREWS	Joseph Andrews	Norfolk, Va.	1800
JAnthony	Joseph Anthony, Jr.	Philadelphia	1783
JASD PHILIPS	James D. Philips	Cincinnati, Ohio	1829
J&AS	J. & A. Simmons	New York	1805
J&A SIMMONS	J. & A. Simmons	New York	1805
Jas Thomson NY 1837	James Thomson	New York	1834
J AUSTIN J AUSTIN	Josiah Austin	Charlestown, Mass.	1745

JAVAIN	Henry J. Javain	Charleston, S. C.	1835
JB	John Bedford	Fishkill, N. Y.	1782
JB	James Black	Philadelphia	1795
JB NY	John Boyce	New York	1801
JB	John Brown	Philadelphia	1785
J&B	Johnson & Ball	Baltimore, Md.	1790
J.BALDWIN	Jabez C. Baldwin	Boston	1800
J·BALL JOHN BALL	John Ball	Concord, Mass.	1763
J.BARTON	Joseph Barton	Stockbridge, Mass.	1790
JBEATON	James B. Eaton	Boston	1805
J.Bedford	John Bedford	Fishkill, N. Y.	1782
JBELL	Joseph Bell	New York	1817
J.B.GINOCHIO	John B. Ginochio P.M.	New York	1837
JBJONES	John B. Jones	Boston	1813
J.B.JONES & CO	John B. Jones & Co.	Boston	1838
J.B.M°FADDEN	J. B. M'Fadden	Pittsburgh, Pa.	1840
JBOUTIER	John Boutier	New York	1805
J.Brock	John Brock	New York	1833
JB THAXTER	Joseph B. Thaxter	Hingham, Mass.	1815
J BUTLER	James Butler	Boston	1734
J.Byrne	James Byrne	Philadelphia	1784

JC	Joseph Clark	Danbury, Conn.	1791
J.C J·C	John Coburn	Boston	1750
J·C	Joseph Cook	Philadelphia	1785
JC	Joseph Coolidge, Jr.	Boston	1770
JC	Jonathan Crosby	Boston	1764
J.CAMPBELL	John Campbell	Fayetteville, N. C.	1829
J.C.B&C°	J. C. Blackman & Co.	Bridgeport, Conn.	1835
J.C.BALDWIN	Jabez C. Baldwin	Boston	1800
J.C.FARR	John C. Farr	Philadelphia	1824
J.CHURCH	Joseph Church	Hartford, Conn.	1815
J.C.JENCKES	John C. Jenckes	Providence, R. I.	1798
J.CLARK	Joseph Clark	Danbury, Conn.	1791
J·CLARKE JClarke	Jonathan Clarke	Newport, R. I.	1734
J.C.M	John C. Moore S.M.	New York	1835
J.COBURN	John Coburn	Boston	1750
J.CONNING MOBILE	J. Conning	Mobile, Ala.	1840
J.COOK	John Cook	New York	1795
J.COPP	Joseph Copp	New London, Conn.	1757
J.CRAWFORD	John Crawford	New York	1815
J.CURRY J PHILA	John Curry	Philadelphia	1831
J.D	John David, Jr.	Philadelphia	1785

JD JD	John Denise	New York	1798
JD	Joseph Dubois	New York	1790
JDAVIS	Joshua G. Davis	Boston	1796
J·DAY	John Day	Boston	1820
JDECKER	James Decker S.M.	Troy, N. Y.	1833
JDMASON	J. D. Mason	Philadelphia	1830
JDODGE	John Dodge	Catskill, N. Y.	1818
J·DOLL	J. Doll	New York	1820
JDRAPER	Joseph Draper	Wilmington, Del.	1825
JDSTOUT	J. D. Stout	New York	1817
J·DUBOIS	Joseph Dubois	New York	1790
JE	Joseph Edwards, Jr.	Boston	1758
JE JE	Jeremiah Elfreth	Philadelphia	1752
J Easton 2d JEASTON	James Easton	Nantucket, R. I.	1828
JEFFREY R BRACKETT	Jeffrey R. Brackett	Boston	1840
JEHU & W L WARD PHILA	Jehu & W. L. Ward	Philadelphia	1837
JENNINGS & LANDER	Jennings & Lander P.M.	New York	1848
JERWIN	James Erwin B.M.	Baltimore, Md.	1809
J E STANWOOD	J. E. Stanwood	Philadelphia	1850
JEWAN	John Ewan S.M.	Charleston, S. C.	1823
JEWOOD	J. E. Wood	New York	1845

Mark	Name	Location	Date
JEYLAND	James Eyland	Charleston, S. C.	1820
JF	John Fitch	Trenton, N. J.	1774
JF	Josiah Flagg	Boston	1765
JF T.RICHARDS	Foster & Richards	New York	1815
J FAIRCHILD	Joseph Fairchild	New Haven, Conn.	1824
J FITCH AUBURN	James Fitch	Auburn, N. Y.	1821
J FOSTER	John Foster S.M.	New York	1811
J FRANK	Jacob Frank	Philadelphia	1793
J F REEVES 1015	J. F. Reeves	Baltimore, Md.	1835
J F ROBINSON	John F. Robinson	Wilmington, Del.	1844
JG	John Gardner	New London, Conn.	1760
J·G	John Gibbs	Providence, R. I.	1790
JG	James Gough	New York	1769
J GALE	John L. Gale	New York	1819
J.GARDNER	John Gardner	New London, Conn.	1760
J. Gaskins J.Gaskins	J. Gaskins	Norfolk, Va.	1830
J.GIBBS	John Gibbs	Providence, R. I.	1790
JGL	Jacob G. Lansing	Albany, N. Y.	1765
J.GLibby	Jacob G. L. Libby	Boston	1820
J.GOODHUE	John Goodhue	Salem, Mass.	1822
J GORHAM	Jabez Gorham	Providence, R. I.	1815

J Gorham & Son	Jabez Gorham & Son	Providence, R. I.	1842
J.GOULD 10.15	James Gould B.M.	Baltimore, Md.	1816
J.GUTHRE	James Guthre	Wilmington, Del.	1822
JH	John Hancock	Boston	1760
JH	John Heath	New York	1761
J.HAMILL NY	James Hamill	New York	1816
J.HANCOCK	John Hancock	Boston	1760
J.HANSELL	J. Hansell	Valley Forge, Pa.	1825
J.HART	Judah Hart	Middletown, Conn.	1799
J.HART	Jonathan Hart	Canandaigua, N. Y.	1810
J.H.C	John H. Connor	New York	1835
J.H.CLARK	J. H. Clark	New York	1815
J.H.CONNOR	John H. Connor	New York	1835
J.H.CONNOR G.EOFF	Eoff & Connor	New York	1833
J.HEATH	John Heath	New York	1761
J.HILL	James Hill	Boston	1770
J.H.MORSE	J. H. Morse	Boston	1795
J.HOBARTH	Joshua Hobart	New Haven, Conn.	1810
J.HODGE HADLEY	John Hodge	Hadley, Mass.	1800
J.HOLLISTER PURE COIN	Julius Hollister	Oswego, N. Y.	1846
J.Howell	James Howell	Philadelphia	1802

Mark	Name	Location	Date
J.HUGHES	Jeremiah Hughes	Annapolis, Md.	1805
J&IC	John & James Cox	New York	1817
J&IC&C	John & James Cox	New York	1831
J.&I.COX N.Y.	John & James Cox	New York	1817
J.HLEWIS	J. H. Lewis	Albany, N. Y.	1810
JJackson	Joseph Jackson S.M.	Baltimore, Md.	1803
J.JBANGS	John J. Bangs	Cincinnati, Ohio	1825
J JENCKES	John C. Jenckes	Providence, R. I.	1798
J J.LOW	John J. Low	Boston	1825
JJ.LOW&CO	J. J. Low & Co.	Boston	1830
JJMonell CMWilliams	J. J. Monell & C. M. Williams	New York	1825
J.JONES	John B. Jones	Boston	1813
J.J.S	John J. Staples, Jr.	New York	1788
JK	James Kendall	Wilmington, Del.	1785
J KEDZIE	J. Kedzie S.M.	Rochester, N. Y.	1830
J.KENDALL	James Kendall	Wilmington, Del.	1785
J.KFELLOWS	James K. Fellows	Lowell, Mass.	1832
J.KITTS	John Kitts	Louisville, Ky.	1838
JL JL	Joseph Loring	Boston	1775
JL	John Lynch	Baltimore, Md.	1786
J.LADOMUS	Jacob Ladomus	Philadelphia	1843

J LEVY	Jones Levy	New York	1835
J. G	John L. Gale	New York	1819
J. GALE	John L. Gale	New York	1819
J. MOFFAT	J. L. Moffat	New York	1815
J. L. MOORE	Jared L. Moore P.M.	New York	1835
J. ORD	Jabez C. Lord P.M.	New York	1825
JLoring	Joseph Loring	Boston	1775
J LOWE	Joshua Lowe	New York	1823
JLownes	Joseph Lownes	Philadelphia	1780
J SMITH	John Leonard Smith	Syracuse, N. Y.	1850
J. W	John L. Westervelt	Newburgh, N. Y.	1845
J. NCH	John Lynch	Baltimore, Md.	1786
JM	J. Merchant	New York	1795
J·M J·M	Joseph Moulton	Newburyport, Mass.	1765
JMBARROWS	James Madison Barrows	Tolland, Conn.	1828
JMF	John McFarlane	Boston	1796
JM℃FARLANE	John McFarlane	Boston	1796
J·MERCHANT	J. Merchant	New York	1795
JMEREDITH	Joseph P. Meredith	Baltimore, Md.	1824
JMHOFFMAN	James M. Hoffman	Philadelphia	1820
JOHN B AKIN	John B. Akin	Danville, Ky.	1850

JOHN BALL	John Ball	Concord, Mass.	1763
JOHN BIGELOW · PURE COIN	John Bigelow	Boston	1830
JOHN B SCOTT	John B. Scott	New York	1820
JOHN BURT	John Burt	Boston	1712
JOHN C FARR	John C. Farr	Philadelphia	1824
JOHN H TYLER & CO	John H. Tyler & Co.	Boston	1840
JOHNSON · Johnson	Samuel Johnson	New York	1780
JOHSON & REAT	Johnson & Reat	Richmond, Va.	1810
J.O.&JR.POTTER	J. O. & J. R. Potter	Providence, R. I.	1810
J.MOOD · J MOOD	John Mood	Charleston, S. C.	1816
J MOTT	James S. Mott	New York	1830
J.MOULTON	Joseph Moulton	Newburyport, Mass.	1835
J Murdock	James Murdock	Philadelphia	1779
J.MURPHY · JMURPHY	James Murphy	Boston	1803
Jn Reynolds	John Reynolds	Hagerstown, Md.	1790
JONES BALL & CO	Jones, Ball & Co.	Boston	1850
JONES. BALL & POOR	Jones, Ball & Poor	Boston	1840
JONES & HUTTON	Jones & Hutton	Wilmington, Del.	1840
JONES.LOWS & BALL	Jones, Lows & Ball	Boston	1839
JONES & WARD	Jones & Ward	Boston	1815
J.O.PITKIN	John O. Pitkin	East Hartford, Conn.	1837

JOSEPH RAYNES	Joseph Raynes	Lowell, Mass.	1835
Joseph T. Rice	Joseph T. Rice	Albany, N. Y.	1813
Josiah Gooding	Josiah Gooding	Boston	1840
J·OSGOOD	John Osgood, Jr.	Boston	1817
JOS.M.WALTER	Joseph M. Walter	Baltimore, Md.	1835
J.OTIS	Jonathan Otis	Newport, R. I.	1750
J.O.&W.PITKIN	J. O. & W. Pitkin P.M.	East Hartford, Conn.	1826
J.PEABODY	John Peabody	Enfield, Conn.	1799
J.Pearson	John Pearson	New York	1791
J·PERKINS	Joseph Perkins	Little Rest, R. I.	1770
J.PETERS	James Peters	Philadelphia	1821
J.PETERS & CO	J. Peters & Co.	Philadelphia	1830
J.P.FIRENG BURLINGTON N.J.	J. P. Fireng	Burlington, N. J.	1810
J.&P.MOOD PURE COIN	J. & P. Mood	Charleston, S. C.	1834
JPT JPT JPT	John Proctor Trott	New London, Conn.	1792
J·PT & SON	J. P. Trott & Son	New London, Conn.	1820
J.P.TROTT	John Proctor Trott	New London, Conn.	1792
J.P.W.	Joseph P. Warner	Baltimore, Md.	1830
JR JR JR	Joseph Richardson, Jr.	Philadelphia	1773
JR	Joseph Rogers	Newport, R. I.	1760

J&R J&R	Johnson & Riley	Baltimore, Md.	1785
J.Reeve	Joseph Reeve	Newburgh, N. Y.	1803
J.RIDGEWAY	John Ridgeway	Boston	1813
J.ROGERS	Joseph Rogers	Newport, R. I.	1760
J.RUDD&Cº	J. Rudd & Co.	New York	1831
JS	Joel Sayre	New York	1799
J.S	Joseph Shoemaker	Philadelphia	1793
J.S	John Staniford	Windham, Conn.	1789
J.SARGEANT	Jacob Sargeant	Hartford, Conn.	1785
J.Sayre F	Joel Sayre	New York	1799
J.S.B JSB	John Clark Blackman	Danbury, Conn.	1827
J.S.BIRD	John S. Bird	Charleston, S. C.	1825
J&SBALDWIN	J. & S. Baldwin	Rochester, N. Y.	1800
J.SCHANK m	John A. Schanck	New York	1795
J.S.&CO	Joseph Seymour & Co.	Syracuse, N. Y.	1850
J.Scott J.SCOTT	John B. Scott	New York	1820
Jse OWEN	Jesse Owen	Philadelphia	1794
J.S.FELT	J. S. Felt	Portland, Me.	1825
J.SHAW	John A. Shaw	Newport, R. I.	1819
J.SHEALD	J. S. Heald B.M.	Baltimore, Md.	1810

J.SHOEMAKER	Joseph Shoemaker	Philadelphia	1793
J.SIBLEY	John Sibley	New Haven, Conn.	1810
J.Simmons	James Simmons	New York	1815
J.S.MOTT	J. S. Mott	New York	1790
J.S.SHARRARD	J. S. Sharrard	Shelbyville, Ky.	1850
J.STOCKMAN	Jacob Stockman	Philadelphia	1828
J.STODDER	Jonathan Stodder, Jr.	New York	1825
JStow	John Stow	Wilmington, Del.	1772
J.T	Jonathan Trott	Boston	1758
J TANGUY	John Tanguy	Philadelphia	1801
J.&TD	John & Tunis Denise	New York	1798
JTOUZELL	John Touzell	Salem, Mass.	1756
J.T.R	Joseph T. Rice	Albany, N. Y.	1813
J.TRICE Albany	Joseph T. Rice	Albany, N. Y.	1813
J.TROTT JTrott	Jonathan Trott	Boston	1758
J.W	John Waite	South Kingston, R. I.	1763
J.W	John Walraven	Baltimore, Md.	1792
JW	James Ward	Hartford, Conn.	1798
J.W	Joseph Warner	Wilmington, Del.	1775
J.W	John Wendover	New York	1694
J.W	Joseph Wyatt	Philadelphia	1797

J.W.ABBOTT	John W. Abbott	Portsmouth, N. H.	1839
J.WAITE	John Waite	South Kingston, R. I.	1763
J.WALLEN	John Wallen	Philadelphia	1763
J.WALTER	Jacob Walter B.M.	Baltimore, Md.	1815
J.WARD HARTFORD	James Ward	Hartford, Conn.	1798
J.WARNER	Joseph Warner	Wilmington, Del.	1775
J.WATSON	James Watson	Philadelphia	1830
JWB	Joseph W. Boyd	New York	1820
J.WBEEBE ✿ ❂ ❀	James W. Beebe S.M.	New York	1835
J.W.BEEBE & CO	J. W. Beebe & Co.	New York	1844
J.W.CORTELYOU	J. W. Cortelyou	New Brunswick, N. J.	1805
J.WEBB	James Webb B.M.	Baltimore, Md.	1810
J.WENTWORTH	Jason Wentworth	Lowell, Mass.	1846
J.W.F.	John W. Faulkner	New York	1835
J.W.FAULKNER	John W. Faulkner	New York	1835
J.W.FORCE	Jabez W. Force	New York	1819
J.Williams	John Williams	Philadelphia	1793
J.WOOD	John Wood	New York	1770
J.ZANE	Jesse S. Zane	Wilmington, Del.	1796
K B	Krider & Biddle	Philadelphia	1850

K.C.&J.	Kidney, Cann & Johnson	New York	1850
K&D	Kidney & Dunn	New York	1844
KEELER	Joseph Keeler	Norwalk, Conn.	1810
Kimberly KIMBERLY	William Kimberly	New York	1790
Kirk KIRK	Samuel Kirk B.M.	Baltimore, Md.	1815
KIRK&SMITH	Kirk & Smith B.M.	Baltimore, Md.	1817
K&S.	Kirk & Smith B.M.	Baltimore, Md.	1817
KL	Knight Leverett	Boston	1736
K.Leverett	Knight Leverett	Boston	1736
KE KE	Koenraet Ten Eyck	Albany, N. Y.	1703
LAFAR	John J. Lafar	Charleston, S. C.	1805
Lamothe	John Lamothe	New Orleans, La.	1822
LANG	Richard Lang	Salem, Mass.	1770
LANG	Jeffery Lang	Salem, Mass.	1733
LANGE	William Lange	New York	1844
L.B LB	Loring Bailey	Hingham, Mass.	1801
L.B	Luther Bradley	New Haven, Conn.	1798
L.B LB	Lewis Buichle	Baltimore, Md.	1798
L.B.CANDEE &CO.	L. B. Candee & Co.	Woodbury, Conn.	1830
L BROCK NEW YORK	L. Brock	New York	1830
L.Browne LBROWNE	Liberty Browne	Philadelphia	1801

L Buichle	Lewis Buichle	Baltimore, Md.	1798
L.CARY	Lewis Cary	Boston	1815
L'COUVERTIE	Louis Couvertie	New Orleans, La.	1822
L·CURTIS	Lewis Curtis	Farmington, Conn.	1797
LEACH	Charles Leach	Boston	1789
LEMAR	Benjamin Lemar	Philadelphia	1775
LEONARD	Samuel T. Leonard	Chestertown, Md.	1805
LeTelier	John Le Telier	Philadelphia	1770
Lewis & Smith	Lewis & Smith	Philadelphia	1805
LF LF	Lewis Fueter	New York	1770
L.FUETER N.YORK	Lewis Fueter	New York	1770
L&G	Lincoln & Green	Boston	1810
LH	Lewis Heck	Lancaster, Pa.	1760
LH STERLING	Littleton Holland	Baltimore, Md.	1800
L.HECK	Lewis Heck	Lancaster, Pa.	1760
L.H.Miller&Co	L. H. Miller & Co.	Baltimore, Md.	1840
LHOLLAND	Littleton Holland	Baltimore, Md.	1800
Libby Boston	Jacob G. L. Libby	Boston	1820
LIBERTY·BROWNE	Liberty Browne	Philadelphia	1801
LIDDEN	John Lidden	St. Louis, Mo.	1850
LINCOLN&FOSS	Lincoln & Foss	Boston	1850

LINCOLN & READ	Lincoln & Read	Boston	1835
L. KIMBALL	Lewis A. Kimball	Buffalo, N. Y.	1837
LLupp LLupp	Louis Lupp	New Brunswick, N. J.	1800
L. M. & A. C. ROOT	L. M. & A. C. Root	Pittsfield, Mass.	1830
LOCKWOOD	James Lockwood	New York	1799
LOMBARD	B. E. Lombard	Charleston, S. C.	1828
Longley Longley	Henry Longley	New York	1810
Longley & Dodge	Longley & Dodge	Charleston, S. C.	1810
LOVETT	Robert Lovett	Philadelphia	1818
LOWELL & SENTER	Lowell & Senter	Portland, Me.	1830
L. PONCET	Louis Poncet	Baltimore, Md.	1800
LOW & CO	John J. Low & Co.	Boston	1830
LOWER	Joseph Lower	Philadelphia	1806
LOWS, BALL & CO	Lows, Ball & Co.	Boston	1840
LRyerson	Lou Ryerson	York, Pa.	1760
LSB SB	Lucas Stoutenburgh	Charleston, S. C.	1718
L. BOUDO	Louis Boudo	Charleston, S. C.	1810
LW	Lemuel Wells	New York	1790
L. & W STANDARD	Leonard & Wilson	Philadelphia	1847
L. Walker	L. Walker	Boston	1825
L. W. CLARK	Lewis W. Clark	Watertown, N. Y.	1832

Mark	Name	Location	Year
L.W. & Co	Lemuel Wells & Co.	New York	1794
LYNCH	John Lynch	Baltimore, Md.	1786
LYNG N·YORK	John Burt Lyng	New York	1759
M&A Utica	Murdock & Andrews	Utica, N. Y.	1822
MARQUAND & CO	Marquand & Co.	New York	1820
MARSHALL & TEMPEST	Marshall & Tempest	Philadelphia	1813
MATHER & NORTH	Mather & North	New York	1825
MATT SKINNER	Matt Skinner	Philadelphia	1752
M·B MB	Miles Beach	Hartford, Conn.	1775
M&B M·B	Merriman & Bradley	New Haven, Conn.	1817
Mc CONNELL	Hugh McConnell	Philadelphia	1813
Mc.CONNELL	Thomas McConnell	Wilmington, Del.	1806
Mc CLYMAN	John McClyman	New York	1805
Mc Clymon	William McClymon	Schenectady, N. Y.	1800
Mc Mullin & Black	McMullin & Black	Philadelphia	1811
M&D	Moulton & Davis	Newburyport, Mass.	1824
M. De Young	Michael De Young	Baltimore, Md.	1816
MEAD & ADRIANCE	Mead & Adriance	Ithaca, N. Y.	1831
MEADOWS & CO	Meadows & Co.	Philadelphia	1831
MERRIMAN	Marcus Merriman	New Haven, Conn.	1787
Σ·ω	Michael Gibney	New York	1844

M.G MG	Miles Gorham	New Haven, Conn.	1790
M.GORHAM	Miles Gorham	New Haven, Conn.	1790
MH	Marquette Hastier	New York	1771
M.I	Munson Jarvis	Stamford, Conn.	1765
MILLER	William Miller	Philadelphia	1810
Minott Minott	Samuel Minott	Boston	1764
Minott IA	Minott & Austin	Boston	1765
Minott WS	Minott & Simpkins	Boston	1769
MITCHELL	Henry Mitchell	Philadelphia	1844
MJ	Munson Jarvis	Stamford, Conn.	1765
ML	Mathias Lemar	Philadelphia	1790
MM M.M	Marcus Merriman S.M.	New Haven, Conn.	1787
MM MM MM	Myer Myers	New York	1745
M.M&Co 🐦	Marcus Merriman & Co.	New Haven, Conn.	1806
M.M.LAWRENCE	Martin M. Lawrence	New York	1832
M.MILLER	Mathew Miller P.M.	Charleston, S. C.	1807
M.MORSE	Moses Morse	Boston	1816
MONK	James Monk	Charleston, S. C.	1800
MONTEITH 10-15	Robert Monteith B.M.	Baltimore, Md.	1825
MOOD	Peter Mood	Charleston, S. C.	1790
MOORE	Jared L. Moore	New York	1835

MOORE & BREWER	Moore & Brewer	New York	1835
MOORE & FERGUSON	Moore & Ferguson	Philadelphia	1801
MORSE	Moses Morse	Boston	1816
MOSELEY	David Moseley	Boston	1775
MOSES	Jacob Moses	Birmingham, Ala.	1768
MOTTS	W. & J. Mott	New York	1789
MOULTON	Ebenezer Moulton	Boston	1795
MOULTON	Joseph Moulton	Newburyport, Mass.	1765
MP M·P	Matthew Petit S.M.	New York	1811
M.P ⊙♠⊙	Maltby Pelletreau P.M.	New York	1813
M.P.STICKNEY	M. P. Stickney	Newburyport, Mass.	1820
MR MR MR	Moody Russell	Barnstable, Mass.	1715
M&R	McFee & Reeder	Philadelphia	1793
MS	Moreau Sarrazin	Charleston, S. C.	1734
MULFORD & WENDELL	Mulford & Wendell P.M.	Albany, N. Y.	1842
MUMFORD	Henry B. Mumford	Providence, R. I.	1813
MURDOCK	John Murdock	Philadelphia	1779
Musgrove Musgrave	James Musgrave	Philadelphia	1795
MWHITNEY	M. F. Whitney	New York	1823
MWING	Moses Wing	Windsor, Conn.	1785
M.W.JOHSON	Maycock W. Johnson	Albany, N. Y.	1815

Myers *Myers*	Myer Myers	New York	1745
N·A	Nathaniel Austin	Boston	1760
N·ANDRUS&C°	N. Andrus & Co.	New York	1834
N·B	Nathaniel Bartlett	Concord, Mass.	1760
N·B	Nicholas Burdock	Philadelphia	1797
N·B	Nathaniel Burr	Fairfield, Conn.	1780
N·BARTLETT	Nathaniel Bartlett	Concord, Mass.	1760
N·BOGERT	Nicholas J. Bogert	New York	1801
N·C N·C N·C	Nathaniel Coleman	Burlington, N. J.	1790
N·COLEMAN	Nathaniel Coleman	Burlington, N. J.	1790
N·DODGE N·DODGE	Nehemiah Dodge	Providence, R. I.	1795
N·EASTON	Nathaniel Easton	Nantucket, Mass.	1815
N·E·CRITTENDEN	Newton E. Crittenden	Cleveland, Ohio	1847
Newman ★	Timothy H. Newman	Groton, Mass.	1800
N·FRANCIS	Nathaniel Francis	New York	1804
N·GEFFROY	Nicholas Geffroy	Newport, R. I.	1795
N·H	Nathaniel Helme	Little Rest, R. I.	1782
N·H	Nicholas Hutchins	Baltimore, Md.	1810
N·H&CO	N. Harding & Co.	Boston	1842
NICHOLS	William S. Nichols	Newport, R. I.	1808
N·HAIGHT	Nelson Haight	Newburgh, N. Y.	1839

N HARDING	Newell Harding	Boston	1822
N HAYDEN	Nathaniel Hayden	Charleston, S. C.	1832
N Hobbs	Nathan Hobbs	Boston	1815
N·Hurd N·Hurd	Nathaniel Hurd	Boston	1755
NICHOLS	Basset Nichols	Providence, R. I.	1815
NICHOLS	William S. Nichols	Newport, R. I.	1808
N.J.BOGERT	Nicholas J. Bogert	New York	1801
N·L	Nathaniel Leach	Boston	1789
N·LANG	Nathaniel Lang	Salem, Mass.	1760
N.LE HURAY	Nicholas LeHuray	Philadelphia	1809
N LE HURAY JR	Nicholas LeHuray, Jr.	Philadelphia	1821
NM NM NM	Nathaniel Morse	Boston	1709
N MATSON	Newell Matson	Oswego, N. Y.	1845
N MUNROE	Nathaniel Munroe	Baltimore, Md.	1815
N N	Nehemiah Norcross	Boston	1796
N N.WEAVER	Nicholas N. Weaver	Utica, N. Y.	1815
N OLMSTED	Nathaniel Olmsted	Farmington, Conn.	1808
NORTON & SEYMOUR	Norton & Seymour	Syracuse, N. Y.	1850
NOXON	Martin Noxon	Edenton, N. C.	1800
N·PRATT	Nathan Pratt	Essex, Conn.	1792
N.ROTH – UTICA	Nelson Roth	Utica, N. Y.	1837

NR	Nicholas Roosevelt	New York	1738
NS	Nathaniel Shipman	Norwich, Conn.	1790
N·SHIPMAN	Nathaniel Shipman	Norwich, Conn.	1790
N·STORRS	Nathan Storrs	Northhampton, Mass.	1792
N.TAYLOR & CO	N. Taylor & Co.	New York	1825
N&T.FOSTER	Nathaniel & Thomas Foster	Newburyport, Mass.	1820
NV	Nathaniel Vernon	Charleston, S. C.	1802
NV	Nicholas Van Rensselaer	New York	1765
N·VERNON	Nathaniel Vernon	Charleston, S. C.	1802
N·VERNON & CO	N. Vernon & Co.	Charleston, S. C.	1803
NR NR	Nicholas Roosevelt	New York	1738
OAKES K	Frederick Oakes S.M.	Hartford, Conn.	1810
O.D.Seymour	Oliver D. Seymour	Hartford, Conn.	1843
O.KUCHER	O. Kuchler	New Orleans, La.	1850
OP	Otto Paul De Parisien	New York	1763
OPDP	Otto Paul De Parisien	New York	1763
O·PIERCE	O. Pierce	Boston	1824
OREED PHILA·	Osman Reed	Philadelphia	1831
O.REED & CO W	O. Reed & Co.	Philadelphia	1841
O·RICH BOSTON	Obadiah Rich	Boston	1830
O·ROBINSON	O. Robinson	New Haven, Conn.	1800

Mark	Name	Place	Date
O.&S.	Oakes & Spencer	Hartford, Conn.	1814
OSMON.REED & CO	Osmon Reed & Co.	Philadelphia	1841
OTIS Otis NEWPORT	Jonathan Otis	Newport, R. I.	1750
Ott	George Ott	Norfolk, Va.	1806
OWEN	Jesse Owen	Philadelphia	1794
O.W.Towson A	Obadiah W. Towson B.M.	Baltimore, Md.	1813
OWTOWSON	Obadiah W. Towson B.M.	Baltimore, Md.	1813
PA PA	Pygan Adams	New London, Conn.	1735
PALMER&BACHELDER	Palmer & Bachelder	Boston	1850
PANCOAST	Samuel Pancoast	Philadelphia	1785
PARISEN	Otto Paul De Parisien	New York	1763
PARKMAN Parkman	John Parkman	Boston	1738
PARRY	Martin Parry	Portsmouth, N. H.	1780
PB	Phillip Becker	Lancaster, Pa.	1764
PB	Phineas Bradley	New Haven, Conn.	1770
P.B.&C	Pelletreau, Bennett & Cooke	New York	1815
P.&B	Pangborn & Brinsmaid	Burlington, Vt.	1833
P.B.SADTLER&SON	P. B. Sadtler & Son	Baltimore, Md.	1850
PChitry N.YORK	Peter Chitry	New York	1814
PD	Phillip Dally	New York	1779
PD PD	Peter David	Philadelphia	1730

Mark	Name	Place	Date
P.DANA	Peyton Dana	Providence, R. I.	1821
P.DAVID P.DAVID	Peter David	Philadelphia	1730
PDR PDR	Peter De Riemer	New York	1763
P.DUBOIS BUFFALO	Philo Dubois	Buffalo, N. Y.	1842
PEIRCE	John Pierce	Boston	1810
PF	Peter Feurt	Boston	1732
P.FIELD JR	Peter Field, Jr.	New York	1805
P.G PG	Peter Getz	Lancaster, Pa.	1782
PG	Philip Goelet	New York	1731
P.GARRETT	Philip Garrett	Philadelphia	1811
P.Getz	Peter Getz	Lancaster, Pa.	1782
P.GRIFFIN	Peter Griffen	Albany, N. Y.	1825
P.G.TANNER	Perry G. Tanner S.M.	Utica, N. Y.	1842
PH P.H	Philip Hulbeart	Philadelphia	1750
PH	Philip Huntington	Norwich, Conn.	1795
PhilipSyng	Philip Syng, Jr.	Philadelphia	1726
P.Howell P.HOWELL	Paul Howell	New York	1810
PIERPONT	Benjamin Pierpont	Boston	1756
PITKIN	John O. Pitkin	East Hartford, Conn.	1837
PITMAN Pitman	Sanders Pitman	Providence, R. I.	1775
Pitts	Richard Pitts	Philadelphia	1744

Peter Van Inburgh	New York	1710
Philip Jones	Wilmington, Del.	1843
Peter Kirkwood	Chestertown, Md.	1790
Peter Leret	Philadelphia	1779
Paul Little	Portland, Me.	1760
Peter Lupp	New Brunswick, N. J.	1787
Platt & Brother	New York	1825
Peter Leret	Philadelphia	1779
Peter L. Krider	Philadelphia	1850
Peter Martin	New York	1756
Peter Mood	Charleston, S. C.	1790
Parry & Musgrave	Philadelphia	1793
Peter Martin	New York	1756
Pardon Miller	Providence, R. I.	1810
Peter Mood	Charleston, S. C.	1790
Peter Oliver	Boston	1705
Peter Olivier	Philadelphia	1790
Thomas Pons	Boston	1789
John Potwine	Boston	1721
Peter Perreau	Philadelphia	1797
Peter P. Hayes	Poughkeepsie, N. Y.	1826

PQ PQ P.Q			Peter Quintard		New York	1731
PR			Paul Revere		Boston	1725
PR PR			Paul Revere, Jr.		Boston	1757
P.REVERE			Paul Revere		Boston	1725
P.REVERE PRevere			Paul Revere		Boston	1725
P.RIKER NYORK			Peter Riker		New York	1797
P.S ⬤ ⬤ PS			Philip B. Sadtler	B.M.	Baltimore, Md.	1800
PS) PP PS			Philip Syng, Jr.		Philadelphia	1726
PS			Philip Syng		Philadelphia	1715
P.Sadtler P.B.SADTLER			Philip B. Sadtler	B.M.	Baltimore, Md.	1800
P.SAYRE			Paul Sayre		Southampton, N. Y.	1785
P.STACY			Philemon Stacy, Jr.		Boston	1819
P.&U			Pelletreau & Upson		New York	1818
PURSE Purse			William Purse		Charleston, S. C.	1798
Putnam&Low			Putnam & Low		Boston	1822
PV PV			Peter Vergereau		New York	1720
P.V.B PVB ⬤			Peter Van Beuren		New York	1795
P.V.BEUREN			Peter Van Beuren		New York	1795
PVD PVD PVD			Peter Van Dyke		New York	1705
P.WHITE			Peregrine White		Woodstock, Conn.	1774
R&A.C			R. & A. Campbell	B.M.	Baltimore, Md.	1835

R&A.CAMPBELL	R. & A. Campbell B.M.	Baltimore, Md.	1835
R.A.LYTLE 1015	R. A. Lytle B.M.	Baltimore, Md.	1825
RB	Roswell Bartholomew	Hartford, Conn.	1805
RB RB	Robert Brookhouse	Salem, Mass.	1800
R.BEAUVAIS	René Beauvais	St. Louis, Mo.	1838
RBROWN ★ 10~15	Robert Brown	Baltimore, Md.	1813
R.BROWN&SON	R. J. Brown & Son	Boston	1833
RC	Robert Campbell B.M.	Baltimore, Md.	1819
RC	Richard Conyers	Boston	1688
RD	Robert Douglas	New London, Conn.	1766
RD	Richard Van Dyke	New York	1750
R.E RE	Robert Evans	Boston	1798
REEVES	Enos Reeves	Charleston, S. C.	1784
RE.SMITH	Richard E. Smith	Louisville, Ky.	1827
R.EVANS	Robert Evans	Boston	1798
REVERE REVERE	Paul Revere	Boston	1757
RF	Rufus Farnam	Boston	1796
R·F RF	Robert Fairchild	Durham, Conn.	1740
R.FAIRCHILD	Robert Fairchild	Durham, Conn.	1740
R.FARNAM	Rufus Farnam	Boston	1796
RG	Robert Gray	Portsmouth, N. H.	1830

RG	Rufus Greene	Boston	1730
RG	Rene Grignon	Oxford, Mass.	1691
R&G	Riggs & Griffith B.M.	Baltimore, Md.	1816
RGray	Robert Gray	Portsmouth, N. H.	1830
R·GREENE RGreene	Rufus Greene	Boston	1730
RH RH RH	Richard Humphreys	Philadelphia	1772
R.HBAILEY	Roswell H. Bailey	Woodstock, Vt.	1825
R&HFARNAM	R. & H. Farnam	Boston	1807
RHMAYNARD	R. H. Maynard	Buffalo, N. Y.	1825
RHumphreys	Richard Humphreys	Philadelphia	1772
Rice	Joseph Rice	Baltimore, Md.	1784
RICHARDS	Samuel R. Richards, Jr.	Philadelphia	1793
RICHARDS&WILLIAMSON	Richards & Williamson	Philadelphia	1797
RICHMOND	Franklin Richmond	Providence, R. I.	1815
RIGGS Riggs	George W. Riggs B.M.	Baltimore, Md.	1810
RKEYWORTH	Robert Keyworth	Washington, D. C.	1833
R&L	Roberts & Lee	Boston	1772
RLANG	Richard Lang	Salem, Mass.	1770
RM PureCoin	Reuben Merriman	Cheshire, Conn.	1810
RM	Robert Monteith B.M.	Baltimore, Md.	1825
R.MERRIMAN	Reuben Merriman	Cheshire, Conn.	1810

Mark	Name	Place	Date
R.NIXON	Richard Nixon	Philadelphia	1820
ROBERT J.BROWN	Robert J. Brown	Boston	1813
ROBT GRAY	Robert Gray	Portsmouth, N. H.	1830
ROCKWELL ROCKWELL	Edward Rockwell	New York	1807
Rockwell	Thomas Rockwell	Norwalk, Conn.	1775
ROGERS	Daniel Rogers	Newport, R. I.	1774
R·P	Richard Pitts	Philadelphia	1744
RPARRY	Rowland Parry	Philadelphia	1790
RPUTNEY	Reuben H. Putney	Sackets Harbor, N. Y.	1816
RR RR	Richard Riggs	Philadelphia	1810
RR	Robert Ross	Frederica, Del.	1789
RRAIT	Robert Rait	New York	1830
RRBROWN	R. R. Brown	Baltimore, Md.	1830
RROSS	Robert Ross	Frederica, Del.	1789
RS RS	Robert Sanderson	Boston	1638
RS IH RS IH	Hull & Sanderson	Boston	1652
R Shepherd	Robert Shepherd	Albany, N. Y.	1805
R STARR	Richard Starr	Boston	1807
R.STILLMAN	Richard Stillman	Philadelphia	1805
R·SWAN	Robert Swan	Andover, Mass.	1795
RUSSEL	Jonathan Russell	Ashford, Conn.	1804

Richard Rutter	Baltimore, Md.	1790
Richard Vincent	Baltimore, Md.	1799
Richard Van Dyke	New York	1750
Robert Wilson	New York	1805
R. & W. Wilson	Philadelphia	1831
R. & W. Wilson	Philadelphia	1831
Samuel Alexander	Philadelphia	1797
Samuel Avery	Preston, Conn.	1786
Simmons & Alexander	Philadelphia	1800
Samuel Alexander	Philadelphia	1797
Henry Salisbury S.M.	New York	1831
Salisbury & Co.	New York	1835
Samuel Kirk B.M.	Baltimore, Md.	1815
Samuel Burt	Boston	1750
Samuel Avery	Preston, Conn.	1786
John Sayre	New York	1792
S. Ayres	Lexington, Ky.	1805
Standish Barry	Baltimore, Md.	1784
Samuel Bartlett	Boston	1775
Stephen Bourdet	New York	1730
Samuel Buel	Middletown, Conn.	1777

SB	Samuel Burrill	Boston	1733
SB S-BURT	Samuel Burt	Boston	1750
S&B	Shepherd & Boyd	Albany, N. Y.	1810
S.BAKER	Stephen Baker	New York	1830
S.Ball	Sheldon Ball	Buffalo, N. Y.	1821
S.BARRETT ✪	Samuel Barrett	Nantucket, Mass.	1775
S·BARTLETT	Samuel Bartlett	Boston	1775
S.BELL	S. W. Bell	Philadelphia	1837
S·Bowne S·Bowne	Samuel Bowne	New York	1780
S.BRAMHALL	S. Bramhall	Plymouth, Mass.	1800
S.BROWN	Samuel C. Brown S.M.	New York	1825
S·Burrill S·Burrill	Samuel Burrill	Boston	1733
S&B.BROWER	S. & B. Brower	Albany, N. Y.	1810
S.C	Samuel Casey	South Kingstown, R. I.	1750
S:CASEY	Samuel Casey	South Kingstown, R. I.	1750
S.C.& Co	Simon Chaudron & Co.	Philadelphia	1807
S&C	Storrs & Cooley	Utica, N. Y.	1827
SC & CO	Stephen Castan & Co.	Philadelphia	1819
SCHANCK ⓐ ⓜ	John A. Schanck	New York	1795
S.COLEMAN	Samuel Coleman	Burlington, N. J.	1805

Mark	Name	Place	Date
Coley	Simeon Coley	New York	1767
S.COLLINS	Seldon Collins, Jr.	Utica, N. Y.	1837
S COVIL & KINSEY	Scovil & Kinsey	Cincinnati, Ohio	1830
S.D S.D	Samuel Drowne	Portsmouth, N. H.	1770
S.DAVIS	Samuel Davis	Plymouth, Mass.	1801
S.D.BROWER	S. D. Brower S.M.	Troy, N. Y.	1832
S.DODGE ★	Seril Dodge	Providence, R. I.	1793
S.D.ROCKWELL NEW YORK	S. D. Rockwell	New York	1830
S.Drowne S.DROWNE	Samuel Drowne	Portsmouth, N. H.	1770
S.E S.E	Samuel Edwards	Boston	1729
S.E	Stephen Emery	Boston	1775
S.Emery	Stephen Emery	Boston	1775
SETH.EASTMAN	Seth Eastman	Concord, N. H.	1820
SEYMOUR & HOLLISTER	Seymour & Hollister	Hartford, Conn.	1845
SE YOUNG LACONIA	S. E. Young	Laconia, N. H.	1840
SF	Samuel Ford	Philadelphia	1797
SG	S. Garre	New York	1825
SG	Samuel Gilbert	Hebron, Conn.	1798
SG	Samuel Gray	New London, Conn.	1710
S.GARRE	S. Garre	New York	1825
S.GRAY	Samuel Gray	Boston	1732

SH SH	Stephen Hardy	Portsmouth, N. H.	1805
SH	Samuel Haugh	Boston	1696
S·H	Stephen Hopkins	Waterbury, Conn.	1745
SHAW & DUNLEVY	Shaw & Dunlevy	Philadelphia	1833
SHEPHERD	Robert Shepherd	Albany, N. Y.	1805
SHEPHERD & BOYD	Shepherd & Boyd	Albany, N. Y.	1810
SHIPP & COLLINS	Shipp & Collins	Cincinnati, Ohio	1850
S.Howell	Silas W. Howell	Albany, N. Y.	1798
S·HOYT PEARL ST	S. Hoyt	New York	1817
S.HOYT & CO	S. Hoyt & Co.	New York	1842
S.HUNTINGTON	S. Huntington	Portland, Me.	1850
S Hussey	Stephen Hussey	Easton, Md.	1818
S HUTCHINSON	Samuel Hutchinson	Philadelphia	1828
SIBLEY	Clark Sibley	New Haven, Conn.	1800
S.ILEA	Samuel J. Lea B.M.	Baltimore, Md.	1815
SIMMONS & ALEXANDER	Simmons & Alexander	Philadelphia	1800
Simes	William Simes	Portsmouth, N. H.	1800
Simpkins	William Simpkins	Boston	1730
S.J	Samuel Johnson	New York	1780
S.J.LEA	Samuel J. Lea B.M.	Baltimore, Md.	1815

Samuel Kirk B.M.	Baltimore, Md.	1815
Samuel Keplinger B.M.	Baltimore, Md.	1812
Thomas Skinner	Marblehead, Mass.	1740
Samuel Kirk B.M.	Baltimore, Md.	1815
Samuel W. Lee	Providence, R. I.	1815
Samuel T. Leonard	Chestertown, Md.	1805
Joshua Slidell	New York	1765
Stephen L. Preston	Newburgh, N. Y.	1850
Samuel Merriman	New Haven, Conn.	1795
Samuel Minott	Boston	1764
Sylvester Morris	New York	1745
Sibley & Marble	New Haven, Conn.	1801
Simeon Marble	New Haven, Conn.	1800
Samuel Merriman	New Haven, Conn.	1795
Smith & Grant	Louisville, Ky.	1827
S. N. Story	Worcester, Mass.	1845
Samuel Pancoast	Philadelphia	1785
Samuel Parmelee	Guilford, Conn.	1760
Samuel Phillips	Salem, Mass.	1680
Samuel Parmelee	Guilford, Conn.	1760
Saunders Pitman	Providence, R. I.	1775

S.P.SQUIRE	S. P. Squire	New York	1835
SQUIRE & BROTHER	Squire & Brother	New York	1846
SQUIRE & LANDER	Squire & Lander	New York	1840
SR	Samuel R. Richards, Jr.	Philadelphia	1793
S&R	Sayre & Richards	New York	1802
SREED	Stephen Reed	New York	1805
SReeves	Stephen Reeves	Cohansey Bridge, N. J.	1767
SRICHARDS	Stephen Richards	New York	1815
SRICHARDS	Samuel R. Richards, Jr.	Philadelphia	1793
SRichards SW	Richards & Williamson	Philadelphia	1797
SS	Silas W. Sawin	New York	1825
SS	Samuel Soumaine	Annapolis, Md.	1740
SS SS	Simeon Soumaine	New York	1706
S.SIMMONS	S. Simmons	Philadelphia	1797
S&SWILSON	S. & S. Wilson	Philadelphia	1805
ST ST ST NYork	Samuel Tingley	New York	1754
S&T	Shethar & Thompson	Litchfield, Conn.	1801
S&T.T.WILMOT	Samuel & Thomas T. Wilmot	Charleston, S. C.	1837
Standish Barry	Standish Barry	Baltimore, Md.	1784
STANIFORD Staniford	John Staniford	Windham, Conn.	1789
STANLEY S BALDWIN	Stanley S. Baldwin	New York	1820

Mark	Name	Location	Date
STANTON	Zebulon Stanton	Stonington, Conn.	1775
STEBBINS	Thomas E. Stebbins	New York	1830
STEBBINS&CO	T. E. Stebbins & Co.	New York	1835
STEBBINS&HOWE	Stebbins & Howe	New York	1832
STEPHENSON	Thomas Stephenson	Buffalo, N. Y.	1835
STEVENS&LAKEMAN	Stevens & Lakeman	Salem, Mass.	1825
STEWART IOS	John Stewart	New York	1791
STingley NYork	Samuel Tingley	New York	1754
STOCKMAN&PEPPER	Stockman & Pepper	Philadelphia	1828
STODDER&FROBISHER	Stodder & Frobisher	Boston	1816
Stollenwerck	Stollenwerck & Co.	New York	1800
Stollenwerck&Bros	Stollenwerck & Bros.	New York	1805
Storm&Son	A. G. Storm & Son	Poughkeepsie, N. Y.	1823
Storrs & Cook	Storrs & Cook	Northampton, Mass.	1827
Storrs&Cooley. Utica	Storrs & Cooley	Utica, N. Y.	1827
Stuart	John Stuart	Providence, R. I.	1720
SV SV	Samuel Vernon	Newport, R. I.	1705
WSPELLETREAU SVANWYCK	Pelletreau & Van Wyck	New York	1815
SVANWYCK	Stephen Van Wyck	New York	1805
SV.LUPP	S. V. Lupp	New Brunswick, N. J.	1815
SW S	Samuel Warner	Philadelphia	1797

Mark	Name	Place	Year
SW	Samuel Waters	Boston	1803
SW SW R	Simon Wedge B.M.	Baltimore, Md.	1798
SW S W	Silas White	New York	1791
SW SW	Samuel Williamson	Philadelphia	1794
S&W	Simmons & Williamson	Philadelphia	1797
Swan SWAN	William Swan	Boston	1740
S.Warner	Samuel Warner	Philadelphia	1797
S.WATERS	Samuel Waters	Philadelphia	1803
S.WEDGE S.Wedge	Simon Wedge B.M.	Baltimore, Md.	1798
S.WHITE	Silas White	New York	1791
S.W.Howell S.W.Howell	Silas W. Howell	Albany, N. Y.	1798
S.WILLIAMS	Stephen Williams	Providence, R. I.	1799
S.WILLIS	Stillman Willis	Boston	1813
S.WILMOT	Samuel Wilmot	New Haven, Conn.	1800
S&WILSON	Storm & Wilson	Poughkeepsie, N. Y.	1802
SWL I W	S. W. Lee	Providence, R. I.	1815
S.W.LEE	S. W. Lee	Providence, R. I.	1815
SY	S. Yates	Albany, N. Y.	1810
SYATES	S. Yates	Albany, N. Y.	1810
T.A TA	Thomas Arnold	Newport, R. I.	1760
TA.DAVIS	Thomas A. Davis	Boston	1825

T&AE·WARNER	Thomas & A. E. Warner	Baltimore, Md.	1805
T·ARNOLD	Thomas Arnold	Newport, R. I.	1760
TAYLOR & LAWRIE	Taylor & Lawrie	Philadelphia	1837
B **B**	Thauvet Besley	New York	1727
TB	Timothy Bontecou	New Haven, Conn.	1725
T·B	Timothy Bontecou, Jr.	New Haven, Conn.	1760
T.B	Theophilus Bradbury	Newburyport, Mass.	1815
TB	Timothy Brigden	Albany, N. Y.	1813
TB **U**	Thomas Burger	New York	1805
T&B	Trott & Brooks	New London, Conn.	1798
T·B *Burger*	Thomas & John Burger	New York	1805
T.BRUFF	Thomas Bruff	Easton, Md.	1785
TB Simpkins	Thomas B. Simpkins	Boston	1750
T.BYRNES	Thomas Byrnes	Wilmington, Del.	1793
TC	Thomas Carson	Albany, N. Y.	1815
T C	Thomas Clark	Boston	1764
TC	Thomas Colgan	New York	1771
T&C	Trott & Cleveland	New London, Conn.	1792
T.CAMPBELL	Thomas Campbell	New York	1800
J.C.C	Thomas Chester Coit	Norwich, Conn.	1812
T.C.GARRETT	Thomas C. Garrett	Philadelphia	1829

Mark	Name	Location	Date
TC&H	Thomas Chadwick & Heims	Albany, N. Y.	1815
TClark	Thomas Clark	Boston	1764
TCOHEN	Thomas Cohen	Chillicothe, Ohio	1814
TCOLGAN	Thomas Colgan	New York	1771
T.CONLYN	T. Conlyn	Philadelphia	1845
T.COVERLY	Thomas Coverly	Newport, R. I.	1760
TD	Timothy Dwight	Boston	1675
T·DANE	Thomas Dane	Boston	1745
JDBussy	Thomas D. Bussey	Baltimore, Md.	1792
TDD	Tunis D. Dubois	New York	1797
T·D·DUBOIS	Tunis D. Dubois	New York	1797
TE	Thomas Stevens Eayres	Boston	1785
TE TE TE	Thomas Edwards	Boston	1725
TE	Thomas Knox Emery	Boston	1802
T·EATON	Timothy Eaton	Philadelphia	1793
TEdwards	Thomas Edwards	Boston	1725
T·Emery T·KEMERY	Thomas Knox Emery	Boston	1802
TENNEY 251BWAY	William I. Tenney	New York	1840
TERRY	Geer Terry	Enfield, Conn.	1800
T.E.S	Thomas E. Stebbins	New York	1830
T.F	Thomas Fletcher	Philadelphia	1813

TFisher	Thomas Fisher	Philadelphia	1797
T·FLETCHER	Thomas Fletcher	Philadelphia	1813
TFOSTER	Thomas Foster	Newburyport, Mass.	1820
TG	Timothy Gerrish	Portsmouth, N. H.	1775
T·Gerrish	Timothy Gerrish	Portsmouth, N. H.	1775
T·GRANT	Thomas Grant	Marblehead, Mass.	1754
TH TH *TH*	Thomas Hammersley	New York	1756
T&H C ⊡ ⊡	Taylor & Hinsdale	New York	1807
Th·Farnam	Thomas Farnam	Boston	1825
THIBAULT	Francis & Felix Thibault	Philadelphia	1807
THBAULT BROTHERS	Thibault & Brothers	Philadelphia	1810
TH·MARSHALL	Thomas H. Marshall	Albany, N. Y.	1832
T·H·Newman	Timothy H. Newman	Groton, Mass.	1800
Tiley	James Tiley	Hartford, Conn.	1765
TITCOMB	Francis Titcomb	Newburyport, Mass.	1813
T·J·MEGEAR	Thomas J. Megear	Wilmington, Del.	1830
TK	Thaddeus Keeler	New York	1805
TK	Thomas Kettle	Charlestown, Mass.	1784
TK TK	Thomas Kinney	Norwich, Conn.	1807
TKE	Thomas Knox Emery	Boston	1802
TKEELER	Thaddeus Keeler	New York	1805

T·KEITH	Timothy Keith	New York	1805
T·K·EMERY	Thomas Knox Emery	Boston	1802
TKMARSH PARIS	Thomas K. Marsh	Paris, Ky.	1830
T·LYNDE	Thomas Lynde	Worcester, Mass.	1771
TM TM	Thomas Millner	Boston	1715
TMILNE	Thomas Milne	New York	1795
TN TN	Thomas Norton	Farmington, Conn.	1796
TPARKMAN	Thomas Parkman	Boston	1793
TPARROTT	T. Parrott	Boston	1775
TPDROWN	T. P. Drown	Portsmouth, N. H.	1803
TPERKINS	T. Perkins	Boston	1810
TR	Thomas Revere	Boston	1789
T·R	Thomas Richards P.M.	New York	1815
TR WSP	Richards & Pelletreau	New York	1825
T&R	Tanner & Rogers	Newport, R. I.	1750
TRICHARDS	Thomas Richards	New York	1815
TRKING	Thomas R. King B.M.	Baltimore, Md.	1819
TS	Thomas Savage	Boston	1689
TS TS	Thomas Shields	Philadelphia	1765
TS TS	Thomas Skinner	Marblehead, Mass.	1740
TS	Thomas Sparrow	Annapolis, Md.	1764

T.SARGEANT	Thomas Sargeant	Springfield, Mass.	1816
TSB	Tobias Stoutenburgh	New York	1721
T.SIMPKINS	Thomas Barton Simpkins	Boston	1750
T.STEBBINS	Thomas Stebbins	New York	1830
T.Steele	T. S. Steele	Hartford, Conn.	1800
T.Steele & Co	T. Steele & Co.	Hartford, Conn.	1815
T.T	Thomas Townsend	Boston	1725
T.T.WILMOT	Thomas T. Wilmot	Charleston, S. C.	1840
T.U **N.York**	Thomas Underhill	New York	1779
T.U **V**	Underhill & Vernon	New York	1787
T.V.R	Tunis Van Riper	New York	1813
T.W	Thomas Whartenby	Philadelphia	1811
T.W **STERLING**	Thomas H. Warner B.M.	Baltimore, Md.	1805
T.WARNER **STERLING**	Thomas H. Warner B.M.	Baltimore, Md.	1805
T.W.KEITH	T. & W. Keith	Worcester, Mass.	1829
T.Y	Thomas You	Charleston, S. C.	1753
U&B	Ufford & Burdick	New Haven, Conn.	1812
V&C	Van Voorhis & Coley	New York	1786
V&Co	Vansant & Co.	Philadelphia	1850
VERNON	Nathaniel Vernon S.M.	Charleston, S. C.	1802
VILLARD **Villard**	R. H. L. Villard	Georgetown, D. C.	1833

V.LAFORME	Vincent LaForme	Boston	1850
VL&B PUREGOIN	Vincent LaForme & Bro.	Boston	1850
V.MARTIN	Valentine Martin	Boston	1842
VV&S VV&S V&S	Van Voorhis & Schanck	New York	1791
VVSCHANCK& McCALL	Van Voorhis, Schanck & McCall	Albany, N. Y.	1800
V&W	Van Ness & Waterman	New York	1835
WA	William Anderson	New York	1746
W.ADAMS NEW-YORK	William L. Adams	New York	1831
Walraven	John Walraven	Baltimore, Md.	1792
WARD HARTFORD	James Ward	Hartford, Conn.	1798
WARD.67.MARKET.ST	John Ward	Middletown, Conn.	1805
WARD & BARTHOLOMEW	Ward & Bartholomew	Hartford, Conn.	1804
WARDEN	Abijah B. Warden	Philadelphia	1842
W.A.RASCH	W. A. Rasch	New Orleans, La.	1830
WARFORD	Joseph Warford	Albany, N. Y.	1810
WATSON & BROWN	Watson & Brown	Philadelphia	1836
W.A.WILLIAMS	William A. Williams	Alexandria, Va.	1809
WB	William Bartram	Philadelphia	1769
WB WB	William Ball, Jr.	Baltimore, Md.	1785
WB WB	William Breed	Boston	1750
W&B W&B.	Ward & Bartholomew	Hartford, Conn.	1804

WBAILEY	William Bailey	Utica, N. Y.	1818
WBall WBALL	William Ball, Jr.	Baltimore, Md.	1785
W.B.HEYER W.B.Heyer	William B. Heyer	New York	1798
W.B.HEYER & J.GALE	Heyer & Gale	New York	1807
W.B.N	William B. North	New Haven, Conn.	1810
W B NORTH & CO	W. B. North & Co.	New York	1823
WBreed	William Breed	Boston	1750
W.BROWN	William Brown	Albany, N. Y.	1849
WBURR	William Burr	Providence, R. I.	1793
WBURT	William Burt	Boston	1747
W.& BYRNES	Woodcock & Byrnes	Wilmington, Del.	1793
WC WC	William Clark	New Milford, Conn.	1775
WC WC	William Cleveland	Norwich, Conn.	1791
WC WC	William Cowell	Boston	1703
W.C	William Cowell, Jr.	Boston	1734
WC	William Cross	Boston	1695
W.CARIO WCARIO	William Cario	Boston	1738
W.CARRINGTON	William Carrington	Charleston, S. C.	1830
W.C.DUSENBURY	W. C. Dusenbury	New York	1819
WColey	William Coley	New York	1767
W.CORNELL	Walter Cornell	Providence, R. I.	1780

W.COWAN	William D. Cowan	Philadelphia	1808
W.Cowell	William Cowell, Jr.	Boston	1734
W.D.RAPP STANDARD	W. D. Rapp	Philadelphia	1828
Weaver	Emmor T. Weaver	Philadelphia	1808
WEBB	Edward Webb	Boston	1705
WELLES BOSTON	George Welles	Boston	1805
WELLES & CO	Welles & Co.	Boston	1816
WELLES & GELSTON	Welles & Gelston	New York	1840
WENTWORTH & CO	Wentworth & Co.	New York	1850
WF WF	William Faris	Annapolis, Md.	1757
WF NEW YORK	William Forbes S.M.	New York	1830
W.F.Hill	William F. Hill	Boston	1810
W.FORBES NY	William Forbes S.M.	New York	1830
W.G	William Gale S.M.	New York	1820
WG	William Ghiselin	Philadelphia	1751
WG	William W. Gilbert	New York	1767
W.G	William Gowdey	Charleston, S. C.	1757
WG	William Gowen	Medford, Mass.	1777
WG	William Grant, Jr.	Philadelphia	1785
W.G	William Gurley	Norwich, Conn.	1804
W & G BOSTON	Woodward & Grosjean	Boston	1847

W.GALE	William Gale S.M.	New York	1820
W.GALE & SON	William Gale & Son	New York	1823
W.GETHEN	William Gethen	Philadelphia	1797
W.G.Forbes **W.G Forbes**	William G. Forbes	New York	1773
W.Gilbert	William W. Gilbert	New York	1767
W.GOWEN **W.Gowen**	William Gowen	Medford, Mass.	1777
W.GRANT **W Grant**	William Grant, Jr.	Philadelphia	1785
W GRIGG	William Grigg	New York	1765
W.GRISWOLD	William Griswold	Middletown, Conn.	1820
W.G&S	William Gale & Son	New York	1823
W & G SHARP	W. & G. Sharp	Philadelphia	1848
WH	William Hamlin	Providence, R. I.	1795
WH	William Haverstick	Philadelphia	1781
WH	William Heurtin	New York	1731
WH **WH**	William Hollingshead	Philadelphia	1754
WH **WH**	William Homes	Boston	1739
WH	William Homes, Jr.	Boston	1783
W.H	William Hughes	Baltimore, Md.	1785
⊖ ◆ ◑	Wood & Hughes	New York	1846
W·HART	William Hart	Philadelphia	1818
WHARTENBY	Thomas Whartenby	Philadelphia	1811

Mark	Name	Location	Year
W·HADWEN	William Hadwen	Nantucket, Mass.	1820
WHEELER &BROOKS	Wheeler & Brooks	Livonia, N. Y.	1830
WHITE	Amos White	East Haddam, Conn.	1766
WHITING	Charles Whiting .	Norwich, Conn.	1750
Whitlock	Thomas B. Whitlock	New York	1805
Whitney	Eben Whitney	New York	1805
WHITNEY & HOYT	Whitney & Hoyt	New York	1828
Whittemore	William Whittemore	Portsmouth, N. H.	1735
W·Homes	William Homes	Boston	1739
W·J WI	William Jones	Marblehead, Mass.	1715
WILLARD	James Willard	East Windsor, Conn.	1815
William Osborn	William Osborn	Providence, R. I.	1840
WILLIAMSON	Samuel Williamson	Philadelphia	1794
WILMOT	Samuel Wilmot	New Haven, Conn.	1800
WISHART	Hugh Wishart P.M.	New York	1784
WI·TENNEY NY	William I. Tenney P.M.	New York	1840
W·J	William B. Johonnot S.M.	Middletown, Conn.	1787
W·K	William Kimberley	New York	1790
W·K B· W·K B·	Benjamin Wynkoop	New York	1698
W·K C	Cornelius Wynkoop	New York	1724
W KENDRICK	William Kendrick	Louisville, Ky.	1840

WL	William Little	Newburyport, Mass.	1775
W·M	William Moulton	Newburyport, Mass.	1750
W·M **W·M**	William Moulton	Newburyport, Mass.	1796
WMANNERBACK	William Mannerback	Reading, Pa.	1825
W·MB **READING**	William Mannerback	Reading, Pa.	1825
WM.B.Durgin	William B. Durgin	Concord, N. H.	1850
WᵐBROWN **IO5**	William Brown B.M.	Baltimore, Md.	1810
WMᶜP	William McParlin B.M.	Annapolis, Md.	1805
WM GALE JR	William Gale, Jr.	New York	1825
WM H McDOWELL	William H. McDowell	Philadelphia	1819
WᵐHWHITLOCK	William H. Whitlock	New York	1805
WᵐH.EWAN	William H. Ewan P.M.	Charleston, S. C.	1849
WM.MCDOUGALL	William McDougall	Meredith, N. H.	1825
W.MILLER	William Miller	Philadelphia	1810
W.MITCHELL	William Mitchell	Richmond, Va.	1820
WM.J.PITKIN	William J. Pitkin	East Hartford, Conn.	1820
WᵐL.PITKIN	William L. Pitkin	East Hartford, Conn.	1820
W.MORRELL	William M. Morrell	New York	1828
W.MOULTON	William Moulton	Newburyport, Mass.	1750
WᵐROGERS	William Rogers	Hartford, Conn.	1822
WMROGERS & SON	William Rogers & Son	Hartford, Conn.	1850

Mark	Name	Location	Date
WM ROOT	W. M. Root	Pittsfield, Mass.	1840
W.M.ROUSE	William M. Rouse	Charleston, S. C.	1835
WM SAVAGE	William M. Savage	Glasgow, Ky.	1805
Wᵐ SMITH	William Smith	New York	1770
Wᵐ S Willis	William S. Willis	Boston	1830
WᵐThomson	William Thomson	New York	1810
Wᵉ W·WHITE	William W. White	New York	1805
W NEEDELS	William Needles	Easton, Md.	1807
W.N.ROOT & BROTHER	W. N. Root & Brother	New Haven, Conn.	1850
Wolcott & Gelston	Wolcott & Gelston	Boston	1820
WOLFE & WRIGGINS	Wolfe & Wriggins	Philadelphia	1837
WOOD & HUGHES	Wood & Hughes	New York	1846
WOODCOCK	Bancroft Woodcock	Wilmington, Del.	1754
Woods Woods	Freeman Woods	New York	1791
Woodward	Antipas Woodward	Middletown, Conn.	1791
W.P	William Parham	Philadelphia	1785
W.P WP	William Pollard	Boston	1715
WP	William Poole	Wilmington, Del.	1790
W PEARCE VA. NORFOLK	William Pearce	Norfolk, Va.	1820
W.P. & H STANTON	W. P. & H. Stanton	Rochester, N. Y.	1826
W.PITKIN	Walter Pitkin	East Hartford, Conn.	1830

Mark	Name	Place	Date
W.PITKIN C.C.NORTON	Pitkin & Norton	Hartford, Conn.	1825
WR WR	William Roe	Kingston, N. Y.	1795
WR WR	William Rouse	Boston	1660
W.ROE	William Roe	Kingston, N. Y.	1795
W.ROE & STOLLENWERCK	W. Roe & Stollenwerck	New York	1800
W.ROGERS	William Rogers	Hartford, Conn.	1822
WRP	W. R. Pitman	New Bedford, Mass.	1835
WS	William Simes	Portsmouth, N. H.	1800
WS WS	William Simpkins	Boston	1730
WS	William Swan	Boston	1740
W.Sanford	William Sanford	New York	1817
W SEAL	William Seal	Philadelphia	1816
W.SIMES W.SIMES	William Simes	Portsmouth, N. H.	1800
W.Simpkins W.SIMPKINS	William Simpkins	Boston	1730
WS Minott	Minott & Simpkins	Boston	1769
W.S.N	William S. Nicholas	Newport, R. I.	1808
W.SP	William S. Pelletreau	Southampton, N. Y.	1810
W.S.PELLETREAU	William S. Pelletreau	Southampton, N. Y.	1810
W.S.PELLETREAU S.VAN WYCK	Pelletreau & Van Wyck	New York	1815
W.SP TR	Pelletreau & Richards	New York	1825
W SWAN	William Swan	Boston	1740
W.T	William Taylor	Philadelphia	1775

WT	Walter Thomas	New York	1769
WT	William Thompson	Baltimore, Md.	1795
W.TERRY	Wilbert Terry	Enfield, Conn.	1785
W.Thomson	William Thomson	New York	1810
WV	William Vilant	Philadelphia	1725
W.V.B	William Van Beuren	New York	1790
W.W	William Ward	Litchfield, Conn.	1757
WW	William Whetcroft	Annapolis, Md.	1766
WW	William Whittemore	Portsmouth, N. H.	1735
W·W	William Wilson	Abingdon, Md.	1785
W.W IT	Wilson & Toy	Abingdon, Md.	1790
W·WAITE	William Waite	Wickford, R. I.	1760
W.WALKER	William Walker	Philadelphia	1793
WWARD WWard	William Ward	Litchfield, Conn.	1757
WWG	W. W. Gaskins	Norfolk, Va.	1806
WWHANNAH	W. W. Hannah P.M.	Hudson, N. Y.	1840
WWWHITE	William W. White	Philadelphia	1805
WYER&FARLEY	Wyer & Farley	Portland, Me.	1828
WYNKOOP	Jacobus Wynkoop	Kingston, N. Y.	1765
W.Young	William Young	Philadelphia	1761
YOU	Daniel You	Charleston, S. C.	1743

Mark	Name	Place	Year
YOUNG	Ebenezer Young	Hebron, Conn.	1778
YOUNG	Alexander Young	Camden, S. C.	1807
ZAHM & JACKSON	Zahm & Jackson	New York	1830
	Zalmon Bostwick	New York	1846
Z.B Z+B	Zachariah Brigden	Boston	1760
Z BOSTWICK	Zalmon Bostwick	New York	1846
Z.BRADLEY	Zebul Bradley	New Haven, Conn.	1810
Z.Brigden	Zachariah Brigden	Boston	1760
ZIBA FERRIS	Ziba Ferris	Wilmington, Del.	1810
Z S	Zebulon Stanton	Stonington, Conn.	1775
Z.SMITH Z.Smith	Zebulon Smith	Maine	1820

Chapter III

LOCATIONS OF SILVERSMITHS' SHOPS

THE LOCATIONS of the shops of the early American silversmiths as indicated on these maps of New York, Philadelphia, and Boston are intended to show as nearly as possible the places where the craftsmen made the many beautiful and valuable examples, still extant, of their workmanship. The writer makes no claim to accuracy in these locations for the reason that, except in very few instances, it is impossible to denote other than an approximate site of the houses and shops — because most of the early notices are no more explicit than: "Nigh the New Dutch Church"; "At Burling's Slip"; "In Third Street"; "At the North End," etc., and because even the original early records, from which many of the data have been gathered, have been found to occasionally conflict. These properties have been found chiefly in old deeds, early wills, and newspaper advertisements, and in various publications on the early American silversmiths.

It is difficult to know when the homes and shops were together or apart. It is, however, safe to say that the earliest craftsmen plied their trade in an ell or outbuilding connected with their living quarters and that it is probable that this custom was prevalent through the eighteenth century in many, if not most, cases.

The late 18th century shops, even those with street names and house numbers, except in a few instances, cannot be indicated with any degree of certainty because of inability to identify the numbering of that day with the system in use today. It will, of course, be understood that public places such as the Gaol in Philadelphia were removed prior to the establishment of the shop of certain silversmiths occupying the space as indicated. Those locations with street names and no numbering are difficult to place because of descriptions such as "On the corner of Maiden Lane and Crown." This puts it entirely up to the compiler to decide upon which of the four corners the shop was and in some cases other than corner property, which side of the street. There are some who advertise as "Maiden Lane and

Queen Street" in one year and in the next year the same silversmith advertised on "Lower End of Maiden Lane." These two addresses were probably one and the same. In numerous such instances, it has been assumed that the shop had not been moved. In others, no such liberty has been taken. This is explained for those readers who may question the existing difference in checking with published lists. There are some contemporary craftsmen omitted among the early as well as among the later. This is due to inability to ascertain their property in some cases and to the fact that later they had become too numerous so that only the best known among the later ones were included.

Changes were made in the names of the streets after the maps were printed which explains a difference in the address given in the index with that on the map. For instance: Prior to and subsequently to the Holland map of New York, Pearl Street began at the Battery and extended only to Whitehall Street. From there to Hanover Square, it was called Dock Street. From Hanover Square the continuation of the early Pearl Street was called Queen Street. Later the entire length of the street was given the name of Pearl Street which curves around opening into Broadway above Chambers Street (Frankford Street on the map). Therefore, silversmiths whose addresses were Pearl Street, after the change, are marked on the map on Queen Street. The same changes occur as well on various streets in Philadelphia and Boston. To complicate matters, in addition to the legitimate changes, several of the streets were called by other than their true names: i.e. Beekman Street was commonly called Chapel Street. This was because St. George's Chapel was on Beekman Street. There was a properly named Chapel Street on the west side of Broadway. In locating the shop of a William Smith, whose address was given as Chapel Street, a place was given him on Chapel Street, but later he was removed to Beekman Street when certain facts, stumbled upon accidently, showed his property was actually on Beekman Street. This incident again occurred in the case of Joseph Pinto whose property was found to have been on Bayard Street. The Bayard farm, then quite far from the center of the active settlement, was marked off in streets: Bayard Street, Judith, Elizabeth, etc. Naturally Joseph Pinto was placed on Bayard Street. As he was one of the active craftsmen of his day, it was perplexing that he should have settled so far out in the country. However, since his property was recorded as such, he was allowed to remain there — a considerable distance from his fellow workers. Later, however, when it was found that Duke Street was commonly called Bayard Street because the estate of the well-known Samuel Bayard, a prominent and prosperous inhabitant and a member of an eminent family of New Amsterdam, was on Duke Street, Joseph Pinto was rescued from his lonely habitation in the distant farm country (not far above where City Hall stands today) and given a place on Duke Street where he rightfully belonged with other craftsmen of his period.

Another well-known silversmith, John Burt Lyng, it appeared, had two addresses, one on Broadway opposite the Lutheran Church, and the other in The Great George Street. Holland's map shows a short street called King George Street and another longer one called George Street. Believing that the longer of the two streets was probably referred to as "The Great George Street" to differentiate between them, John Burt Lyng was placed on George Street. Later, as the research continued, a description of a piece of property was noted thus: "On the corner of Little Queen Street and The Great George Street." The latter, then could have been none other than Broadway so again a removal was made. Again and again these complications arose making necessary quite a number of changes. Kip Street is another which has caused some uncertainty due to a description in an early deed which differs somewhat from Kip Street as marked on Holland's map. It is generally known that Nassau Street was formerly Kip Street.

When reasonable, though not positive, evidence of certain properties has been found, a few of the silversmiths' shops have been marked on the map in more than one place rather than make a definite choice of the two. This occurs but rarely. The earliest and most important of these were Jesse Kip of New York, and Johannes Nys of Philadelphia. Jesse Kip was given a second location — the first on Kip Street, the second on William — because of convincing evidence. Johannes Nys' shop was on Carpenter's Alley in Philadelphia. Two locations are given him on the map both taken from reliable sources — one giving Carpenter's Alley near the corner of Fourth Street between Chestnut and Walnut — the other giving it on the east side of Front above Walnut — so Johannes Nys will be found in both places.

Gerrit Onckelbag owned several large tracts of land. These are not all indicated on the map because some of them were in outlying districts. The Jacob Boelen property on Queen Street above Burling Slip is questionable. Certain research material revealed such strong facts pointing in that direction as to seem justifiable to place him there. His Broadway property is one of the few very early sites so clearly described in deeds that it has been possible to mark this one of his shops on the map with assurance.

On the other hand, with no assurance, the Cowells of Boston are given their location in the South End of Boston. The research material at hand failed in description of the Cowell property more detailed than "the South End of Boston." Not knowing just where the "South End of Boston" began nor just how much of the city was considered the "South End," and also not wanting to omit such early and well-known, as well as expert craftsmen, as the Cowell family of silversmiths, a spot was selected near some of the other silversmiths of their period and there they will be found on the map although they may be some distance from their true location.

Vast research and close study of all material gathered has been required to establish as accurate locations as possible before making final indication on these maps. It is hoped that the readers will make generous allowances for the decision in the choice as shown.

The maps used were: New York, 1776 by Holland; Boston, by Osgood Carleton, supplied through the courtesy of The Horace Brown Map Collection, Yale University Library; the Philadelphia map, 1762 by Benjamin Eastman after Thomas Holmes, supplied through the courtesy of The Historical Society of Pennsylvania.

HELEN BURR SMITH

NEW YORK SILVERSMITHS
1660 - 1750

	Working	*Location*

B

Bancker, Adrian	1725	Bridge St. near Queen St. (formerly Wynkoop St.—also Brugh St.)
Becker, Fredrick	1725	Beekman St. (commonly called Chapel St.—also George St.)
Besley, Thauvet	1727	Golden Hill (John St. from William to Pearl)
Blanck, Jurian, Sr.	1660	South side of Pearl St. between State and Whitehall Sts.
Blanck, Jurian, Jr.	1666	Broadway
Boelen, Henricus	1718	Rotten Row (Hunter's Key) West side of Broadway between Little Queen and Crown Sts. (now Cedar and Liberty)
Boelen, Jacob	1680	Rotten Row (Hunter's Key) West side of Broadway between Little Queen and Crown Sts. (now Cedar and Liberty) Queen St. head of Burling's Slip
Bogardus, Everadus	1698	Corner of Princess and Broad Sts. (sold to Onckelbag)
Bourdet, Stephen	1730	Corner of John and William Sts.
Brevoort, John	1742	Fly Market

C

Cario, Michael	1728	Crown and Pearl Sts.

D

DePeyster, William	1730	Queen St. to Fletcher St.

F

Fielding, George	1731	Broad and Princess Sts.

G

Goelet, Philip	1731	Narrow St. west side of Broadway Broad St.

H

Hastier, John	1726	Queen St. in 1735
Hendricks, Ahasuerus	1678	Smith St.

Heurtin, William	1731	Golden Hill (John St. from William to Pearl)
Hutton, John	1720	Smith St.

K

Kierstede, Cornelius	1696	Queen and Cliff Sts.
Kip, Jesse	1682	Kip St. (Nassau) Smith St. between Princess and Garden Sts.

L

LeRoux, Bartholomew	1687	Broadway near Beaver Lane
LeRoux, Bartholomew	1738	Broadway near Beaver Lane
LeRoux, Charles	1710	Beekman St. near Peck's Slip Gold St.

M

Mariusgroen, Jacob	1701	Pearl St.
Myers, Myer	1745	Water St. Princess St. Greenwich St. Meal Market King St.

O

Onckelbag, Gerrit	1691	Smith St. between Princess and Garden Sts. Princess and Broad Sts. (bought in 1704 from Everadus Bogardus)

P

Pelletreau, Elias	1750	Golden Hill (John St. from William to Pearl Sts.)

Q

Quintard, Peter	1731	"Near the New Dutch Church"

R

Ridout, George	1745	"Near the Ferry Stairs"
Robert, Christopher	1731	Queen St. Broadway at Bowling Green
Roosevelt, Nicholas	1738	Thames Street on the wharf

S

Schaats, Bartholomew	1695	Near the Meal Market

Soumaine, Simeon	1706	Dock Street
Stoutenburgh, Tobias	1721	Broadway near the Spring Garden

V

Vanderburgh, Cornelius	1675	High St. (Duke St.) In the Fort
Vanderheul, Hendrick	1733	Queen St. and Smith's Fly (near Burling Slip)
Vander Spiegel, Jacobus	1689	Rotten Row Queen St. near Burling Slip
Van Dyck, Richard	1750	Hanover Square
Vergereau, Peter	1720	"Queen St. commonly called Smith's Valley"

W

Wynkoop, Benjamin	1698	Smith's Fly and Queen St.
Wynkoop, Cornelius	1726	West side of Smith St.

NEW YORK SILVERSMITHS
1750 - 1800

	Working	*Location*

A

Ackley, Francis M.	1797	Warren St. New St.
Alstyne, Jeronimus	1787	Maiden Lane
Andras, William	1795	40 William St.
Archie (Archer), John	1759	Dock St.

B

Bay, A. S.	1786	William St.
Bayley, Simeon A.	1789	Maiden Lane Old Slip Queen St.
Bennet, James	1773	Corner of Crown and Queen Sts.
Boelen, Jacob II	1755	Rotten Row (Hunter's Key)
Bowne, Samuel	1780	81 John St.
Brasher, A.	1790	Queen St. north of Crown and Maiden Lane.
Brasher, Ephraim	1766	Cherry St.
Bruff, Charles Oliver	1763 1769 1772	Maiden Lane near Fly Market Rotten Row opposite Fly Market Upper end of Maiden Lane near Broadway

Buché, Peter	1795	Fly Market
Burger, John	1780	{ Water St. (southeast of Cherry St.) Queen St. north of Cherry St. James St. and Rutgers St.

C

Coen, Daniel Bloom	1787	{ Maiden Lane Gold St.
Coley, Simeon	1767	Near the Merchant's Coffee House by the Ferry Stairs
Cook, John	1795	Ann St.

D

Dally, Phillip (with Jabez Halsey)	1779 1787	Queen St. Queen St.
Dawson, John	1769	Rotten Row
DeParisien, Otto Paul	{ April { May	1763 1769 1774 fire 1774 removed to	Smith St. at Crown St. Near Peck's Slip Smith's Fly Dock St.
DeRiemer, Peter	1763	Cortlandt St.
Dubois, Joseph	1790	{ 81 John St. Great Dock St.
Dubois, Tunis	1797	{ 90 John St. (1797) Pearl St.
Duche, Benne Roche	1795	{ Maiden Lane Beekman St. Nassau St.
Dunn, Cary	1765	{ Crown St. near New Dutch Church Maiden Lane and William St.

F

Forbes, Abraham G.	1769	Broadway
Forbes, William G.	1773	Broadway
Fournequet, Louis	1795	{ Ann St. William St.

Fueter, Daniel Christian	1754	{ James St. (St. James St.)
		Back of Hendrick Vanderwater's near Brew
		   House of Harmanus Bleecker
		Bayard St. (Duke St. commonly called
		   Bayard)
		Broadway

Fueter, Lewis	1770	Bayard St. (with father)

G

Gilbert, William W.	1767	{ Broadway opposite Trinity Church Below Peck's Slip on Front St.

Gordon, James	1795	Cliff St. and Ann St.
Gough, James	1769	Beaver St.
Grigg, William	1765	{ Maiden Lane and William St. { Broadway and Van Gelder's Alley
Guercy, Dominick	1795	{ Maiden Lane { William St.

H

Halsey, Jabez (with Phillip Dally)	1789	Queen St.
Halstead, Benjamin	1764	Maiden Lane and Nassau St. Also Broad St.
Hammersley, Thomas	1756	{ Near the Exchange in Dock St. { Hanover Square
Heath, John	1761	Wall St.
Heyer, William B.	1798	Warren St.

J

Johnson, Samuel	1780	Crown St. (Liberty St.)

K

Kimberly, William	1790	Crown St. and Fly Market

L

Lent, John	1787	{ 20 Beekman St. { 61 Beekman St. { 69 Maiden Lane
Lyng, John Burt	1759	Broadway opposite Lutheran Church

M

Maverick, Peter Rushton	1772	Crown St.
Mears, Samson	1762	Pearl St. (House of Andrew Breasted)

O

Ogilvie, Gabriel	1791	Beaver St.

P

Pinto, Joseph	1758	Bayard St. (Duke St.)

R

Reeves, Stephen	1776	Burling Slip in Queen St.
Richardson, Thomas	1769	Fly Market
Ritter, Michael	1786	Fly Market
Roberts, Michael	1786	Hanover Square

S

Sayre, Joel	1799	Pearl St. Maiden Lane West side of William St.
Sayre, John	1792	Pearl St.
Schaats, Bartholomew, II	1784	"Near City Hall" Federal Hall Nassau St.
Schanck, Garret	1791	Fair St. (now Fulton)
Schanck, John (with Garret)	1797	Water St. (north of Peck's Slip)
Skinner, Abraham	1756	Near Dock St. between Ferry Stair and Rotten Row
Smith, James	1794	Fair St. Water St.
Smith, William	1770	Chapel St. (Beekman)

T

Targee, John	1797	Gold St. Water St.
Tingley, Samuel	1754	The Fly Rotten Row

U

Underhill & Vernon (Thomas) (John)	1787	Water St.

V

Van Beuren, Peter	1795	Maiden Lane Pearl St.
Van Beuren, William	1790	Cortland St. Maiden Lane
Van Voorhis, Daniel	1782	Hanover Square Queen St. North Pearl St. Broadway
Van Voorhis & Coley	1786	Hanover Square
Vernon, John	1787	Gold St. John St. Water St. with Underhill

W

Wenman, Barnard	1789	Fly Market "Fournequet's Place on William St."

Wishart, Hugh	1784	Wall St. Market St. William St. Liberty St. (formerly Crown) Maiden Lane Pearl St.
Woods, Freeman	1791	Smith St.
Wood, John	1770	Lower end of Maiden Lane and Upper end of Fly Market

BOSTON SILVERSMITHS

1650-1800

	Working	*Location*
		A
Allen, John	1695	Cornhill (with John Edwards)
		B
Belknap, Samuel	1789	30 Cornhill St.
Blowers, John	1738	School St.
Boyer, Daniel	1750	Opposite Governor's House between Marlborough and School Sts.
Brigden, Zachariah	1760	Cornhill
Burt, Benjamin	1750	Fish St.
Burt, John	1712	
Butler, John	1758	Corner of Clark's Ship Yard
		C
Churchill, Jesse	1795	88 Newbury St.
Coburn, John	1750	King St. Head of Town Dock
Coney, John	1676	Court St. near Scollay Square Town Dock near Faneuil Hall Ann St. (now North)
Cowell, John	1728	South End of Boston
Cowell, William, Sr.	1703	South End of Boston
Cowell, William, Jr.	1734	South End of Boston
		D
Dawes, Wm.	1765	Ann St. (with Wm. Homes, Jr.)

Dummer, Jeremiah	1666	Present State and Congress Sts. (where Exchange Bldg. stands)

E

Eastwick, Thomas	1743	{Dock Square {William's Court in Cornhill
Edwards, John	1691	{Cornhill (with John Allen) {6 Dock Square
Edwards, Joseph, Jr.	1758	Cornhill
Edwards, Thomas	1725	Cornhill
Emery, Stephen	1775	5 Union St.

F

Farnam, Rufus	1796	42 Cornhill St.
Foster, Joseph	1785	{171 Ann St. {Fish St.

G

Gray, John	1713	Near Old State Meeting House
Gray, Samuel	1732	Cornhill—South side of Town House
Griffith, David	1789	26 Newbury St.

H

Hanners, George, Sr.	1720	Head of Town Dock
Henchman, Daniel	1753	Cornhill opposite Old Brick Meeting House
Homes (Holmes), Wm. Sr.	1739	Near the Draw Bridge
Homes, Wm. Jr.	1783	Ann St. near the Draw Bridge, with Wm. Dawes
Hull, John	1645	Newbury St. north of Mill St. (Summer St.) with Robert Sanderson
Hurd, Jacob	1723	{Summer and Bedford St. on Washington {South side of Town House {Atkinson St.
Hurd, Nathaniel	1755	Exchange Place or corner of State and Congress Sts.

L

Leach, Charles	1789	Ann St.
Leach, Nathaniel	1789	Kilby St.
Loring, Joseph	1775	Union St.

	Working	*Location*

M

Minott, Samuel	1764	Ann St. Fish St. Opposite William's Court—Cornhill Northward of Draw Bridge (with Wm. Simpkins)
Mors, (Morse) Obadiah	1733	King St.

P

Parker, Daniel	1750	Merchant's Row Union St.
Pierpont, Benjamin	1756	Newbury St.
Potwine, John	1721	Newbury St.

R

Revere, Edward	1796	Back St.
Revere, Paul, Jr.	1757	50 Cornhill St. Clark's Wharf
Revere, Paul, Sr.	1725	At Town Dock Hutchinson's Wharf
Revere, Joseph	1796	Clark's Wharf (with father, Paul, Jr.)
Revere, Thomas	1789	Newbury St.
Ridgeway, James S.	1789	Friend St. Cambridge St.

S

Sanderson, Robert	1638	Newbury St. north of Mill St. (Summer St.) (with Hull)
Simpkins, William	1730	Near Draw Bridge
Simpkins, Thomas Barton	1750	Fish St.
Smith, Joseph	1765	Newbury St.

T

Trott, Jonathan	1758	South End
Turner, James	1744	Near Town House—Cornhill

W

Webb, Barnabas	1756	Back St. (1761) Near the Market (1756) Ann St. (1762)

PHILADELPHIA SILVERSMITHS
1695 - 1800

Working		*Location*

A

Alexander, Samuel	1797	17 So. Second St. 33 So. Second St. 132 Letitia St.
Alford, Thomas	1762	Front St. between Chestnut and Market Sts.
Allen, James	1720	Market St.
Allen, Robert	1775	215 So. Third St.
Andrews, Abraham	1795	69 Race St.
Andrews, Henry	1800	65 So. Second St.
Andrews, Jeremiah	1776	Second St. near Market (between Chestnut and Walnut Sts.)
Anthony, Joseph, Jr.	1783	Market St., two doors east of the Indian King 45 Market St. 74 Market St. 94 High St. Bank St. 76 South side of Market St. between Second and Third Sts.
Ashmead, William	1797	122 Race St.

B

Ball, William, Jr.	1785	Market St., also Front St.
Bardon, Stephen	1785	Corner of South and Third Sts.
Bartram, Wm.	1769	Front St. at Golden Cup and Crown
Bayly, John	1755	Lower end of Front St. near Draw Bridge Corner of Front and Chestnut Sts. Cherry Alley
Beck, Thomas	1774	Chestnut between Second and Third Sts.
Berard, Andrew	1797	Corner of Arch and Eighth Sts.
Best, Joseph	1723	High St.
Black, James	1795	89 So. Second St. 123 Chestnut St.
Boone, Jeremiah	1791	133 Chestnut St. 30 So. Second St.
Bordeaux, Augustine	1798	319 So. Second St.
Boudinot, Elias	1730	Next door to Post Office on Market St. (between Third and Fourth Sts.) Second St.

Bouvar, Joseph	1797	83 Vine St.
Brooks, Samuel	1793	29 So. Front St.
Brown, John	1785	⎧Third between Spruce and Union Sts. ⎩36 No. Front St.
Burns, Anthony	1785	Chestnut between Second and Front Sts.

C

Carman, John	1771	Corner of Second and Chestnut Sts.
Chaudron, Simon	1798	⎧12 So. Third St. ⎩5 So. Third St.
Cooke, Joseph	1785	⎧Second St. between Market and Chestnut ⎱ Sts. (corner of Black Horse Alley) ⎰38 South side of Market St. between Front ⎩ and Second Sts.

D

David, John	1763	⎧Chestnut and Second Sts. ("next door to ⎱ Second St. corner in Chestnut") ⎩Fourth door from Draw Bridge
David, Peter	1730	⎧Front St. ⎩Second St.
Davy, Adam	1795	Coombs Alley and North Second St.
Dawson, William	1793	55 So. Second St.
Delagrow, Andrew	1795	4 No. Second St.
Descuret, Lewis	1799	55 So. Second St.
Dickerson, Jonathan,	1794	73 High St.
Dorsey, Joshua	1793	22 No. Third St.
Dowig, Geo. Christophe.	1765	⎧Second between Arch and Race Sts. ⎩Front near Coffee House
Douglass, Jeremott William	1790	257 So. Front St.
Doutiemer, Gille	1791	121 No. Front St.
Drewry, George	1763	Walnut St.—four doors below Second St.
Dubois, Abraham	1777	⎧Second St.—four doors below Arch St. ⎩65 No. Second St.
Dumoutet, John Baptiste	1793	⎧17 Elm St. ⎨79 No. Third St. ⎩55–57 So. Second St.
Dupuy, Daniel	1745	⎧A little below the Friends Meeting House ⎨ on Second St. ⎩114 Sassafras St. (Race St.)
Dupuy, Daniel, Jr.	1785	16 So. Second St.
Dupuy, John	1770	Same as father and brother, Daniel

Dutens, Charles J.	1751	Next to Indian King in Market St.

E

Eaton, Timothy	1793	9 Cherry St.
Elfreth, Jeremiah	1752	No. Second near Arch St.

F

Ford, Samuel	1797	39 Arch St.
Frank, Jacob	1793	{Front between Market and Arch Sts. {2 No. Front St.

G

Gee, Joseph	1785	Front between Arch and Race Sts.
Geley, Peter	1793	{4 So. Second St. {73 Arch St.
Georgeon, Bernard	1794	{74 So. Second St. {74 Elm St.
Germon, John	1782	{33 No. Third St. {Quarry St.
Gethen, William	1797	{14 Coombs Alley {172 So. Front St.
Ghiselin, William	1751	A little below the Church in Second St. (Old Christ Church)
Girreau, Stephen	1785	Chestnut St. between Second and Front Sts.
Grant, William, Jr.	1785	{115 No. Third St. {Green and Third Sts.
Griscom, George	1791	35 Wood St.
Guerin, Anthony	1791	{No. Front St. {52 Race St.

H

Hall, David	1765	Second St. near Chestnut St.
Halstead, Benjamin	1785	Arch St. between Second and Third Sts.
Harper, David	1755	With Duten on Market St. next to Indian King
Haverstick, William	1781	76 No. Second St. between Arch and Race Sts.
Head, Joseph	1798	Lombard and 7th Sts.
Hollingshead, William	1754	Corner Arch and Second Sts.
Holton, John	1794	39 Race St.
Humphreys, Richard	1772	{54 High St. {Front St.—7 doors below Coffee House {Front St. near Draw Bridge

J

Jenkins, John	1777	16 Green St. Corner Chestnut and Front Sts.

L

Leacock, John	1748	Sign of the Cup in Water St. Front St. opposite Norris' Alley
Lemar, Mathias	1790	81 Market St. Strawberry St. Front St. corner of Chestnut St.
Lemar, Benjamin	1775	Front St. between Chestnut and Walnut Sts.
Letelier, John	1770	Second St. between Market and Chestnut Sts. Opposite Coffee House 172 No. Front St.
Lownes, Joseph	1780	Front St. between Walnut and Spruce Sts. 130 So. Front St. near Draw Bridge 124 So. Front St. 191 So. Third St.
Lyng, John	1734	Market St. against Market House, next to The Crown

M

M'Fee, John	1796	22 Coombs' Alley
M'Fee and Reeder	1793	38 No. Front St.
M'Mullin, John	1790	120 So. Front St.
Miles, John	1785	Spruce between 5th and 6th Sts.
Mills, Edmund	1785	Corner Third and Vine Sts.
Mills, John	1793	15 Walnut St.
Milne, Edmund	1757	Next to Indian King in Market St. Market and Second Sts.
Murdock, John	1779	Front between Walnut and Spruce Sts.
Musgrave, James	1795	Chestnut and Third Sts. 42 So. Second St. 74 Spruce St.
Myers, John	1785	13 No. Second St. 71 No. Second St. North side of Market St. between Second and Third Sts.

N

Nys, Johannis	1695	Front St. and Carpenter's Alley

O

Olivier, Peter	1790	6 Strawberry St.

P

Pancoast, Samuel	1785	Front St. between Walnut and Spruce Sts.
Parham, William	1785	Front St. between Walnut and Spruce Sts. 104 Swanson St.
Parker, Richard	1785	36 South side of Chestnut St.
Pascall, William	1695	Second and Walnut Sts.
Perreau, Peter	1797	220 No. Front St.
Pinchin, William	1779	Front St. opposite Gray's Alley 3 So. Front St. 20 Seventh St. Mulberry St.
Pitt, Richard	1744	Front St.
Poincignon, Francis	1795	55 No. Third St.
Pratt, Henry	1730	Front St. between Walnut and Chestnut Sts corner of Taylor's Alley

R

Reeder, Abner	1793	38 No. Front St.
Richards, Samuel R. Jr.	1793	136 So. Front St.
Richardson, Francis	1710	At corner of Letitia Court in Market St.
Richardson, Joseph	1732	50 So. Front St.
Richardson, Joseph, Jr.	1773	50 So. Front St.
Richardson, Joseph & Nathaniel	1771	50 So. Front St.
Richardson, Richard	1793	50 So. Front St.
Robinson, Anthony W.	1798	23 Strawberry St.

S

Saint Martin, Anthony	1796	85 So. Front St.
Schaffield, Jeremiah	1785	Front St. between Union and Pine Sts.
Sénémand, John B.	1798	79 Elm St. 37 Union St.
Shields, Thomas	1765	3rd door above the Draw Bridge in Front St. 7th house above Draw Bridge in Front St.
Shoemaker, Joseph	1793	12 No. Front St. 24 Pewter Platter Alley 38 No. Front St.
Smith, Samuel	1785	Front St. between Walnut and Spruce Sts.
Stedman, Alexander	1793	288 So. Second St. 117 Callow Hill St.
Swan, Robert	1799	77 So. Second St.

Syng, John	1734	Market St. against the Market House
Syng, Philip Sr.	1715	Near Market Place
Syng, Philip, Jr.	1726	Front St.—seven doors below Coffee House

V

Van Voorhis, Daniel	1782	West side of Front St.—6 doors below Coffee House

W

Walker, William	1793	2 Quarry St.
Walker, William and George	1795	76 No. Second St.
Warner, Samuel	1797	Pewter Platter Alley
Webb, Charles	1738	Front St. with Peter David
Williams, John	1793	91 No. Front St.
Williams, Samuel	1796	70 So. Front St.
Wiltberger, Christian	1793	{ 33 So. Second St. { Second St.—3 doors above Arch St.

Y

Yetton, Randal	1739	Front St. opposite Gray's Alley
Young, William	1761	Three doors above corner of Front and Market Sts.

REFERENCES

American Silversmiths and Their Marks—Stephen G. C. Ensko, 1927

Dom. Selyns Records

Early land deeds and wills

Manuscript Collection of Harrold E. Gillingham

Market Street—Joseph Jackson

Minutes of the Common Council of the City of New York

New York Genealogical and Biographical Society

Pennsylvania Magazine of History and Biography

Scharf & Westcott's History of Philadelphia

The Arts and Crafts in New England, 1704-1775—George Francis Dow, 1927

The Arts and Crafts in Philadelphia, Maryland and South Carolina, Series I, 1721-1785 (1929). Series II, 1786-1800 (1932)—Alfred Cox Prime

The Arts and Crafts in New York, 1726-1776—Rita Susswein-Gottesman

Numerous others and references listed in Bibliography with asterisks

MAPS: Showing locations of Silversmiths in:

New York 1660-1750

New York 1750-1800

Boston 1650-1800

Philadelphia 1695-1800

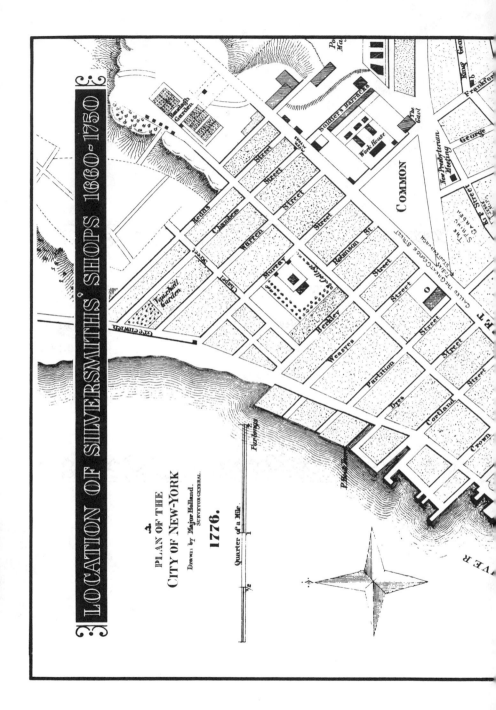

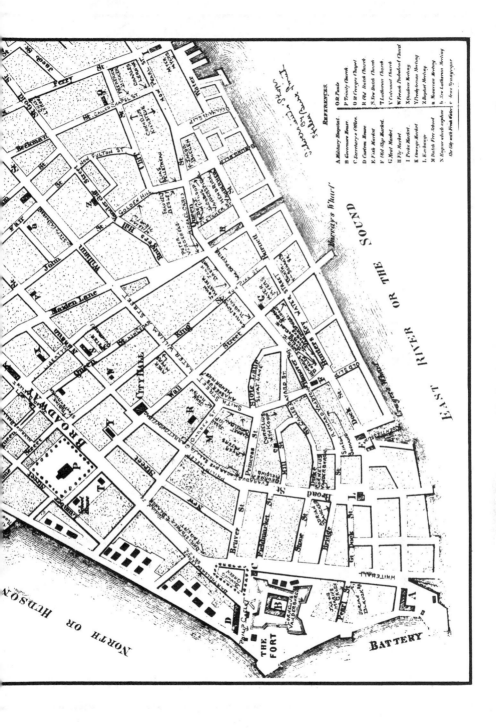

REFERENCES

A Military Hospital.
B Governours House.
C Secretary's Office.
D Custom House.
E Fish Market.
F Old Slip Market.
G Meat Market.
H Fly Market.
I Poshe Market.
K Oswego Market.
L Exchange.
M Dutch Free School.
N Esquire which supplies
the City with Fresh Water.

O St Pauls.
P Trinity Church.
Q St Georges Chapel.
R Old Dutch Church.
S New Dutch Church.
T Lutheran Church.
V Calvenist Church.
W French Protestant Church.
X Quakers Meeting.
Y Presbyterian Meeting.
Z Baptist Meeting.
a Moravian Meeting.
b New Lutheran Meeting.
c Jews Synagogue.

EAST RIVER OR THE SOUND

NORTH OR HUDSON

BATTERY

THE FORT

BROADWAY

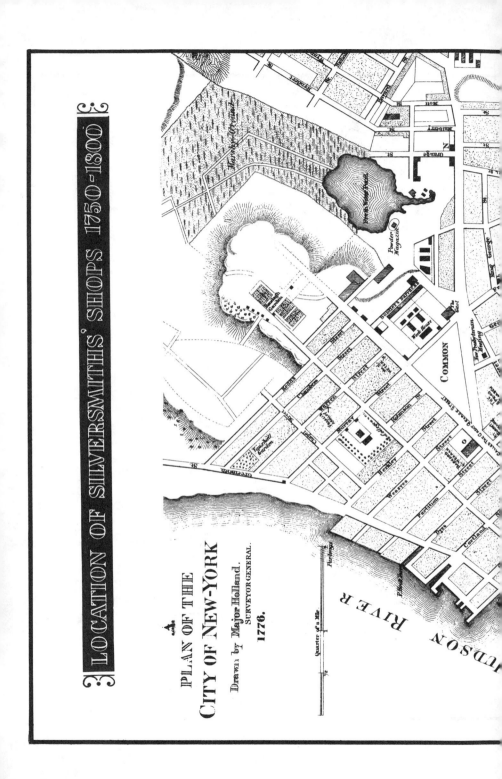

LOCATION OF SILVERSMITHS' SHOPS 1750-1800

A
PLAN OF THE
CITY OF NEW-YORK

Drawn by Major Holland.
SURVEYOR GENERAL.
1776.

Quarter of a Mile

HUDSON RIVER

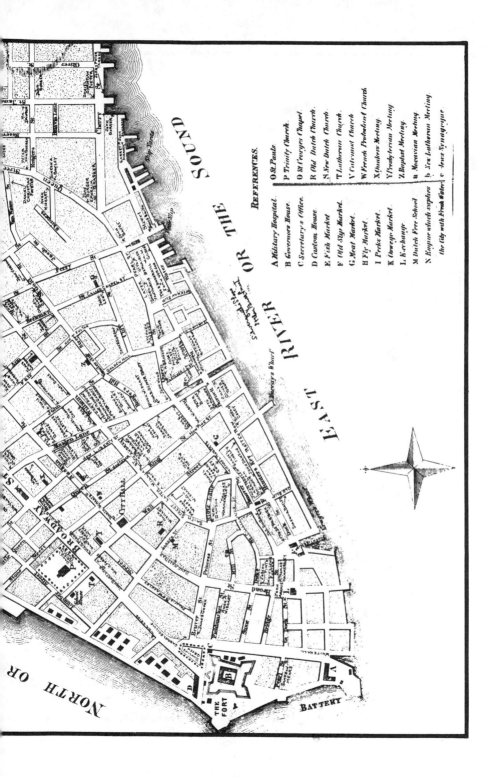

REFERENCES.

A Military Hospital.
B Governors House.
C Secretary's Office.
D Custom House.
E Fish Market.
F Old Slip Market.
G Meat Market.
H Fly Market.
I Peck's Market.
K Oswego Market.
L Exchange.
M Dutch Free School.
N Exquire which supplies
   the city with Fresh Water.

O St. Pauls.
P Trinity Church.
Q St George's Chapel.
R Old Dutch Church.
S New Dutch Church.
T Lutheran Church.
V Calvinist Church.
W French Protestant Church.
X Quakers Meeting.
Y Presbyterian Meeting.
Z Baptist Meeting.
a Moravian Meeting.
b New Lutheran Meeting.
c Jews Synagogue.

NORTH OR

NORTH RIVER

EAST RIVER

OR THE SOUND

THE FORT
BATTERY

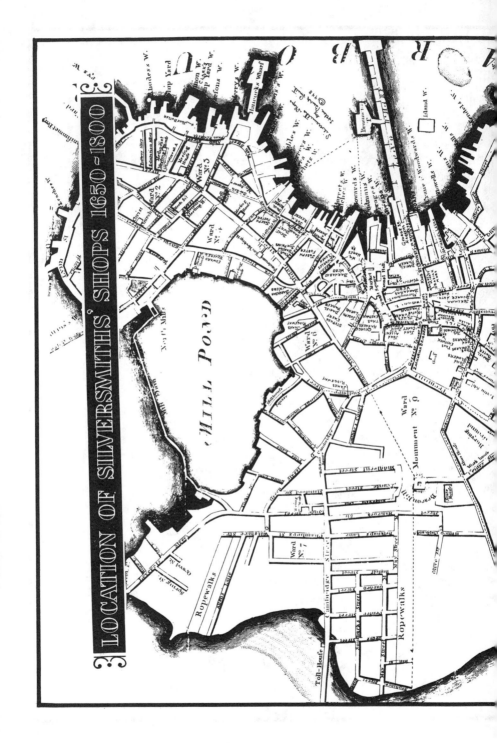

LOCATION OF SILVERSMITHS' SHOPS 1650~1800

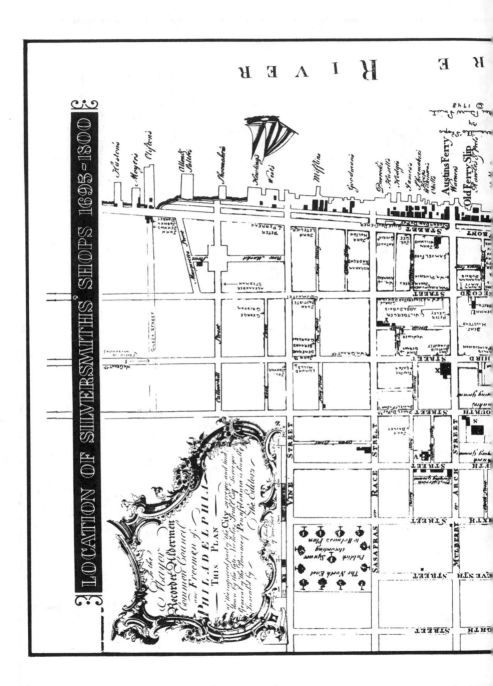

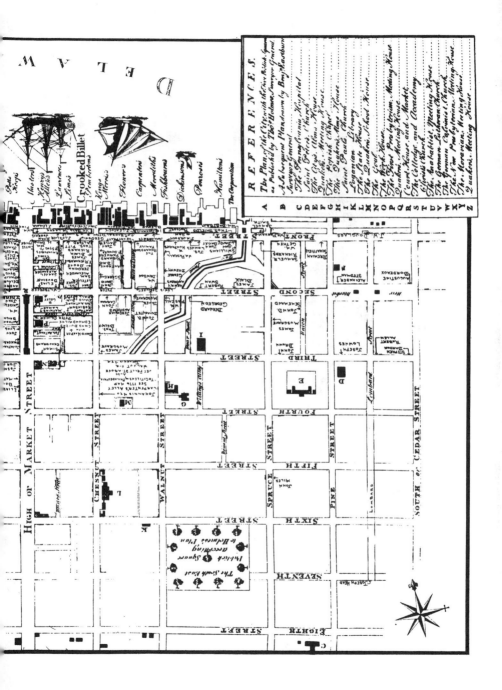

Paul Revere House in North Square, Boston 1770

BIBLIOGRAPHY

This list of publications of early American silver covers the subject from 1832 to 1948. The chronological arrangement is offered to show the development of everspreading interest in this absorbing study. For original research more information will be found in old public records, newspapers, directories, town histories, and other sources too numerous to mention and include here.

BOOK AND EXHIBITION CATALOGUES

*CATALOGUE OF ALBANY'S BICENTENNIAL LOAN EXHIBITION AT ALBANY ACADEMY. 1886.

OLD PLATE, ECCLESIASTICAL, DECORATIVE, AND DOMESTIC. Its Makers and Marks by J. H. Buck, New York. 1888.

THE LIFE OF COLONEL PAUL REVERE. By Elbridge Henry Goss. Two Volumes. 1891.

PAUL REVERE AND HIS ENGRAVING. By William Loring Andrews. 1901.

OLD PLATE. Its Makers and Marks by J. H. Buck, New and Enlarged Edition, New York. 1903.

CATALOGUE OF THE ANTIQUE SILVER. By the Mary Floyd Tallmadge Chapter, Daughters of the American Revolution, Litchfield, Connecticut. 1903.

*AMERICAN SILVER. The Work of 17th and 18th Century Silversmiths. Exhibited at the Museum of Fine Arts, Boston. 1906. Introduction by R. T. Haines Halsey.

THE HUDSON-FULTON CELEBRATION. Catalogue of an Exhibition held at the Metropolitan Museum of Art. Volume II. New York. 1909.

CATALOGUE OF THE LOAN EXHIBITION ON THE TWO HUNDRED AND FIFTIETH ANNIVERSARY OF THE FOUNDING OF THE TOWN OF NORWICH, CONNECTICUT, 1659-1909. Faith Trimbull Chapter, D.A.R.

*THE METROPOLITAN MUSEUM OF ART. Catalogue of an Exhibition of Silver used in New York, New Jersey and The South with a Note on Early New York Silversmiths by R. T. Haines Halsey. New York. 1911.

EARLY SILVERSMITHS OF CONNECTICUT. By George Munson Curtis. 1911.

*AMERICAN CHURCH SILVER, of the Seventeenth and Eighteenth Centuries with a few Pieces of Domestic Plate Exhibited at the Museum of Fine Arts, Boston. 1911. Introduction by George Munson Curtis. Explanation of terms by Florence V. Paull.

COPLEY SOCIETY RETROSPECTIVE EXHIBITION OF DECORATIVE ARTS. Copley Hall, Boston, Mass. 1911.

*THE OLD SILVER OF AMERICAN CHURCHES. By E. Alfred Jones. National Society of Colonial Dames of America. 1913.

*EARLY SILVER OF CONNECTICUT AND ITS MAKERS. By George Munson Curtis. Meriden. 1913.

WORCESTER ART MUSEUM EXHIBITION OF OLD SILVER OWNED IN WORCESTER COUNTY. Colonial Dames of America. 1913.

MAKERS OF EARLY AMERICAN SILVERSMITHS AND THEIR MARKS. By Robert Ensko. New York. 1915.

THE SPOON FROM EARLIEST TIMES. International Silver Company. 1915.

LIST OF EARLY AMERICAN SILVERSMITHS AND THEIR MARKS. By Hollis French. Walpole Society, Boston. 1917.

*HISTORIC SILVER OF THE COLONIES AND ITS MAKERS. By Francis Hill Bigelow. 1917.

EXHIBITION OF OLD AMERICAN AND ENGLISH SILVER. Pennsylvania Museum. Philadelphia. 1917.

WADSWORTH ATHENAEUM IN HARTFORD. Catalogue of Exhibition of American Silver. Colonial Dames of America. 1919, 1945.

*LIST OF PHILADELPHIA SILVERSMITHS AND ALLIED ARTIFICERS FROM 1682 TO 1850. By Maurice Brix. Philadelphia. 1920.

*THE METROPOLITAN MUSEUM OF ART. American Silver of the XVII and XVIII Centuries. A study based on The Clearwater Collection by C. Louise Avery with a Preface by R. T. Haines Halsey. 1920.

A COLLECTION OF EARLY AMERICAN SILVER. Tiffany & Co. 1920.

*THE PENNSYLVANIA MUSEUM BULLETIN. Special Silver Catalogue. 1921. Introduction by Dr. Samuel W. Woodhouse, Jr.

EXHIBITION OF EARLY AMERICAN SILVER, Assembled by the Washington Exhibition Committee of the National Art Museum, Washington, D. C. 1925.

ABEL BUELL OF CONNECTICUT, SILVERSMITH, TYPE FOUNDER AND ENGRAVER. By Lawrence C. Wroth. 1926.

*AMERICAN SILVERSMITHS AND THEIR MARKS I. By Stephen G. C. Ensko. New York. 1927.

ARTISTS AND CRAFTSMEN OF ESSEX COUNTY. By Henry Wyckoff Belknap. The Essex Institute, Salem, Mass. 1927.

*THE ARTS AND CRAFTS IN NEW ENGLAND, 1704-1775. By George Francis Dow. 1927.

*THE SILVERSMITHS OF LITTLE REST. By William Davis Miller. Kingston, Rhode Island. 1928.

OLD SILVER OF EUROPE AND AMERICA. By E. Alfred Jones. 1928.

*THE ARTS AND CRAFTS IN PHILADELPHIA, MARYLAND AND SOUTH CAROLINA, 1721-1785, SERIES I. By Alfred Coxe Prime. The Walpole Society. 1929.

*EARLY AMERICAN SILVER. By C. Louise Avery. New York. 1930.

*MARYLAND SILVERSMITHS, 1715-1830. With Illustrations of Their Silver and Their Marks and with a Facsimile of the Design Book of William Faris, by J. Hall Pleasants and Howard Sill. Baltimore, Maryland. 1930.

PAUL REVERE. By Emerson Taylor. 1930.

EARLY NEW YORK SILVER. By C. Louise Avery. 1931. The Metropolitan Museum of Art.

CATALOGUE OF SILVER OWNED BY NICHOLAS SEVER, A.B. 1701, IN 1928. By Richard Waiden Hale. Fogg Art Museum of Harvard University. 1931.

*JOHN CONEY, SILVERSMITH, 1665-1722. By Hermann Frederick Clarke with Introduction by Hollis French. Boston. 1932.

*THE ARTS AND CRAFTS IN PHILADELPHIA, MARYLAND AND SOUTH CAROLINA, 1786-1800, SERIES II. By Alfred Coxe Prime. The Walpole Society. 1932.

*JEREMIAH DUMMER, COLONIAL CRAFTSMAN AND MERCHANT, 1645-1718. By Hermann Frederick Clarke and Henry Wilder Foote, with Foreword by E. Alfred Jones. Boston. 1935.

*CONNECTICUT TERCENTENARY, 1635-1935. EARLY CONNECTICUT SILVER, 1700-1830. The Gallery of Fine Arts, Yale University. Introduction by John Marshall Phillips. 1935.

CATALOGUE OF SILVER EXHIBITION, Held at the Art Museum of the Rhode Island School of Design. Introduction by William Davis Miller. 1936.

HARVARD TERCENTENARY EXHIBITION. 1936.

THE SILVERSMITHS OF UTICA. By George B. Cutten. 1936.

CONTEMPORARY INDUSTRIAL AND HANDWROUGHT SILVER. Brooklyn Museum, New York. 1937.

*AMERICAN SILVERSMITHS AND THEIR MARKS II. By Stephen G. C. Ensko. New York. 1937.

MARKS OF EARLY AMERICAN SILVERSMITHS. By Ernest M. Currier. Edited by Kathryn C. Buhler. 1938.

*THE ARTS AND CRAFTS IN NEW YORK, 1726-1776. By Rita S. Gottesman. New-York Historical Society. 1938.

*EARLY AMERICAN SILVERSMITHS, VOLUMES I-II. Articles in The New York Sun, Antiques Section; Magazine "Antiques," by Helen Burr Smith. 1938-1948.

*THREE CENTURIES OF HISTORIC SILVER. By Mrs. Alfred C. Prime. The Pennsylvania Society of the Colonial Dames of America. 1938.

THREE CENTURIES OF EUROPEAN AND AMERICAN DOMESTIC SILVER. M. H. de Young Memorial Museum, San Francisco, Calif. 1938.

*MASTERPIECES OF NEW ENGLAND SILVER, 1650-1800. Introduction by John Marshall Phillips, The Gallery of Fine Arts, Yale University. 1939.

*JACOB HURD AND HIS SONS, NATHANIEL AND BENJAMIN, SILVERSMITHS, 1702-1781. By Hollis French, with Foreword by Kathryn C. Buhler. 1939.

*SILVERSMITHS OF DELAWARE AND OLD CHURCH SILVER IN DELAWARE, 1700-1850. By Jessie Harrington. 1939.

*JOHN HULL, BUILDER OF, THE BAY COLONY. By Hermann Frederick Clarke. 1940.

PAUL REVERE AND THE WORLD HE LIVED IN. By Esther Forbes. 1942.

*SOUTH CAROLINA SILVERSMITHS, 1690-1860. By E. Milby Burton. 1942.

*THE PHILIP LEFFINGWELL SPALDING COLLECTION OF EARLY AMERICAN SILVER. By Edwin J. Hipkiss. 1943.

EARLY OHIO SILVERSMITHS AND PEWTERERS, 1787-1847. By Rhea M. Knittle. 1943.

TEN SILVERSMITHS FAMILIES OF NEW YORK STATE. By George B. Cutten. 1946.

THE SILVERSMITHS OF NORTH CAROLINA. By George B. Cutten. 1948.

†THE MABLE BRADY GARVAN COLLECTION. Art Gallery, Yale University. By John Marshall Phillips.

†EDWARD WINSLOW, SILVERSMITH. By John Marshall Phillips.

†NEW ENGLAND SILVERSMITHS. By John Marshall Phillips.

†SILVERSMITHS OF VIRGINIA. By George Barton Cutten.

†Future publications.
*References, Chapter III.

ARTICLES IN JOURNALS AND MAGAZINES

AMERICAN ANTIQUARIAN SOCIETY, John Hull, Colonial Merchant, 1624-1683. Hermann J. Clarke. 1937.

"ANTIQUES" MAGAZINE: (*The following articles appeared*)
SOME CHARLESTON SILVERSMITHS AND THEIR WORK. Jennie Haskell Rose. April 1928.
TWO PHILADELPHIA SILVERSMITHS (ANTHONY SIMMONS AND SAMUEL ALEXANDER). Dr. Samuel W. Woodhouse, Jr. April 1930.
CAPTAIN ELIAS PELLETREAU, LONG ISLAND SILVERSMITH. Mabel C. Weaks —Part I, May 1931; Part II, June 1931.
JOHN DE NYS, PHILADELPHIA SILVERSMITH. Dr. Samuel W. Woodhouse, Jr. May 1932.
JOHN POTWINE, SILVERSMITH OF MASSACHUSETTS AND CONNECTICUT. Elizabeth B. Potwine. September 1935.
CORNELIUS VANDERBURGH—SILVERSMITH OF NEW YORK. Mrs. Russel Hastings. Part I, January 1936; Part II, February 1936.
A SILVERSMITH OF THE GENESEE TRAIL (JOHN CHEADELL OR CHEDELL, NEW YORK STATE, NINETEENTH CENTURY). M. W. Richardson. June 1936.
JOHN NYS VS. JAN NIEU KIRKE. December 1936.

PETER VAN DYCK OF NEW YORK, GOLDSMITH, 1684-1750. Mrs. Russel Hastings. Part I, May 1937; Part II, June 1937.
RENE GRIGNON, SILVERSMITH. Ada R. Chase. July 1938.
JOHN FITCH: JACK OF MANY TRADES. Harrold E. Gillingham. February 1939.
ASA BLANCHARD, EARLY KENTUCKY SILVERSMITH. Margaret M. Bridwell. March 1940.
THE MOULTON SILVERSMITHS. Stephen Decatur. January 1941.
CHARLES OLIVER BRUFF, SILVERSMITH. J. Hall Pleasants and Howard Sill. June 1941.
DANIEL GREENOUGH, EARLY NEW HAMPSHIRE SILVERSMITH. Frank O. Spinney. June 1942.
*THE TEN EYCK SILVERSMITHS. George Barton Cutten. December 1942.
*IDENTIFYING THE MYSTERIOUS IK: JESSE KIP, NEW YORK GOLDSMITH. John Marshall Phillips. July 1943.
AN INGENIOUS YANKEE CRAFTSMAN (BENJAMIN C. GILMAN, NEW HAMPSHIRE). Frank O. Spinney. September 1943.
SILVERSMITHS OF LANCASTER, PENNSYLVANIA. Carl Drepperd. August 1944.
*ISAAC HUTTON, SILVERSMITH, CITIZEN OF ALBANY. John Davis Hatch, Jr. January 1945.
SILVERSMITHS OF ALEXANDRIA (VIRGINIA). February 1945.
KENTUCKY SILVER AND ITS MAKERS. Lockwood Barr. July 1945.
*AN UNRECORDED GOLDSMITH. Jeremiah Elfreth, Jr. of Philadelphia, Carl M. Williams. January 1947.
SILVERSMITHS OF ST. LOUIS: Part I—January 1947 by Ruth Hunter Roach; Part II —March 1947 by Ruth Hunter Roach.
KENTUCKY SILVER. Margaret M. Bridwell. November 1947.

COUNTRY LIFE IN AMERICA. Old American Silver, 5 Parts, February 1913— January 1915. Luke Vincent Lockwood.
HARPER'S MAGAZINE, OLD SILVER. Theodore S. Woolsey. 1896.
THE FILSON CLUB HISTORICAL QUARTERLY, Kentucky Silversmiths Before 1850. Margaret M. Bridwell. 1942.
THE MARYLAND HISTORICAL MAGAZINE, William Faris, 1728-1804. Lockwood Barr. 1941.
THE NEW ENGLAND MAGAZINE, Early American Artists and Mechanics. No. I Nathaniel Hurd, July 1932. No. II Paul Revere, October 1932.
NEW JERSEY HISTORICAL SOCIETY, Silversmiths of New Jersey. Julia Sabine. July 1943.
THE PENNSYLVANIA MAGAZINE OF HISTORY AND BIOGRAPHY, The Cost of Old Silver. Harrold E. Gillingham. 1930. Caesar Ghiselin, Philadelphia's First Gold and Silversmith, 1693-1733. Harrold E. Gillingham. 1933. Indian Silver Ornaments. Harrold E. Gillingham. 1934.

* * *

BULLETINS AND COLLECTIONS OF:

American Collector,
Art Institute of Chicago, Illinois,
Baltimore Museum of Art, Maryland,
Boston Transcript,
Brooklyn Institute of Arts and Sciences, New York,
Charleston Museum, South Carolina,
Christian Science Monitor,
Cleveland Museum of Art, Ohio,
Detroit Institute of Arts, Michigan,
M. H. de Young Memorial Museum, San Francisco, California,
Metropolitan Museum of Art, New York,
Museum of Art, Boston, Mass.,
Museum of the City of New York, New York,

New York Historical Society, New York,
Pennsylvania Museum of Art,
Rhode Island School of Design Museum, Rhode Island,
Santa Barbara Museum, California,
The New York Sun, Antiques Section,
Wadsworth Athaeneum, Avery and Morgan Memorials, Hartford, Connecticut,
Wilmington Society of Fine Arts, Delaware,
Worcester Art Museum, Massachusetts,
Yale University Art Gallery,
Historical Societies,
Newspapers, Town Histories,
Genealogical and Biographical Societies,
Almanacs, City Directories, and other sources.

A CATALOG OF SELECTED

DOVER BOOKS

IN ALL FIELDS OF INTEREST

A CATALOG OF SELECTED DOVER
BOOKS IN ALL FIELDS OF INTEREST

DRAWINGS OF REMBRANDT, edited by Seymour Slive. Updated Lippmann, Hofstede de Groot edition, with definitive scholarly apparatus. All portraits, biblical sketches, landscapes, nudes. Oriental figures, classical studies, together with selection of work by followers. 550 illustrations. Total of 630pp. 9⅛ × 12¼.
21485-0, 21486-9 Pa., Two-vol. set $25.00

GHOST AND HORROR STORIES OF AMBROSE BIERCE, Ambrose Bierce. 24 tales vividly imagined, strangely prophetic, and decades ahead of their time in technical skill: "The Damned Thing," "An Inhabitant of Carcosa," "The Eyes of the Panther," "Moxon's Master," and 20 more. 199pp. 5⅜ × 8½. 20767-6 Pa. $3.95

ETHICAL WRITINGS OF MAIMONIDES, Maimonides. Most significant ethical works of great medieval sage, newly translated for utmost precision, readability. Laws Concerning Character Traits, Eight Chapters, more. 192pp. 5⅜ × 8½.
24522-5 Pa. $4.50

THE EXPLORATION OF THE COLORADO RIVER AND ITS CANYONS, J. W. Powell. Full text of Powell's 1,000-mile expedition down the fabled Colorado in 1869. Superb account of terrain, geology, vegetation, Indians, famine, mutiny, treacherous rapids, mighty canyons, during exploration of last unknown part of continental U.S. 400pp. 5⅜ × 8½. 20094-9 Pa. $6.95

HISTORY OF PHILOSOPHY, Julián Marías. Clearest one-volume history on the market. Every major philosopher and dozens of others, to Existentialism and later. 505pp. 5⅜ × 8½. 21739-6 Pa. $8.50

ALL ABOUT LIGHTNING, Martin A. Uman. Highly readable non-technical survey of nature and causes of lightning, thunderstorms, ball lightning, St. Elmo's Fire, much more. Illustrated. 192pp. 5⅜ × 8½. 25237-X Pa. $5.95

SAILING ALONE AROUND THE WORLD, Captain Joshua Slocum. First man to sail around the world, alone, in small boat. One of great feats of seamanship told in delightful manner. 67 illustrations. 294pp. 5⅜ × 8½. 20326-3 Pa. $4.95

LETTERS AND NOTES ON THE MANNERS, CUSTOMS AND CONDI-TIONS OF THE NORTH AMERICAN INDIANS, George Catlin. Classic account of life among Plains Indians: ceremonies, hunt, warfare, etc. 312 plates. 572pp. of text. 6⅛ × 9¼. 22118-0, 22119-9 Pa. Two-vol. set $15.90

ALASKA: The Harriman Expedition, 1899, John Burroughs, John Muir, et al. Informative, engrossing accounts of two-month, 9,000-mile expedition. Native peoples, wildlife, forests, geography, salmon industry, glaciers, more. Profusely illustrated. 240 black-and-white line drawings. 124 black-and-white photographs. 3 maps. Index. 576pp. 5⅜ × 8½. 25109-8 Pa. $11.95

THE BOOK OF BEASTS: Being a Translation from a Latin Bestiary of the Twelfth Century, T. H. White. Wonderful catalog real and fanciful beasts: manticore, griffin, phoenix, amphivius, jaculus, many more. White's witty erudite commentary on scientific, historical aspects. Fascinating glimpse of medieval mind. Illustrated. 296pp. 5⅜ × 8¼. (Available in U.S. only) 24609-4 Pa. $5.95

FRANK LLOYD WRIGHT: ARCHITECTURE AND NATURE With 160 Illustrations, Donald Hoffmann. Profusely illustrated study of influence of nature—especially prairie—on Wright's designs for Fallingwater, Robie House, Guggenheim Museum, other masterpieces. 96pp. 9¼ × 10¾. 25098-9 Pa. $7.95

FRANK LLOYD WRIGHT'S FALLINGWATER, Donald Hoffmann. Wright's famous waterfall house: planning and construction of organic idea. History of site, owners, Wright's personal involvement. Photographs of various stages of building. Preface by Edgar Kaufmann, Jr. 100 illustrations. 112pp. 9¼ × 10. 23671-4 Pa. $7.95

YEARS WITH FRANK LLOYD WRIGHT: Apprentice to Genius, Edgar Tafel. Insightful memoir by a former apprentice presents a revealing portrait of Wright the man, the inspired teacher, the greatest American architect. 372 black-and-white illustrations. Preface. Index. vi + 228pp. 8¼ × 11. 24801-1 Pa. $9.95

THE STORY OF KING ARTHUR AND HIS KNIGHTS, Howard Pyle. Enchanting version of King Arthur fable has delighted generations with imaginative narratives of exciting adventures and unforgettable illustrations by the author. 41 illustrations. xviii + 313pp. 6⅛ × 9¼. 21445-1 Pa. $6.50

THE GODS OF THE EGYPTIANS, E. A. Wallis Budge. Thorough coverage of numerous gods of ancient Egypt by foremost Egyptologist. Information on evolution of cults, rites and gods; the cult of Osiris; the Book of the Dead and its rites; the sacred animals and birds; Heaven and Hell; and more. 956pp. 6⅛ × 9¼. 22055-9, 22056-7 Pa., Two-vol. set $20.00

A THEOLOGICO-POLITICAL TREATISE, Benedict Spinoza. Also contains unfinished *Political Treatise*. Great classic on religious liberty, theory of government on common consent. R. Elwes translation. Total of 421pp. 5⅜ × 8½. 20249-6 Pa. $6.95

INCIDENTS OF TRAVEL IN CENTRAL AMERICA, CHIAPAS, AND YUCATAN, John L. Stephens. Almost single-handed discovery of Maya culture; exploration of ruined cities, monuments, temples; customs of Indians. 115 drawings. 892pp. 5⅜ × 8½. 22404-X, 22405-8 Pa., Two-vol. set $15.90

LOS CAPRICHOS, Francisco Goya. 80 plates of wild, grotesque monsters and caricatures. Prado manuscript included. 183pp. 6⅝ × 9⅝. 22384-1 Pa. $4.95

AUTOBIOGRAPHY: The Story of My Experiments with Truth, Mohandas K. Gandhi. Not hagiography, but Gandhi in his own words. Boyhood, legal studies, purification, the growth of the Satyagraha (nonviolent protest) movement. Critical, inspiring work of the man who freed India. 480pp. 5⅜ × 8½. (Available in U.S. only) 24593-4 Pa. $6.95

ILLUSTRATED DICTIONARY OF HISTORIC ARCHITECTURE, edited by Cyril M. Harris. Extraordinary compendium of clear, concise definitions for over 5,000 important architectural terms complemented by over 2,000 line drawings. Covers full spectrum of architecture from ancient ruins to 20th-century Modernism. Preface. 592pp. 7½ × 9⅝. 24444-X Pa. $14.95

THE NIGHT BEFORE CHRISTMAS, Clement Moore. Full text, and woodcuts from original 1848 book. Also critical, historical material. 19 illustrations. 40pp. 4⅝ × 6. 22797-9 Pa. $2.25

THE LESSON OF JAPANESE ARCHITECTURE: 165 Photographs, Jiro Harada. Memorable gallery of 165 photographs taken in the 1930's of exquisite Japanese homes of the well-to-do and historic buildings. 13 line diagrams. 192pp. 8⅜ × 11¼. 24778-3 Pa. $8.95

THE AUTOBIOGRAPHY OF CHARLES DARWIN AND SELECTED LETTERS, edited by Francis Darwin. The fascinating life of eccentric genius composed of an intimate memoir by Darwin (intended for his children); commentary by his son, Francis; hundreds of fragments from notebooks, journals, papers; and letters to and from Lyell, Hooker, Huxley, Wallace and Henslow. xi + 365pp. 5⅜ × 8. 20479-0 Pa. $6.95

WONDERS OF THE SKY: Observing Rainbows, Comets, Eclipses, the Stars and Other Phenomena, Fred Schaaf. Charming, easy-to-read poetic guide to all manner of celestial events visible to the naked eye. Mock suns, glories, Belt of Venus, more. Illustrated. 299pp. 5¼ × 8¼. 24402-4 Pa. $7.95

BURNHAM'S CELESTIAL HANDBOOK, Robert Burnham, Jr. Thorough guide to the stars beyond our solar system. Exhaustive treatment. Alphabetical by constellation: Andromeda to Cetus in Vol. 1; Chamaeleon to Orion in Vol. 2; and Pavo to Vulpecula in Vol. 3. Hundreds of illustrations. Index in Vol. 3. 2,000pp. 6⅛ × 9¼. 23567-X, 23568-8, 23673-0 Pa., Three-vol. set $38.85

STAR NAMES: Their Lore and Meaning, Richard Hinckley Allen. Fascinating history of names various cultures have given to constellations and literary and folkloristic uses that have been made of stars. Indexes to subjects. Arabic and Greek names. Biblical references. Bibliography. 563pp. 5⅜ × 8½. 21079-0 Pa. $7.95

THIRTY YEARS THAT SHOOK PHYSICS: The Story of Quantum Theory, George Gamow. Lucid, accessible introduction to influential theory of energy and matter. Careful explanations of Dirac's anti-particles, Bohr's model of the atom, much more. 12 plates. Numerous drawings. 240pp. 5⅜ × 8½. 24895-X Pa. $4.95

CHINESE DOMESTIC FURNITURE IN PHOTOGRAPHS AND MEASURED DRAWINGS, Gustav Ecke. A rare volume, now affordably priced for antique collectors, furniture buffs and art historians. Detailed review of styles ranging from early Shang to late Ming. Unabridged republication. 161 black-and-white drawings, photos. Total of 224pp. 8⅜ × 11¼. (Available in U.S. only) 25171-3 Pa. $12.95

VINCENT VAN GOGH: A Biography, Julius Meier-Graefe. Dynamic, penetrating study of artist's life, relationship with brother, Theo, painting techniques, travels, more. Readable, engrossing. 160pp. 5⅜ × 8½. (Available in U.S. only) 25253-1 Pa. $3.95

HOW TO WRITE, Gertrude Stein. Gertrude Stein claimed anyone could understand her unconventional writing—here are clues to help. Fascinating improvisations, language experiments, explanations illuminate Stein's craft and the art of writing. Total of 414pp. 4⅜ × 6⅜. 23144-5 Pa. $5.95

ADVENTURES AT SEA IN THE GREAT AGE OF SAIL: Five Firsthand Narratives, edited by Elliot Snow. Rare true accounts of exploration, whaling, shipwreck, fierce natives, trade, shipboard life, more. 33 illustrations. Introduction. 353pp. 5⅜ × 8½. 25177-2 Pa. $7.95

THE HERBAL OR GENERAL HISTORY OF PLANTS, John Gerard. Classic descriptions of about 2,850 plants—with over 2,700 illustrations—includes Latin and English names, physical descriptions, varieties, time and place of growth, more. 2,706 illustrations. xlv + 1,678pp. 8½ × 12¼. 23147-X Cloth. $75.00

DOROTHY AND THE WIZARD IN OZ, L. Frank Baum. Dorothy and the Wizard visit the center of the Earth, where people are vegetables, glass houses grow and Oz characters reappear. Classic sequel to *Wizard of Oz*. 256pp. 5⅜ × 8. 24714-7 Pa. $4.95

SONGS OF EXPERIENCE: Facsimile Reproduction with 26 Plates in Full Color, William Blake. This facsimile of Blake's original "Illuminated Book" reproduces 26 full-color plates from a rare 1826 edition. Includes "The Tyger," "London," "Holy Thursday," and other immortal poems. 26 color plates. Printed text of poems. 48pp. 5¼ × 7. 24636-1 Pa. $3.50

SONGS OF INNOCENCE, William Blake. The first and most popular of Blake's famous "Illuminated Books," in a facsimile edition reproducing all 31 brightly colored plates. Additional printed text of each poem. 64pp. 5¼ × 7. 22764-2 Pa. $3.50

PRECIOUS STONES, Max Bauer. Classic, thorough study of diamonds, rubies, emeralds, garnets, etc.: physical character, occurrence, properties, use, similar topics. 20 plates, 8 in color. 94 figures. 659pp. 6⅛ × 9¼. 21910-0, 21911-9 Pa., Two-vol. set $15.90

ENCYCLOPEDIA OF VICTORIAN NEEDLEWORK, S. F. A. Caulfeild and Blanche Saward. Full, precise descriptions of stitches, techniques for dozens of needlecrafts—most exhaustive reference of its kind. Over 800 figures. Total of 679pp. 8⅛ × 11. Two volumes. Vol. 1 22800-2 Pa. $11.95
Vol. 2 22801-0 Pa. $11.95

THE MARVELOUS LAND OF OZ, L. Frank Baum. Second Oz book, the Scarecrow and Tin Woodman are back with hero named Tip, Oz magic. 136 illustrations. 287pp. 5⅜ × 8½. 20692-0 Pa. $5.95

WILD FOWL DECOYS, Joel Barber. Basic book on the subject, by foremost authority and collector. Reveals history of decoy making and rigging, place in American culture, different kinds of decoys, how to make them, and how to use them. 140 plates. 156pp. 7⅞ × 10¾. 20011-6 Pa. $8.95

HISTORY OF LACE, Mrs. Bury Palliser. Definitive, profusely illustrated chronicle of lace from earliest times to late 19th century. Laces of Italy, Greece, England, France, Belgium, etc. Landmark of needlework scholarship. 266 illustrations. 672pp. 6⅛ × 9¼. 24742-2 Pa. $14.95

ILLUSTRATED GUIDE TO SHAKER FURNITURE, Robert Meader. All furniture and appurtenances, with much on unknown local styles. 235 photos. 146pp. 9 × 12. 22819-3 Pa. $7.95

WHALE SHIPS AND WHALING: A Pictorial Survey, George Francis Dow. Over 200 vintage engravings, drawings, photographs of barks, brigs, cutters, other vessels. Also harpoons, lances, whaling guns, many other artifacts. Comprehensive text by foremost authority. 207 black-and-white illustrations. 288pp. 6 × 9. 24808-9 Pa. $8.95

THE BERTRAMS, Anthony Trollope. Powerful portrayal of blind self-will and thwarted ambition includes one of Trollope's most heartrending love stories. 497pp. 5⅜ × 8½. 25119-5 Pa. $8.95

ADVENTURES WITH A HAND LENS, Richard Headstrom. Clearly written guide to observing and studying flowers and grasses, fish scales, moth and insect wings, egg cases, buds, feathers, seeds, leaf scars, moss, molds, ferns, common crystals, etc.—all with an ordinary, inexpensive magnifying glass. 209 exact line drawings aid in your discoveries. 220pp. 5⅜ × 8½. 23330-8 Pa. $3.95

RODIN ON ART AND ARTISTS, Auguste Rodin. Great sculptor's candid, wide-ranging comments on meaning of art; great artists; relation of sculpture to poetry, painting, music; philosophy of life, more. 76 superb black-and-white illustrations of Rodin's sculpture, drawings and prints. 119pp. 8⅜ × 11¼. 24487-3 Pa. $6.95

FIFTY CLASSIC FRENCH FILMS, 1912-1982: A Pictorial Record, Anthony Slide. Memorable stills from Grand Illusion, Beauty and the Beast, Hiroshima, Mon Amour, many more. Credits, plot synopses, reviews, etc. 160pp. 8¼ × 11. 25256-6 Pa. $11.95

THE PRINCIPLES OF PSYCHOLOGY, William James. Famous long course complete, unabridged. Stream of thought, time perception, memory, experimental methods; great work decades ahead of its time. 94 figures. 1,391pp. 5⅜ × 8½. 20381-6, 20382-4 Pa., Two-vol. set $19.90

BODIES IN A BOOKSHOP, R. T. Campbell. Challenging mystery of blackmail and murder with ingenious plot and superbly drawn characters. In the best tradition of British suspense fiction. 192pp. 5⅜ × 8½. 24720-1 Pa. $3.95

CALLAS: PORTRAIT OF A PRIMA DONNA, George Jellinek. Renowned commentator on the musical scene chronicles incredible career and life of the most controversial, fascinating, influential operatic personality of our time. 64 black-and-white photographs. 416pp. 5⅜ × 8¼. 25047-4 Pa. $7.95

GEOMETRY, RELATIVITY AND THE FOURTH DIMENSION, Rudolph Rucker. Exposition of fourth dimension, concepts of relativity as Flatland characters continue adventures. Popular, easily followed yet accurate, profound. 141 illustrations. 133pp. 5⅜ × 8½. 23400-2 Pa. $3.95

HOUSEHOLD STORIES BY THE BROTHERS GRIMM, with pictures by Walter Crane. 53 classic stories—Rumpelstiltskin, Rapunzel, Hansel and Gretel, the Fisherman and his Wife, Snow White, Tom Thumb, Sleeping Beauty, Cinderella, and so much more—lavishly illustrated with original 19th century drawings. 114 illustrations. x + 269pp. 5⅜ × 8½. 21080-4 Pa. $4.50

SUNDIALS, Albert Waugh. Far and away the best, most thorough coverage of ideas, mathematics concerned, types, construction, adjusting anywhere. Over 100 illustrations. 230pp. 5⅜ × 8½. 22947-5 Pa. $4.50

PICTURE HISTORY OF THE NORMANDIE: With 190 Illustrations, Frank O. Braynard. Full story of legendary French ocean liner: Art Deco interiors, design innovations, furnishings, celebrities, maiden voyage, tragic fire, much more. Extensive text. 144pp. 8⅜ × 11¾. 25257-4 Pa. $9.95

THE FIRST AMERICAN COOKBOOK: A Facsimile of "American Cookery," 1796, Amelia Simmons. Facsimile of the first American-written cookbook published in the United States contains authentic recipes for colonial favorites—pumpkin pudding, winter squash pudding, spruce beer, Indian slapjacks, and more. Introductory Essay and Glossary of colonial cooking terms. 80pp. 5⅜ × 8½. 24710-4 Pa. $3.50

101 PUZZLES IN THOUGHT AND LOGIC, C. R. Wylie, Jr. Solve murders and robberies, find out which fishermen are liars, how a blind man could possibly identify a color—purely by your own reasoning! 107pp. 5⅜ × 8½. 20367-0 Pa. $2.50

THE BOOK OF WORLD-FAMOUS MUSIC—CLASSICAL, POPULAR AND FOLK, James J. Fuld. Revised and enlarged republication of landmark work in musico-bibliography. Full information about nearly 1,000 songs and compositions including first lines of music and lyrics. New supplement. Index. 800pp. 5⅜ × 8¼. 24857-7 Pa. $14.95

ANTHROPOLOGY AND MODERN LIFE, Franz Boas. Great anthropologist's classic treatise on race and culture. Introduction by Ruth Bunzel. Only inexpensive paperback edition. 255pp. 5⅜ × 8½. 25245-0 Pa. $5.95

THE TALE OF PETER RABBIT, Beatrix Potter. The inimitable Peter's terrifying adventure in Mr. McGregor's garden, with all 27 wonderful, full-color Potter illustrations. 55pp. 4¼ × 5½. (Available in U.S. only) 22827-4 Pa. $1.75

THREE PROPHETIC SCIENCE FICTION NOVELS, H. G. Wells. *When the Sleeper Wakes, A Story of the Days to Come* and *The Time Machine* (full version). 335pp. 5⅜ × 8½. (Available in U.S. only) 20605-X Pa. $5.95

APICIUS COOKERY AND DINING IN IMPERIAL ROME, edited and translated by Joseph Dommers Vehling. Oldest known cookbook in existence offers readers a clear picture of what foods Romans ate, how they prepared them, etc. 49 illustrations. 301pp. 6⅛ × 9¼. 23563-7 Pa. $6.50

SHAKESPEARE LEXICON AND QUOTATION DICTIONARY, Alexander Schmidt. Full definitions, locations, shades of meaning of every word in plays and poems. More than 50,000 exact quotations. 1,485pp. 6½ × 9¼. 22726-X, 22727-8 Pa., Two-vol. set $27.90

THE WORLD'S GREAT SPEECHES, edited by Lewis Copeland and Lawrence W. Lamm. Vast collection of 278 speeches from Greeks to 1970. Powerful and effective models; unique look at history. 842pp. 5⅜ × 8½. 20468-5 Pa. $11.95

THE BLUE FAIRY BOOK, Andrew Lang. The first, most famous collection, with many familiar tales: Little Red Riding Hood, Aladdin and the Wonderful Lamp, Puss in Boots, Sleeping Beauty, Hansel and Gretel, Rumpelstiltskin; 37 in all. 138 illustrations. 390pp. 5⅜ × 8½. 21437-0 Pa. $5.95

THE STORY OF THE CHAMPIONS OF THE ROUND TABLE, Howard Pyle. Sir Launcelot, Sir Tristram and Sir Percival in spirited adventures of love and triumph retold in Pyle's inimitable style. 50 drawings, 31 full-page. xviii + 329pp. 6½ × 9¼. 21883-X Pa. $6.95

AUDUBON AND HIS JOURNALS, Maria Audubon. Unmatched two-volume portrait of the great artist, naturalist and author contains his journals, an excellent biography by his granddaughter, expert annotations by the noted ornithologist, Dr. Elliott Coues, and 37 superb illustrations. Total of 1,200pp. 5⅜ × 8.
Vol. I 25143-8 Pa. $8.95
Vol. II 25144-6 Pa. $8.95

GREAT DINOSAUR HUNTERS AND THEIR DISCOVERIES, Edwin H. Colbert. Fascinating, lavishly illustrated chronicle of dinosaur research, 1820's to 1960. Achievements of Cope, Marsh, Brown, Buckland, Mantell, Huxley, many others. 384pp. 5¼ × 8¼. 24701-5 Pa. $6.95

THE TASTEMAKERS, Russell Lynes. Informal, illustrated social history of American taste 1850's–1950's. First popularized categories Highbrow, Lowbrow, Middlebrow. 129 illustrations. New (1979) afterword. 384pp. 6 × 9.
23993-4 Pa. $6.95

DOUBLE CROSS PURPOSES, Ronald A. Knox. A treasure hunt in the Scottish Highlands, an old map, unidentified corpse, surprise discoveries keep reader guessing in this cleverly intricate tale of financial skullduggery. 2 black-and-white maps. 320pp. 5⅜ × 8½. (Available in U.S. only) 25032-6 Pa. $5.95

AUTHENTIC VICTORIAN DECORATION AND ORNAMENTATION IN FULL COLOR: 46 Plates from "Studies in Design," Christopher Dresser. Superb full-color lithographs reproduced from rare original portfolio of a major Victorian designer. 48pp. 9¼ × 12¼. 25083-0 Pa. $7.95

PRIMITIVE ART, Franz Boas. Remains the best text ever prepared on subject, thoroughly discussing Indian, African, Asian, Australian, and, especially, Northern American primitive art. Over 950 illustrations show ceramics, masks, totem poles, weapons, textiles, paintings, much more. 376pp. 5⅜ × 8. 20025-6 Pa. $6.95

SIDELIGHTS ON RELATIVITY, Albert Einstein. Unabridged republication of two lectures delivered by the great physicist in 1920–21. *Ether and Relativity* and *Geometry and Experience*. Elegant ideas in non-mathematical form, accessible to intelligent layman. vi + 56pp. 5⅜ × 8½. 24511-X Pa. $2.95

THE WIT AND HUMOR OF OSCAR WILDE, edited by Alvin Redman. More than 1,000 ripostes, paradoxes, wisecracks: Work is the curse of the drinking classes, I can resist everything except temptation, etc. 258pp. 5⅜ × 8½. 20602-5 Pa. $4.50

ADVENTURES WITH A MICROSCOPE, Richard Headstrom. 59 adventures with clothing fibers, protozoa, ferns and lichens, roots and leaves, much more. 142 illustrations. 232pp. 5⅜ × 8½. 23471-1 Pa. $3.95

PLANTS OF THE BIBLE, Harold N. Moldenke and Alma L. Moldenke. Standard reference to all 230 plants mentioned in Scriptures. Latin name, biblical reference, uses, modern identity, much more. Unsurpassed encyclopedic resource for scholars, botanists, nature lovers, students of Bible. Bibliography. Indexes. 123 black-and-white illustrations. 384pp. 6 × 9. 25069-5 Pa. $8.95

FAMOUS AMERICAN WOMEN: A Biographical Dictionary from Colonial Times to the Present, Robert McHenry, ed. From Pocahontas to Rosa Parks, 1,035 distinguished American women documented in separate biographical entries. Accurate, up-to-date data, numerous categories, spans 400 years. Indices. 493pp. 6½ × 9¼. 24523-3 Pa. $9.95

THE FABULOUS INTERIORS OF THE GREAT OCEAN LINERS IN HISTORIC PHOTOGRAPHS, William H. Miller, Jr. Some 200 superb photographs capture exquisite interiors of world's great "floating palaces"—1890's to 1980's: *Titanic, Ile de France, Queen Elizabeth, United States, Europa,* more. Approx. 200 black-and-white photographs. Captions. Text. Introduction. 160pp. 8⅞ × 11¾. 24756-2 Pa. $9.95

THE GREAT LUXURY LINERS, 1927–1954: A Photographic Record, William H. Miller, Jr. Nostalgic tribute to heyday of ocean liners. 186 photos of Ile de France, Normandie, Leviathan, Queen Elizabeth, United States, many others. Interior and exterior views. Introduction. Captions. 160pp. 9 × 12. 24056-8 Pa. $9.95

A NATURAL HISTORY OF THE DUCKS, John Charles Phillips. Great landmark of ornithology offers complete detailed coverage of nearly 200 species and subspecies of ducks: gadwall, sheldrake, merganser, pintail, many more. 74 full-color plates, 102 black-and-white. Bibliography. Total of 1,920pp. 8⅝ × 11¼. 25141-1, 25142-X Cloth. Two-vol. set $100.00

THE SEAWEED HANDBOOK: An Illustrated Guide to Seaweeds from North Carolina to Canada, Thomas F. Lee. Concise reference covers 78 species. Scientific and common names, habitat, distribution, more. Finding keys for easy identification. 224pp. 5⅜ × 8½. 25215-9 Pa. $5.95

THE TEN BOOKS OF ARCHITECTURE: The 1755 Leoni Edition, Leon Battista Alberti. Rare classic helped introduce the glories of ancient architecture to the Renaissance. 68 black-and-white plates. 336pp. 8⅜ × 11¼. 25239-6 Pa. $14.95

MISS MACKENZIE, Anthony Trollope. Minor masterpieces by Victorian master unmasks many truths about life in 19th-century England. First inexpensive edition in years. 392pp. 5⅜ × 8½. 25201-9 Pa. $7.95

THE RIME OF THE ANCIENT MARINER, Gustave Doré, Samuel Taylor Coleridge. Dramatic engravings considered by many to be his greatest work. The terrifying space of the open sea, the storms and whirlpools of an unknown ocean, the ice of Antarctica, more—all rendered in a powerful, chilling manner. Full text. 38 plates. 77pp. 9¼ × 12. 22305-1 Pa. $4.95

THE EXPEDITIONS OF ZEBULON MONTGOMERY PIKE, Zebulon Montgomery Pike. Fascinating first-hand accounts (1805–6) of exploration of Mississippi River, Indian wars, capture by Spanish dragoons, much more. 1,088pp. 5⅜ × 8½. 25254-X, 25255-8 Pa. Two-vol. set $23.90

A CONCISE HISTORY OF PHOTOGRAPHY: Third Revised Edition, Helmut Gernsheim. Best one-volume history—camera obscura, photochemistry, daguerreotypes, evolution of cameras, film, more. Also artistic aspects—landscape, portraits, fine art, etc. 281 black-and-white photographs. 26 in color. 176pp. 8⅜ × 11¼. 25128-4 Pa. $12.95

THE DORÉ BIBLE ILLUSTRATIONS, Gustave Doré. 241 detailed plates from the Bible: the Creation scenes, Adam and Eve, Flood, Babylon, battle sequences, life of Jesus, etc. Each plate is accompanied by the verses from the King James version of the Bible. 241pp. 9 × 12. 23004-X Pa. $8.95

HUGGER-MUGGER IN THE LOUVRE, Elliot Paul. Second Homer Evans mystery-comedy. Theft at the Louvre involves sleuth in hilarious, madcap caper. "A knockout."—Books. 336pp. 5⅜ × 8½. 25185-3 Pa. $5.95

FLATLAND, E. A. Abbott. Intriguing and enormously popular science-fiction classic explores the complexities of trying to survive as a two-dimensional being in a three-dimensional world. Amusingly illustrated by the author. 16 illustrations. 103pp. 5⅜ × 8½. 20001-9 Pa. $2.25

THE HISTORY OF THE LEWIS AND CLARK EXPEDITION, Meriwether Lewis and William Clark, edited by Elliott Coues. Classic edition of Lewis and Clark's day-by-day journals that later became the basis for U.S. claims to Oregon and the West. Accurate and invaluable geographical, botanical, biological, meteorological and anthropological material. Total of 1,508pp. 5⅜ × 8½.
21268-8, 21269-6, 21270-X Pa. Three-vol. set $25.50

LANGUAGE, TRUTH AND LOGIC, Alfred J. Ayer. Famous, clear introduction to Vienna, Cambridge schools of Logical Positivism. Role of philosophy, elimination of metaphysics, nature of analysis, etc. 160pp. 5⅜ × 8½. (Available in U.S. and Canada only) 20010-8 Pa. $2.95

MATHEMATICS FOR THE NONMATHEMATICIAN, Morris Kline. Detailed, college-level treatment of mathematics in cultural and historical context, with numerous exercises. For liberal arts students. Preface. Recommended Reading Lists. Tables. Index. Numerous black-and-white figures. xvi + 641pp. 5⅜ × 8½.
24823-2 Pa. $11.95

28 SCIENCE FICTION STORIES, H. G. Wells. Novels, *Star Begotten* and *Men Like Gods,* plus 26 short stories: "Empire of the Ants," "A Story of the Stone Age," "The Stolen Bacillus," "In the Abyss," etc. 915pp. 5⅜ × 8½. (Available in U.S. only)
20265-8 Cloth. $10.95

HANDBOOK OF PICTORIAL SYMBOLS, Rudolph Modley. 3,250 signs and symbols, many systems in full; official or heavy commercial use. Arranged by subject. Most in Pictorial Archive series. 143pp. 8⅛ × 11. 23357-X Pa. $5.95

INCIDENTS OF TRAVEL IN YUCATAN, John L. Stephens. Classic (1843) exploration of jungles of Yucatan, looking for evidences of Maya civilization. Travel adventures, Mexican and Indian culture, etc. Total of 669pp. 5⅜ × 8½.
20926-1, 20927-X Pa., Two-vol. set $9.90

DEGAS: An Intimate Portrait, Ambroise Vollard. Charming, anecdotal memoir by famous art dealer of one of the greatest 19th-century French painters. 14 black-and-white illustrations. Introduction by Harold L. Van Doren. 96pp. 5⅜ × 8½.
25131-4 Pa. $3.95

PERSONAL NARRATIVE OF A PILGRIMAGE TO ALMANDINAH AND MECCAH, Richard Burton. Great travel classic by remarkably colorful personality. Burton, disguised as a Moroccan, visited sacred shrines of Islam, narrowly escaping death. 47 illustrations. 959pp. 5⅜ × 8½.   21217-3, 21218-1 Pa., Two-vol. set $19.90

PHRASE AND WORD ORIGINS, A. H. Holt. Entertaining, reliable, modern study of more than 1,200 colorful words, phrases, origins and histories. Much unexpected information. 254pp. 5⅜ × 8½.   20758-7 Pa. $4.95

THE RED THUMB MARK, R. Austin Freeman. In this first Dr. Thorndyke case, the great scientific detective draws fascinating conclusions from the nature of a single fingerprint. Exciting story, authentic science. 320pp. 5⅜ × 8½. (Available in U.S. only)   25210-8 Pa. $5.95

AN EGYPTIAN HIEROGLYPHIC DICTIONARY, E. A. Wallis Budge. Monumental work containing about 25,000 words or terms that occur in texts ranging from 3000 B.C. to 600 A.D. Each entry consists of a transliteration of the word, the word in hieroglyphs, and the meaning in English. 1,314pp. 6⅝ × 10.
23615-3, 23616-1 Pa., Two-vol. set $27.90

THE COMPLEAT STRATEGYST: Being a Primer on the Theory of Games of Strategy, J. D. Williams. Highly entertaining classic describes, with many illustrated examples, how to select best strategies in conflict situations. Prefaces. Appendices. xvi + 268pp. 5⅜ × 8½.   25101-2 Pa. $5.95

THE ROAD TO OZ, L. Frank Baum. Dorothy meets the Shaggy Man, little Button-Bright and the Rainbow's beautiful daughter in this delightful trip to the magical Land of Oz. 272pp. 5⅜ × 8.   25208-6 Pa. $4.95

POINT AND LINE TO PLANE, Wassily Kandinsky. Seminal exposition of role of point, line, other elements in non-objective painting. Essential to understanding 20th-century art. 127 illustrations. 192pp. 6½ × 9¼.   23808-3 Pa. $4.50

LADY ANNA, Anthony Trollope. Moving chronicle of Countess Lovel's bitter struggle to win for herself and daughter Anna their rightful rank and fortune—perhaps at cost of sanity itself. 384pp. 5⅜ × 8½.   24669-8 Pa. $6.95

EGYPTIAN MAGIC, E. A. Wallis Budge. Sums up all that is known about magic in Ancient Egypt: the role of magic in controlling the gods, powerful amulets that warded off evil spirits, scarabs of immortality, use of wax images, formulas and spells, the secret name, much more. 253pp. 5⅜ × 8½.   22681-6 Pa. $4.00

THE DANCE OF SIVA, Ananda Coomaraswamy. Preeminent authority unfolds the vast metaphysic of India: the revelation of her art, conception of the universe, social organization, etc. 27 reproductions of art masterpieces. 192pp. 5⅜ × 8½.
24817-8 Pa. $5.95

CHRISTMAS CUSTOMS AND TRADITIONS, Clement A. Miles. Origin, evolution, significance of religious, secular practices. Caroling, gifts, yule logs, much more. Full, scholarly yet fascinating; non-sectarian. 400pp. 5⅜ × 8½.
23354-5 Pa. $6.50

THE HUMAN FIGURE IN MOTION, Eadweard Muybridge. More than 4,500 stopped-action photos, in action series, showing undraped men, women, children jumping, lying down, throwing, sitting, wrestling, carrying, etc. 390pp. 7⅞ × 10⅝.
20204-6 Cloth. $21.95

THE MAN WHO WAS THURSDAY, Gilbert Keith Chesterton. Witty, fast-paced novel about a club of anarchists in turn-of-the-century London. Brilliant social, religious, philosophical speculations. 128pp. 5⅜ × 8½.
25121-7 Pa. $3.95

A CEZANNE SKETCHBOOK: Figures, Portraits, Landscapes and Still Lifes, Paul Cezanne. Great artist experiments with tonal effects, light, mass, other qualities in over 100 drawings. A revealing view of developing master painter, precursor of Cubism. 102 black-and-white illustrations. 144pp. 8¾ × 6⅝.
24790-2 Pa. $5.95

AN ENCYCLOPEDIA OF BATTLES: Accounts of Over 1,560 Battles from 1479 B.C. to the Present, David Eggenberger. Presents essential details of every major battle in recorded history, from the first battle of Megiddo in 1479 B.C. to Grenada in 1984. List of Battle Maps. New Appendix covering the years 1967–1984. Index. 99 illustrations. 544pp. 6½ × 9¼.
24913-1 Pa. $14.95

AN ETYMOLOGICAL DICTIONARY OF MODERN ENGLISH, Ernest Weekley. Richest, fullest work, by foremost British lexicographer. Detailed word histories. Inexhaustible. Total of 856pp. 6½ × 9¼.
21873-2, 21874-0 Pa., Two-vol. set $17.00

WEBSTER'S AMERICAN MILITARY BIOGRAPHIES, edited by Robert McHenry. Over 1,000 figures who shaped 3 centuries of American military history. Detailed biographies of Nathan Hale, Douglas MacArthur, Mary Hallaren, others. Chronologies of engagements, more. Introduction. Addenda. 1,033 entries in alphabetical order. xi + 548pp. 6½ × 9¼. (Available in U.S. only)
24758-9 Pa. $11.95

LIFE IN ANCIENT EGYPT, Adolf Erman. Detailed older account, with much not in more recent books: domestic life, religion, magic, medicine, commerce, and whatever else needed for complete picture. Many illustrations. 597pp. 5⅜ × 8½.
22632-8 Pa. $8.50

HISTORIC COSTUME IN PICTURES, Braun & Schneider. Over 1,450 costumed figures shown, covering a wide variety of peoples: kings, emperors, nobles, priests, servants, soldiers, scholars, townsfolk, peasants, merchants, courtiers, cavaliers, and more. 256pp. 8⅜ × 11¼.
23150-X Pa. $7.95

THE NOTEBOOKS OF LEONARDO DA VINCI, edited by J. P. Richter. Extracts from manuscripts reveal great genius; on painting, sculpture, anatomy, sciences, geography, etc. Both Italian and English. 186 ms. pages reproduced, plus 500 additional drawings, including studies for *Last Supper, Sforza* monument, etc. 860pp. 7⅞ × 10¾. (Available in U.S. only) 22572-0, 22573-9 Pa., Two-vol. set $25.90

THE ART NOUVEAU STYLE BOOK OF ALPHONSE MUCHA: All 72 Plates from "Documents Decoratifs" in Original Color, Alphonse Mucha. Rare copyright-free design portfolio by high priest of Art Nouveau. Jewelry, wallpaper, stained glass, furniture, figure studies, plant and animal motifs, etc. Only complete one-volume edition. 80pp. 9⅜ × 12¼. 24044-4 Pa. $8.95

ANIMALS: 1,419 COPYRIGHT-FREE ILLUSTRATIONS OF MAMMALS, BIRDS, FISH, INSECTS, ETC., edited by Jim Harter. Clear wood engravings present, in extremely lifelike poses, over 1,000 species of animals. One of the most extensive pictorial sourcebooks of its kind. Captions. Index. 284pp. 9 × 12. 23766-4 Pa. $9.95

OBELISTS FLY HIGH, C. Daly King. Masterpiece of American detective fiction, long out of print, involves murder on a 1935 transcontinental flight—"a very thrilling story"—NY Times. Unabridged and unaltered republication of the edition published by William Collins Sons & Co. Ltd., London, 1935. 288pp. 5⅜ × 8½. (Available in U.S. only) 25036-9 Pa. $4.95

VICTORIAN AND EDWARDIAN FASHION: A Photographic Survey, Alison Gernsheim. First fashion history completely illustrated by contemporary photographs. Full text plus 235 photos, 1840–1914, in which many celebrities appear. 240pp. 6½ × 9¼. 24205-6 Pa. $6.00

THE ART OF THE FRENCH ILLUSTRATED BOOK, 1700–1914, Gordon N. Ray. Over 630 superb book illustrations by Fragonard, Delacroix, Daumier, Doré, Grandville, Manet, Mucha, Steinlen, Toulouse-Lautrec and many others. Preface. Introduction. 633 halftones. Indices of artists, authors & titles, binders and provenances. Appendices. Bibliography. 608pp. 8⅜ × 11¼. 25086-5 Pa. $24.95

THE WONDERFUL WIZARD OF OZ, L. Frank Baum. Facsimile in full color of America's finest children's classic. 143 illustrations by W. W. Denslow. 267pp. 5⅜ × 8½. 20691-2 Pa. $5.95

FRONTIERS OF MODERN PHYSICS: New Perspectives on Cosmology, Relativity, Black Holes and Extraterrestrial Intelligence, Tony Rothman, et al. For the intelligent layman. Subjects include: cosmological models of the universe; black holes; the neutrino; the search for extraterrestrial intelligence. Introduction. 46 black-and-white illustrations. 192pp. 5⅜ × 8½. 24587-X Pa. $6.95

THE FRIENDLY STARS, Martha Evans Martin & Donald Howard Menzel. Classic text marshalls the stars together in an engaging, non-technical survey, presenting them as sources of beauty in night sky. 23 illustrations. Foreword. 2 star charts. Index. 147pp. 5⅜ × 8½. 21099-5 Pa. $3.50

FADS AND FALLACIES IN THE NAME OF SCIENCE, Martin Gardner. Fair, witty appraisal of cranks, quacks, and quackeries of science and pseudoscience: hollow earth, Velikovsky, orgone energy, Dianetics, flying saucers, Bridey Murphy, food and medical fads, etc. Revised, expanded In the Name of Science. "A very able and even-tempered presentation."—The New Yorker. 363pp. 5⅜ × 8. 20394-8 Pa. $6.50

ANCIENT EGYPT: ITS CULTURE AND HISTORY, J. E Manchip White. From pre-dynastics through Ptolemies: society, history, political structure, religion, daily life, literature, cultural heritage. 48 plates. 217pp. 5⅜ × 8½. 22548-8 Pa. $4.95

SIR HARRY HOTSPUR OF HUMBLETHWAITE, Anthony Trollope. Incisive, unconventional psychological study of a conflict between a wealthy baronet, his idealistic daughter, and their scapegrace cousin. The 1870 novel in its first inexpensive edition in years. 250pp. 5⅜ × 8½.　　　　24953-0 Pa. $5.95

LASERS AND HOLOGRAPHY, Winston E. Kock. Sound introduction to burgeoning field, expanded (1981) for second edition. Wave patterns, coherence, lasers, diffraction, zone plates, properties of holograms, recent advances. 84 illustrations. 160pp. 5⅜ × 8¼. (Except in United Kingdom)　　24041-X Pa. $3.50

INTRODUCTION TO ARTIFICIAL INTELLIGENCE: SECOND, EN-LARGED EDITION, Philip C. Jackson, Jr. Comprehensive survey of artificial intelligence—the study of how machines (computers) can be made to act intelligently. Includes introductory and advanced material. Extensive notes updating the main text. 132 black-and-white illustrations. 512pp. 5⅜ × 8½.　　24864-X Pa. $8.95

HISTORY OF INDIAN AND INDONESIAN ART, Ananda K. Coomaraswamy. Over 400 illustrations illuminate classic study of Indian art from earliest Harappa finds to early 20th century. Provides philosophical, religious and social insights. 304pp. 6⅜ × 9⅜.　　　　　　　　　　　　　25005-9 Pa. $8.95

THE GOLEM, Gustav Meyrink. Most famous supernatural novel in modern European literature, set in Ghetto of Old Prague around 1890. Compelling story of mystical experiences, strange transformations, profound terror. 13 black-and-white illustrations. 224pp. 5⅜ × 8½. (Available in U.S. only)　　25025-3 Pa. $5.95

ARMADALE, Wilkie Collins. Third great mystery novel by the author of *The Woman in White* and *The Moonstone*. Original magazine version with 40 illustrations. 597pp. 5⅜ × 8½.　　　　　　　　　23429-0 Pa. $9.95

PICTORIAL ENCYCLOPEDIA OF HISTORIC ARCHITECTURAL PLANS, DETAILS AND ELEMENTS: With 1,880 Line Drawings of Arches, Domes, Doorways, Facades, Gables, Windows, etc., John Theodore Haneman. Sourcebook of inspiration for architects, designers, others. Bibliography. Captions. 141pp. 9 × 12.　　　　　　　　　　　　　　　　24605-1 Pa. $6.95

BENCHLEY LOST AND FOUND, Robert Benchley. Finest humor from early 30's, about pet peeves, child psychologists, post office and others. Mostly unavailable elsewhere. 73 illustrations by Peter Arno and others. 183pp. 5⅜ × 8½.
　　　　　　　　　　　　　　　　　　　　　　　22410-4 Pa. $3.95

ERTÉ GRAPHICS, Erté. Collection of striking color graphics: *Seasons, Alphabet, Numerals, Aces* and *Precious Stones*. 50 plates, including 4 on covers. 48pp. 9⅜ × 12¼.　　　　　　　　　　　　　　　　23580-7 Pa. $6.95

THE JOURNAL OF HENRY D. THOREAU, edited by Bradford Torrey, F. H. Allen. Complete reprinting of 14 volumes, 1837–61, over two million words; the sourcebooks for *Walden*, etc. Definitive. All original sketches, plus 75 photographs. 1,804pp. 8½ × 12¼.　　　20312-3, 20313-1 Cloth., Two-vol. set $80.00

CASTLES: THEIR CONSTRUCTION AND HISTORY, Sidney Toy. Traces castle development from ancient roots. Nearly 200 photographs and drawings illustrate moats, keeps, baileys, many other features. Caernarvon, Dover Castles, Hadrian's Wall, Tower of London, dozens more. 256pp. 5⅜ × 8¼.
　　　　　　　　　　　　　　　　　　　　　　　24898-4 Pa. $5.95

AMERICAN CLIPPER SHIPS: 1833–1858, Octavius T. Howe & Frederick C. Matthews. Fully-illustrated, encyclopedic review of 352 clipper ships from the period of America's greatest maritime supremacy. Introduction. 109 halftones. 5 black-and-white line illustrations. Index. Total of 928pp. 5⅜ × 8½.
25115-2, 25116-0 Pa., Two-vol. set $17.90

TOWARDS A NEW ARCHITECTURE, Le Corbusier. Pioneering manifesto by great architect, near legendary founder of "International School." Technical and aesthetic theories, views on industry, economics, relation of form to function, "mass-production spirit," much more. Profusely illustrated. Unabridged translation of 13th French edition. Introduction by Frederick Etchells. 320pp. 6⅛ × 9¼. (Available in U.S. only)
25023-7 Pa. $8.95

THE BOOK OF KELLS, edited by Blanche Cirker. Inexpensive collection of 32 full-color, full-page plates from the greatest illuminated manuscript of the Middle Ages, painstakingly reproduced from rare facsimile edition. Publisher's Note. Captions. 32pp. 9⅜ × 12¼.
24345-1 Pa. $4.95

BEST SCIENCE FICTION STORIES OF H. G. WELLS, H. G. Wells. Full novel *The Invisible Man,* plus 17 short stories: "The Crystal Egg," "Aepyornis Island," "The Strange Orchid," etc. 303pp. 5⅜ × 8½. (Available in U.S. only)
21531-8 Pa. $4.95

AMERICAN SAILING SHIPS: Their Plans and History, Charles G. Davis. Photos, construction details of schooners, frigates, clippers, other sailcraft of 18th to early 20th centuries—plus entertaining discourse on design, rigging, nautical lore, much more. 137 black-and-white illustrations. 240pp. 6⅛ × 9¼.
24658-2 Pa. $5.95

ENTERTAINING MATHEMATICAL PUZZLES, Martin Gardner. Selection of author's favorite conundrums involving arithmetic, money, speed, etc., with lively commentary. Complete solutions. 112pp. 5⅜ × 8½.
25211-6 Pa. $2.95

THE WILL TO BELIEVE, HUMAN IMMORTALITY, William James. Two books bound together. Effect of irrational on logical, and arguments for human immortality. 402pp. 5⅜ × 8½.
20291-7 Pa. $7.50

THE HAUNTED MONASTERY and THE CHINESE MAZE MURDERS, Robert Van Gulik. 2 full novels by Van Gulik continue adventures of Judge Dee and his companions. An evil Taoist monastery, seemingly supernatural events; overgrown topiary maze that hides strange crimes. Set in 7th-century China. 27 illustrations. 328pp. 5⅜ × 8½.
23502-5 Pa. $5.95

CELEBRATED CASES OF JUDGE DEE (DEE GOONG AN), translated by Robert Van Gulik. Authentic 18th-century Chinese detective novel; Dee and associates solve three interlocked cases. Led to Van Gulik's own stories with same characters. Extensive introduction. 9 illustrations. 237pp. 5⅜ × 8½.
23337-5 Pa. $4.95

Prices subject to change without notice.

Available at your book dealer or write for free catalog to Dept. GI, Dover Publications, Inc., 31 East 2nd St., Mineola, N.Y. 11501. Dover publishes more than 175 books each year on science, elementary and advanced mathematics, biology, music, art, literary history, social sciences and other areas.